Writing
THE RECORD

The Village Voice and the
Birth of Rock Criticism

DEVON POWERS

University of Massachusetts Press
Amherst & Boston

ISBN 978-1-62534-012-2 (paper); 011-5 (hardcover)
Designed by Jack Harrison
Set in Adobe Minion Pro with ITC Avant Garde Gothic display
Printed and bound by The Maple-Vail Book Manufacturing Group

Library of Congress Cataloging-in-Publication Data

Powers, Devon.
Writing the record : the Village Voice and the birth of rock criticism / Devon Powers.
    pages cm. — (American popular music)
Includes bibliographical references and index.
ISBN 978-1-62534-012-2 (pbk. : alk. paper) — ISBN 978-1-62534-011-5 (hardcover : alk. paper)
1. Village Voice (Greenwich Village, New York, N.Y.) 2. Musical criticism—United States—History.
3. Rock music—United States—History and criticism.   I. Title.
ML3785.P68 2013
781.6609747'1—dc23

                         2012050131

British Library Cataloguing-in-Publication Data
A catalogue record for this book is available from the British Library.

To my parents, Lee and Mandy Powers

CONTENTS

ACKNOWLEDGMENTS

One of the most difficult things I had to confront when writing this book was that what had often felt like a solitary activity—partaken of in the hours between dusk and dawn, scribbled on Post-It notes, floating in data clouds, and gnawing at the back of my mind almost always—would someday become public and tangible, bearing my name. That day has come, dear reader, and I am glad you have started your reading here with the acknowledgments. The publication of this book is, for me, a reason for tremendous celebration, but also one for pause. I admit that I have anxiety, still, that I have not said what it is that I mean, that I have not said all that I could, that I have made a mistake. I have learned that this is the nature of books, though. Even though they are bound, they are never quite finished.

Two things comfort me when the stress of miscommunication and judgment peaks. One is that this book, and any book, is not just a publication; it is also a conversation. As a reader, you are embarking on a conversation with me, one that I hope results in your own scribbled Post-Its and data cloud rants. I thank you, my reader, for spending some time with me thinking about the things I have thought both way too much and barely enough about.

What you are about to read is the record of many conversations that I have had with my own readings, as well as discussions with my friends, colleagues, and family over the ten years this book needed to gestate. It is an acknowledgments cliché to say that writing is never truly solitary, but it's so utterly true that it is worth repeating. My writing is in essence a translation of the energies, ideas, and psychic supports of the people around me, and the love and thanks I have for them could fill an entire book—one that would likely be far easier to write than this one was.

Like many first books, this one began as my doctoral dissertation at New York University. My dissertation adviser, Susan Murray, is as supportive an adviser as I can imagine, whose encouragement, intelligence, good humor, and warmth fueled me during my Ph.D. work and inspired me beyond. Brett Gary, Perry Meisel, and, until her untimely passing, Ellen Willis rounded out my committee. Each of them offered good patience, grand ideas, and dutiful eyes, all the while providing me with pearls of wisdom that have profoundly shaped me as a researcher.

On the march to becoming a book, this work benefited from the insights and criticism of my editor at University of Massachusetts Press, Brian Halley, and the series editors, Jeff Melnick and Rachel Rubin. The anonymous reviewers who read this manuscript in draft form offered incisive readings which were not always easy to hear, but which helped me to make the manuscript better, and to become a better thinker. A portion of chapter 1 originally appeared in *Journalism History,* and I thank Patrick Washburn for accepting that piece and the permission to reprint some of it here; Ian Ingliss, who edited a special issue of *Popular Music and Society,* also provided me a venue to publish an article that overviewed the core of this manuscript's argument. Christopher Vyce greatly assisted me in crafting the proposal for this book and illuminating the obscure process of finding a publisher. Katherine Scheuer and Lindsey Beutin did amazing jobs copyediting the manuscript and proofreading, and the entire staff at the University of Massachusetts Press deserve thanks for their many contributions to the finished project.

Richard Goldstein and Robert Christgau have spent hours of their lives answering my questions, some of which I have since realized were the wrong questions to ask. They are very different men, but both are people whom I greatly respect and I am thankful that I've been able to spend so much time writing about, and learning from, their criticism. Edwin Fancher and Carman Moore also granted me interviews and though I spent less time with them, I found them to be both charming and insightful. Over the years, I've also picked the brains of many other rock critics, including Chuck Eddy, Douglas Wolk, Richard Meltzer, Greg Tate, Anthony DeCurtis, Greil Marcus, Jim DeRogatis, Ann Powers, Jody Rosen, Chris Weingarten, and Michaelangelo Matos. I am awed not just by their encyclopedic knowledge of and investment in popular music, but also by their formidable intellects and graceful, hilarious, and thought-provoking writing. PopMatters.com was the primary vehicle for my own music writing in the early 2000s and a place where I began to float ideas about music criticism, many of which found their way into this book. Thank you to Sarah Zupko and the rest of the PopMatters team from those days for giving me space to think.

Many other teachers, colleagues, and peers have had a hand in shaping this manuscript, and I'm not sure I will be able to name them all. But I am especially grateful for the friendship and support of Melissa Aronczyk, my intellectual foil, cherished friend, and the most perceptive and generous reader I have ever known. The dear Laurel Harris read a good portion of this manuscript over the years and lent not only her insights but also her hawkeyed copyediting skills—something I felt lucky to have as the self-declared queen of typos and comma overuse. I thank Jeremy Morris for identifying places to sharpen and hone my argument during the final stages of writing; from here on out, the first drink is on me. Marion Wrenn, MJ Robinson, Jessie Shimmin, Laina Dawes, Michael Kramer, Kathleen Holscher, Eric Harvey, Cynthia Conti, Joseph Reagle, Michael Zimmer, and Dave Parisi have been involved with this project as allies, instigators, fellow grad students, and shoulders to lean on. I learned a tremendous amount in coursework and correspondence, both formal and informal, with John Gennari, Kembrew McLeod, Siva Vaidhyanathan, and Jonathan Zimmerman. I'm also incredibly indebted to Marita Sturken, Radha Hegde, Aurora Wallace, and Ted Magder, who were amazing to me during my time at NYU Department of Media, Culture, and Communication; and to my current colleagues Brent Luvaas, Jordan McClain, and Susan Stein at Drexel University's Department of Culture and Communication. I send love to my parents, Lee and Mandy Powers, for endowing me with an insatiable appetite for music and the work ethic to always finish what I start.

I've come to the end of these acknowledgments, which means it's time to thank my husband David, who has never known me when I didn't have this book to write. Thank you for putting up with my weird music, long hours, and tears. What will we do now, love?

WRITING THE RECORD

INTRODUCTION
Criticism

The last time I saw Ellen Willis was in the late spring of 2006, when we met to discuss my dissertation, a project I would later revise into this book. Now, I can only remember snippets of our encounter. Out of respect for the graduate students on strike as New York University's administration blocked their efforts to unionize, she insisted we meet off campus, choosing a coffee shop on LaGuardia Place in the Village. I cautiously asked her what she thought about Seymour Krim, a Beat who wrote for the *Voice* in the '50s and had lately become an obsession of mine. Being with her was never entirely comfortable for me; her disarming quietude and extreme smarts did a number on my grad student insecurities. But that day, the chill that had been present at prior meetings warmed just enough for me to feel as though we were finally getting to know each other.

We parted ways that day and emailed a handful of times over the summer as I agonized over finishing my draft. Early in the fall, I sent her a couple of chapters, to which she responded at length. I can't remember anymore when we had intended to meet again. Whatever our plans were then, the fall got away from me, or I wasn't quite ready, or other things took precedence. November arrived very quickly, and just over a week in, I learned that she had passed away.

In the years since, I have rarely talked about Ellen Willis, perhaps even subconsciously avoiding doing so. I can't claim to have known her well, and I regret that I did not know her better. It's hard for me to reconcile myself today with the timid graduate student I was around her; I wish I'd been more confident to explore ideas with her and to express my gratitude for what she taught me. I'm not unique for feeling this way—the death of someone we know often shepherds in dozens of would'ves and could'ves, caught as much in ideas and expectations of the still living as they are about the person deceased. In addition to the common remorse, as a researcher I feel a sense of guilt and sheepishness over the fact that I didn't ask her more about her own rock criticism. Although she was my teacher, I had an embarrassingly shallow knowledge of who she was.

Willis holds the distinction of being the first pop music critic at the *New Yorker* magazine, starting her job there in 1968. She got the position thanks to an essay about Bob Dylan that appeared in *Commentary* as well as in the short-lived *Cheetah* magazine, where she had worked with her friend Richard Goldstein, and her then-boyfriend, Robert Christgau. Goldstein and Christgau were also music journalists—Goldstein began at the *Village Voice* in 1966 and Christgau at *Esquire* in 1967, and the *Voice* in 1969. As the first generation of popular music critics in the United States, they form the nucleus of an intellectual community that forever changed how all of us think, listen, and write about popular music. In inventing the genre of rock criticism, they made it possible to take popular music seriously and to mine it as a repository of ideas. This book endeavors to tell the story of how this community took shape through a deep focus on the *Village Voice,* the publication where much of this writing appeared. From its beginnings in 1955, the *Voice* was a place where writers freely explored alternative cultural forms, and the rock music of the 1960s was no exception. *Voice* critics used rock to grapple with intellectual and social issues but also to exalt it on its own terms. In so doing, they behaved as public intellectuals and deserve a prominent place in the intellectual history of popular music studies and its related disciplines.[1]

Willis did not write for the *Voice* during its first twenty years, the period under close scrutiny in this book, and for this reason she will be among its minor players. I open this introduction with a discussion of her because she has recently come to represent both the opportunities and the challenges that arise in thinking historically about rock criticism. One sustaining lesson I have learned from her life and work is that writing history is a process of both discovering the past and negotiating it with the present. In this and many other ways, she is never very far away from my thinking on these topics, and she was and continues to be one of my most insightful teachers.

Writing Rock Criticism into History

Ellen Willis was born in December 1941 to Jewish, working-class parents, and spent her young years living in the outer boroughs of New York City— first the Bronx, later Queens. Though she claimed her parents never were overt about their political views, Willis inherited their radical inclinations; both parents were in the Communist Party during the 1930s. She completed high school and earned a bachelor's from Barnard in 1962.[2] Newly divorced after a brief marriage, in the early part of 1966 she met Bob Christgau, a journalist who had grown up in the same Queens neighborhood. Quickly, they developed a powerful intellectual and romantic connection. The couple expanded their circle later that year when Christgau reached out to another young, working-class, Jewish writer named Richard Goldstein, who had just published a book about the drug culture among college students. Soon, all three began writing or editing at publications where they could exercise their interest in popular culture, especially rock music. In addition to the *New Yorker,* where Willis wrote until 1975, she was also a contributing editor for *Ms. Magazine* from 1973 until 1975.[3]

Willis turned away from music by the 1980s to write more explicitly on political and gender issues. She also anthologized her work. The first collection, *Beginning to See the Light,* appeared in 1981 to favorable reviews and showcased the pillars of her interests up until that time as rock music, feminism, and cultural politics. Subsequent collections—*No More Nice Girls* in 1992, *Don't Think, Smile: Notes on a Decade of Denial* in 2000—confirmed Willis's sharp insight and deft style. In the meantime, her music writing assumed legendary, if underground, status among music critics; *Billboard*'s Joe Levy, during his editorship of the *Voice*'s music section, used to distribute her copy as an example of superior writing. The 1999 volume *Rock She Wrote: Women Write About Rock, Pop, and Rap,* edited by Ann Powers and Evelyn McDonnell, also exposed some of Willis's writing to new readers, especially the feminist contingent that came of age between the end of the second wave and the beginning of the Riot Grrl movement. Recognized as a pioneer of radical feminism, Willis factors heavily into Alice Echols's 1989 history of the movement, though her name is probably still less well known than that of Shulamith Firestone, her collaborator at Red Stockings, or Valerie Solanas, the erratic but nonetheless inspirational author of the S.C.U.M. Manifesto who famously shot Andy Warhol in 1968.

At the time of this writing, some six years after her death, Willis's reputation as a rock writer and feminist visionary has experienced a profound renewal, precipitated in large part by the 2011 publication of *Out of the Vinyl Deeps,* a collection of her music writing edited by her daughter, writer Nona Willis-Aronowitz. Responses to its appearance have been plentiful and roundly positive.[4] The book has captured the attention of a whole new generation of music writers and brought together a community invested in the ideas her writing proffered. Thanks to its success, a new anthology of

Willis's work is slated to debut in the spring of 2013; there have also been calls to commemorate the writing of other female rock writers, in solo volumes as well as combined collections, such as an updated version of *Rock She Wrote*.

The lionization of Willis's music criticism has been both exciting and well deserved, but its timing is peculiar. It is, on the one hand, proof of the vibrancy of popular music criticism and its maturation from marginal curiosity to animated public sphere. Despite difficulties and missteps in recent years, the popular music industry remains a powerful force, and music celebrities, for better or worse, command extraordinary salaries and attention. In such a world, it is hard to imagine doing without the commentary that critics have come to supply, whether as talking heads on television programs, pundits on the radio, or essayists and obituary writers. Willis's spirit is very much alive among music writers who evaluate popular music's political ideologies right alongside its sound; she naturalized the idea that music criticism is, in the first place, cultural criticism. The renewed adulation of Willis among professional critics has also inspired academics and educators. *Out of the Vinyl Deeps* will be assigned in courses and mined in future research, and will begin to make rock criticism a more regular subject in higher education—something that has already happened to rock music.

At the same time, there has been substantial chagrin in recent years over the state of music criticism, with just cause. Since 2005, the development and widespread adoption of an assortment of computing technologies—easy-to-use blogging software, faster Internet connection speeds with greater bandwidth, websites that can host large music files for marginal cost, and of course, MP3s—have helped to drive the rapid growth of a music blogosphere, described by one commenter as "the new *Rolling Stone;* the new top-40 radio; the new MTV; on crack."[5] In empowering music fans and aspiring tastemakers alike to act as boosters and distributors of music, music blogs surmounted print music criticism's most persistent obstacle: the disconnect between reading a review and sampling the music it discussed. Digital music could race around the web in blatant disregard of release dates and editorial calendars, and a new class of writers—many of them new to music writing—arose to track it, all too willing to match its pace. Social networking and algorithmic technologies geared toward discovering and assessing music have further diversified the environment—from bite-sized Twitter commentary appearing synchronously with concerts, festivals, and award shows; to social networks that magnify the flow of word-of-mouth about bands; to "intelligent" radio stations and streaming services that curate music specifically to an individual's taste and mood. As it had for the recording industry, the transition online disrupted what had become standard critical practice and left its established practitioners grasping for alternative ways to do their jobs.

Similar trends have placed colossal pressures on the print media industry that provides the livelihood for many pop music critics, changing not just how critics worked, but whether they worked at all. Print publications have transformed their arts sections, running shorter pieces or extensive listings in place of longer, more selective reviews.[6] This dovetailed with a more general crisis in print journalism. According to a Pew Project for Excellence in Journalism report, declining advertising revenues, faltering circulation, competition from the Internet, and a substantial economic slowdown had revealed deep flaws in the business models for newspapers and magazines since 2008, demonstrating the need for permanent, radical changes at many old media firms.[7] As a result, a number of publications downsized, offered buyouts, migrated to the Web, or folded in order to cope, putting even the most senior writers at risk.[8]

These contradictory dynamics—that criticism is flourishing but also perilously close to its twilight—indicate a rite of passage as popular music criticism transitions from an alternative media form into a cultural institution. It is a metamorphosis with profound implications. Most obviously but also most importantly, it means that criticism has earned a station in our cultural life, with an impact that extends beyond its practitioners. The recent groundswell of debate, acknowledgment, and acclaim for this criticism is, in part, an effort to determine just how high the cost of losing criticism would be, and who would pay the proverbial price.

Moments of transformation are natural times to come to terms with history; even the most resilient of cultural institutions need nurturing and preserving, and certainly those under threat need it even more. In her renaissance, Willis has become an example of as well as a vessel for historiography, as recollections of the past bump up against the investments and interpretations of the present. Other examples of a historical focus include recent collections from long-time critics such as Chuck Eddy and Chuck Klosterman; reflective newspaper interviews with early critics such as Greil Marcus; and increasing interest in early music criticism among graduate students in a number of disciplines. Beyond the pressures of revisionism, historicization always runs the risk of fossilization; an interest in history cannot replace attending to the everyday realities of professional practice. As the various generations of musical critics fractured by media and time try to make sense of one another, it remains an open question how a genre nearing its fiftieth birthday, born in a different era with different concerns, can honor its foundations while maintaining its acuity. When and under what circumstances does learning from the past blaze the trail toward the future?

What I will call the academicization of popular music criticism opens up some possible answers to this question. I mean academicization in two senses. First, I mean that certain styles of music criticism are obvious in their commitment to theory, scholarship, and philosophical critique. While not all of the attention on Willis has been focused this way—she was also a practiced writer who wrote during a time period that continues to fascinate—many of her admirers take pains to describe her as an intellectual, and in using that word forge a connection to the brand of cultural criticism that most often radiates from the university. Music writers of this stripe, a group which includes Christgau and Goldstein, their peers Richard Meltzer and Greil Marcus, and a number of their later followers, are not straightforwardly reconciled with a world that seems ever more enraptured with quick judgments and brief commentary. Rueful jeremiads about the eclipse of "true" criticism abound. "Audiences, not judges, select winners," mourned Martin Bernheimer in the *Financial Times,* a representative example of the perspective. "Quality is measured by thumbs, up or down. Scholarly analyses have turned into irrelevant extravagances for snobs."[9] Whether or not we agree with this view, it voices the anxieties about to what extent long-form journalism remains economically and culturally viable, and poses some hard questions about who the audience for such criticism might be.

If one component of academicization is the resemblance of much of the most celebrated criticism to "scholarly" analysis, the other is the tangible connections between music critics and the academy. For the last decade of her life, Willis was a professor of cultural journalism at NYU, founding the Cultural Reporting and Criticism concentration in the school's journalism program in 1995. Christgau, Goldstein, and Marcus have also sometimes been employed as college instructors, especially during recent years; many other contemporary critics, such as NPR's Ann Powers and author Simon Reynolds, have tried their hand at college teaching. These entrées into academia sometimes signify troubling trends—the dependency of higher education on adjuncts, or the lengths journalists must take to earn a living as their craft is perpetually undervalued—but they also demonstrate that rock criticism has earned a place in the university. We can see this in more ways than one: several prominent rock critics completed doctorates and made the transition to the professoriate in the 2000s, including Oliver Wang, who has contributed to *Vibe,* the *Village Voice,* and *Rolling Stone,* among many other publications; former *Village Voice* and *Spin* editor Eric Weisbard; and *Village Voice, Blender,* and *Idolator* contributor Jason King. All of these writers have followed a model made practicable by Simon Frith, perhaps the best known rock critic-turned-academic and one of popular music studies' most eminent scholars.

The status of popular music and culture within the academy has changed radically since the mid-twentieth century, marking not just the academicization of criticism, but also the "popularization" of the academy. Scholars now embrace popular culture and music outright within many disciplines, mirroring as well as driving its veneration across the sociocultural spectrum. Moreover, music criticism specifically and critical journalism more generally may themselves be thought of as scholarly endeavors, whether they transpire within universities or not. This is perhaps a rather plain insight—after all, academia has never been alone in generating ideas, and journalism is one way that we learn about the world beyond our immediate experience. A full recognition of the bond between journalistic and scholarly criticism, however, directly challenges many of the assumptions held about and within both professions—for instance, that there are certain points of view, argumentative styles, or concepts that should remain in the lecture hall, or that one camp writes for the public and the other, an esoteric group of experts. Likewise, it implies crucial ways in which their fates converge and interlock and, as such, issues a warning for anyone interested in the health and solvency of cultural criticism.

I approach this subject as a media studies scholar, and I conceive of music and its criticism as media forms that reflect and reinforce not just social, cultural, economic, or political dynamics, but also technological ones. Questions pertaining to mediation—the construction of discourse, the circulation and intermediation of information, and the values and propensities of technology—are both explicit and implicit assumptions of this research. My orientation within media studies also means that this work is integrally, at times wantonly, interdisciplinary; I borrow liberally from critical theory, cultural and intellectual history, literary studies, and cultural studies to offer what I think of as equal parts theoretical and historical intervention into this subject. For some readers these varied methodological perspectives will clash, and for others they may be unorthodox. For example, though this book aims to be an intellectual history, it is not solely focused on the progression of any particular writer's thinking. Rock criticism is not merely the invention of a small number of individuals; it is a genre and the critic has a habitus, for which there are individual and historical but also collective and theoretical explanations.

The small though growing body of scholarly work devoted to rock and popular music criticism emerges from popular music studies, to which my own work owes a great deal. Some of this scholarship, notably that of Simon Frith, dates back to the early 1980s; one of his earliest works, *Sound Effects*, notes that "music papers, indeed, are important even for those people who don't buy them—their readers act as the opinion leaders, the rock interpreters, the ideological gatekeepers for everyone else."[10] More recently, scholars have explored the ability of popular music criticism, especially about rock, to influence taste; to reproduce ideologies, particularly along lines of race and gender; to produce value for music and shape its political reception; and to establish itself as an authoritative journalistic field replete with its own norms.[11] Professional rock critics have also reflected extensively and persuasively about their own practice—keen self-criticism is one of the genre's clearest fingerprints.[12] Given this foundation as well as my own intellectual background, one path toward achieving the aims of this book is to widen the scope of these conversations so that rock criticism might emerge as a more significant object of study within journalism and media studies, as well as join the ranks of scholarship about criticism that already exists in literary studies and history. Besides the obvious fact that both music and music journalism are media, there are compelling motivations for its greater inclusion. The cultural study of media was also expanding during the 1960s, and the writers I research were reading many of the authors who define media studies. We therefore share a common heritage.

Another goal of this work is to build more concrete connections between academe and music journalism and to erode existing barriers. The reasoning for doing so is simple: from the beginning, rock critics concerned themselves with far more than just the quality of notes and rhythms, and work that has to this point understood them primarily for their effect on music only partially appreciates what they accomplished. Here, I emphasize the role of rock critics as knowledge producers whose sociological and humanistic perspectives on music were not limited strictly to the management of taste or the maintenance of their own authority, nor were they ignorant of the wider ideological ramifications of music. Calling them public intellectuals is a stance which locates them within a tradition of bohemian intellectualism and recognizes the dynamic conversations they instigated at precisely the moment often considered the denouement of American letters.

I am sensitive to the fact that my book participates in what is sure to be a bittersweet transition for popular music criticism in the United States. It might even accelerate it, and it will surely produce its own consequences. Given the precarious state of journalistic music criticism today—and, in turn, the threats that exist to cultural study as a whole—I don't see rewriting the narrative of rock music criticism as a choice. I understand it as a strategy. The changes in the direction of popular music and cultural criticism are already afoot. The questions are what direction they will go in and how thoughtfully they will unfold.

Public Intellectuals, Music Critics

It's unclear who, if anyone, uttered the statement "writing about music is like dancing about architecture," but it's become aphoristic because of its supposed truth: that music writing is fundamentally at odds with listening to music. Scholars have also pointed out the hegemony of the visual that has relegated sound to a "second-class" sense and the difficulties of describing aural experience, which would seem to further suggest that writing about sound is a futile exercise.[13] Yet write we do, not just about the formal qualities of music or its emotional effects, but its personas and politics, its movements and moments, its innovation and industry.

Music criticism, at the most basic level, is writing about music that takes an interest—whether it be aesthetic, political, social, or historical—in "reading" that music as a revelatory text. When people bemoan music criticism, they echo complaints about the critical enterprise more generally within the arts and culture, often deplored as superfluous at best, parasitic on or caustic to it at worst. Views such as these have special potency when they combine with the belief that criticism primarily fills a market function, and that critics are little more than mouthpieces for the culture industries. The journalistic critic receives the brunt of this sourness, deemed a mere "reviewer" whose writing more often than not serves as free publicity.[14] Christgau, a career reviewer, even lamented this point when he wrote that "the first tenet of newsroom cynicism is that hard news 'digging' is a more blessed endeavor than feature writing, of which reviewing is the lowliest example."[15]

There is also a strong tradition of championing critics as the independent voices who maintain artistic standards and encourage excellence. From this vantage, Matthew Arnold is criticism's most significant figurehead, who envisioned criticism as an activity that could articulate and promote the culturing effects of the arts. At the extreme of this position is Oscar Wilde, who in the late nineteenth century controversially anointed the critic as an artist in his own right. As the nineteenth century became the twentieth, this commitment to aesthetics developed a more overt social and political mandate, an outgrowth of a flourishing American bohemianism which merged unconventional philosophies, progressive politics, and modernist creativity into a radical if sometimes uneasy coalition. In this union, cultural criticism became the project of "intellectuals": a newly identified caste of people who used critique as a weapon against traditionalism wherever it might be found. The critique of art and society—often both together, and sometimes one in the service of the other—grew across the first three decades of the twentieth century to be a common exercise for the critic-as-intellectual.

Small-circulation "little magazines" such as *Seven Arts,* the *Little Review, The Dial,* and later, *Partisan Review* appeared to house and circulate these ideas, especially around bohemian intellectualism's nucleus of Greenwich Village.

Since the 1980s, a number of prominent scholars have found an ideal in the people and publications practicing criticism during the first half of the last century, with particularly effusive words for intellectuals such as Randolph Bourne, Van Wyck Brooks, Edmund Wilson, and Lewis Mumford. Contemporary scholars cherish and mourn these men for their "outsider" status: in no one's pay, they worked on behalf of truth, aesthetics, and radical political beliefs. In the work of Morris Dickstein, Thomas Bender, Richard Posner, and Russell Jacoby, among others, the professionalization of criticism—and its subsequent sequestering in the university and journalism—undermined the critical sovereignty common during the early twentieth century; laboring within the narrow constrictions of their respective vocations, today's critics exist as toothless, shriveled versions of their earlier selves.[16] In *The Last Intellectuals,* his 1987 book that invigorated the lasting interest (vis-à-vis concern) in "public intellectuals," Jacoby explains:

> Independent intellectuals, who wrote for the educated reader, are dying out; to be sure, often they wrote for small periodicals. Yet these journals participated, if only through hope, in the larger community . . . The contributors viewed themselves as men and women of letters, who sought and prized a sparse prose. They wrote for intellectuals and sympathizers anywhere; small in size, the journals opened out to the world . . . Today, nonacademic intellectuals are an endangered species; industrial development and urban blight have devastated their environment.[17]

Along this line of thinking, the coincidence in the 1950s of massive expansion of the university system, the entrenchment of journalistic objectivity norms, and the dominance of mass culture, particularly television, made public intellectualism—meaningful commentary on social and cultural issues, written for general consumption—a lost art. Notably, then, these charges are often as much about the notion of "the public" as they are about the capacity of intellectualism to reach and affect it. Jacoby contends, for instance, that despite earlier public intellectuals having small audiences, their "sparse prose" and desire to be accessible "out to the world" contrasts sharply with today's academics, content to write in field-specific jargon for tiny subsets of readers. Posner takes this view a step further to claim that intellectuals who do address a large audience are forced to dumb down their ideas.[18]

Two objections to this argument surface immediately—beyond its gross caricature of academic labor. First and foremost is its reification of the idea of the public. Rather than positing an undifferentiated mass existing "out there" to be reached—or, worse, the straw man of Habermas's public sphere—I follow Warner in conceptualizing the public as a "social space created by the reflexive circulation of discourse."[19] A dynamic understanding of the public that places mediation at its center in turn greatly opens up the idea of what counts as a public—particularly important in the realm of culture, where much scholarly work explores the role of social location and interpretation in the reception of cultural production. I will quickly add that those who follow Jacoby are not wrong to desire a wide and diverse readership for thoughtful prose about public issues. But they are mistaken to assume that intellectualism looks and travels as it did in the early twentieth century. This book is aimed to discover one important, though neglected terrain in which publics have indeed come together to consider intellectual concerns.

The second trouble directly follows from this flawed view of publicness. Jacoby spends precious little time thinking about journalistic critics, who by design speak to a larger cohort and must use economical, if not sparse, language to do so. When journalism does appear in this brand of argument—Dickstein's 1992 *Double Agent* is a categorical example—it is by and large considered a different exercise, one concerned with "simply information" rather than ideas. Dickstein does contend that journalistic criticism, at its finest, may resemble the "practical criticism" that is "trained in close reading yet also alert to the ambiguities of consumption."[20] But the rub, for Dickstein as well as others who share this view, is the prudential ends which journalism might serve; not just ideas for ideas' sake, but frequently with the motive of drawing attention or heightening publicity, whether deserved or not. That leaves the pure, useful, legible criticism habitual to the "public intellectual" as a relic of the 1950s, and journalists, like academics, too occupied with workaday concerns to fill the void.

In sum, the belief that public intellectualism has been ailing for more than half a century at best selectively understands the manifestations and potentialities of criticism, both as critics of the early 1900s practiced it and as writers have continued it since the mid-twentieth century. Despite occasional efforts to acknowledge contributions journalists make, its caricature of the critical landscape reproduces a false divide between journalism and academia, "true" criticism and "mere" reviewing, which has resulted in a surprising yet long-lasting dearth of scholarly inquiry into journalistic criticism of all kinds. Moreover, still under the sway of mid-century New York intellectuals like Dwight Macdonald, Clement Greenberg, and Hannah Arendt—the very individuals deemed the "last intellectuals," who felt the most threatened by the onslaught of mass culture—it takes a limited view of what criticism should focus on, where it should appear, and who is its likely audience. Such a bind defines away other kinds of criticism as always-already compromised, the stuff of brash commercialism or detached scholarly pontification. Despite coming from a place that is sympathetic to what critics do, it supports the viewpoints of criticism's detractors through a willful unawareness of journalistic criticism, especially that which focuses on something as mass cultural as popular music.[21]

The irony is that as unsustainable and even destructive as this divide may be, it persists because both academics and journalists acquire authority and legitimacy in part from understanding our interests and labor as more divided than they are. Yet, I believe there is more to gain than to lose in thinking seriously about mutual pursuits and aligned legacies. Keeping this in mind, though the term "public intellectualism" is overused and partially evacuated of meaning, I have selected it because it identifies a brand of criticism and challenges all of us to consider what it means to live up to it. To define it as I have, as meaningful commentary on social and cultural issues for a general audience, is to grapple head-on with the complexities of those terms, and to recognize that neither ideas nor intellectuals are born public, but that they must become public—and that the public itself is an exercise in becoming. Moreover, as Townsley astutely notes, the term "public intellectual" is a "figurative use of words, or a cultural shorthand, that holds, contains, and organizes moral tension about intellectuals and politics in the contemporary United States";[22] to apply it in a way capitulates to the troublesome assumptions that gave rise to the debate in the first place. However, I contend that the best way to unfurl the knotty problems of public intellectualism is not to avoid the term, but to see it for what it is: the most recent iteration of intellectuals' ongoing crises of identity, but one which I reclaim as acutely important given the challenges that face journalism, academia, and other knowledge-centric professions. To quote Christopher Lasch, "the intellectuals' own sense of themselves, not simply as individuals involved in a common undertaking, the somewhat hazardous business of criticism, but as members of a beleaguered minority" is a kind of "class consciousness," and accordingly makes the dilemma of intellectual life of particular, persistent concern.[23] I think he is right, but I cite him not to discount the concerns of the aforementioned scholars as so much handwringing, but rather to take seriously the collective interest intellectuals of all stripes have in their own survival. We might also put to use Hollinger's observation that "any population that has left a record of having addressed 'shared questions'"[24] is a worthy object of study for intellectual history, and that some of the most potent questions, for journalists and academic intellectuals alike, are existential.

To begin to explore how popular music criticism began to address its "shared questions," one might look at jazz critics, who started to push popular music writing into thoughtful, politically oriented directions in the 1950s. Ralph J. Gleason was a pioneer of this practice; he wrote about race and jazz and went on to mentor Jann Wenner, founder and publisher of *Rolling Stone*. Leroi Jones/Amiri Baraka and Nat Hentoff, also writing during the 1950s, likewise used jazz music as a starting point for pressing issues of the day, often penning articles that connected the music to ideas about social change, authenticity, and racism.[25] Their writing would be a strong counterpoint to the "mass culture debates" of the 1940s and 1950s that questioned whether the explosion of popular entertainment negatively affected high art and the political and cultural well-being of the general populace. In this way, early jazz critics began the disintegration of the staunch division between high and low culture that rock criticism would complete. There is much more to say about jazz writing (see Gennari's *Blowin' Hot and Cool* for a groundbreaking analysis), but for my purposes here I mention it to recognize that rock music criticism was not the first genre to attempt to merge sociological and humanistic approaches to culture, nor the first to thoughtfully engage with popular music.

Though the rock and roll of the 1950s also was ripe for this kind of commentary, the existing publications that took an interest in popular music generally did not cover it in this fashion. When trade publications such as *Billboard, Cashbox,* or *Variety* turned their gazes toward rock and roll, they tended to focus on revenues and chart placements rather than the content or context of the music itself.[26] Teen magazines—*Hit Parader, Ingenue, Datebook, 16,* and *Song Hits* among them—did take a more active interest in the music's cultural context, even though they did so through reprinting press releases, photos, and lyrics to the most popular tunes in a fashion that writer and Lester Bangs biographer Jim DeRogatis described as "very little 'real' journalism and absolutely no criticism."[27] (Though my argument in these pages will be elsewhere directed, I would like to qualify any blanket dismissal of the teen books. Read charitably, these magazines engaged their primarily young and female readerships with the burgeoning rock and roll culture, establishing celebrity gossip as its own form of critique. After all, it was teen magazine *Datebook* that in 1966 reprinted the now infamous *London Evening Standard* interview where John Lennon proclaimed "we're more popular than Jesus"[28]—after which the band became an object of controversy and public scorn. I take an interest in other journalistic approaches to the rock of the 1960s, but I strongly believe that this celebrity-oriented perspective, epitomized by a powerful cast of female writers and editors such as Gloria Stavers, Lillian Roxon, and Lisa Robinson, deserves an independent analysis for what it gave to the history of rock music as an object of popular fascination and cultural study.[29])

The sort of rock criticism on which I focus in this book contrasts in a different way with the negative attention rock and roll began to receive during the 1950s and early 1960s. Chuck Berry, Bo Diddley, Elvis Presley, and other rock and rollers of the initial wave of popularity received racist and moralistic ridicule and censure from community groups, government officials, radio DJs, and other genres of musicians, on account of their music's lyrical content, sexual overtones, and sounds. Journalists not only picked up on these stories of moral panic as they unfolded; they also instigated further disparagement of rock and roll through antagonistic framing, which continued as rock and roll transformed into rock music.[30] While to a certain extent this rebellious coding factored into rock's (and by extension, rock criticism's) ideological underpinnings, rejecting the overwhelmingly negative view of the music—not to mention considering it something positive—was oppositional in itself.

Counterhegemonic attitudes began to proliferate publicly in the early to mid-1960s, as folk-rock hybrids and British Invasion bands soared to immense popularity. In the United Kingdom, the Beatles inspired *Melody Maker*, a well-established English trade paper, to take a critical interest in their music.[31] As the band traveled to the other side of the Atlantic, rock writing followed, but U.S. writing differed greatly from and largely ignored its U.K. counterpart. Keenly interested in the relationship between rock music and the wider American culture, U.S.-based writing was notably anti-establishment, its practitioners generally untrained and its home often in new publications expressly founded for this practice. The major exception to this is Jane Scott, a middle-aged journalist who wrote for the teen page of the *Cleveland Plain Dealer*, and whom some affectionately refer to as the "mother" of rock criticism, for the protective, nourishing role she played both in reviewing rock and toward rock artists themselves.

Scott began writing for the *Plain Dealer* in 1964. Two years later, in January 1966, a college freshman named Paul Williams mimeographed and distributed 500 copies of *Crawdaddy!*, a publication which prided itself on its "intelligent writing about pop music."[32] By the end of 1967, the magazine that began with a $40 investment enjoyed a circulation of 20,000, and printed the words of young writers who would soon become recognized names in rock criticism, such as Richard Meltzer, Ed Ward, Sandy Pearlman, and Jon Landau. As one commenter noted, "*Crawdaddy!*'s writers clearly defined the notion (and legitimized it in the process) that rock writing, to be accepted by the young audience, would have to be done by young people, working without an established framework or structure."[33] *Crawdaddy!* also reinterpreted the act of fandom, diverging from celebrity obsession per se or vulgar sales predictions and toward musical and personal reflection.[34] As Williams noted in the first issue,

> The aim of this magazine is readability. We are trying to appeal to people interested in rock 'n' roll, both professionally and casually. If we could predict the exact amount of sales of each record we heard, it would not interest us to do so. If we could somehow pat every single pop artist on the back in a manner calculated to please him and his fans, we would not bother. What we want to do is write reviews and articles that you will not want to put down, and produce a magazine that you will read thoroughly every week.[35]

This spirit, a mélange of DIY can-do and earnest appraisal, kindled within twenty-one-year-old Jann Wenner as well, inspiring him to begin *Rolling Stone* out of San Francisco during the fall of 1967. Intending the magazine to be "not just about music, but also about the things and attitudes that the music embraces,"[36] Wenner explained to the readers of the first issue: "We have begun a new publication reflecting what we see are the changes in rock and roll and the changes related to rock and roll. Because the trade papers have become so inaccurate and irrelevant, and because the fan magazines are an anachronism, fashioned in the mold of myth and nonsense, we hope that we have something here for artists and the industry, and every person who 'believes in the magic that can set you free.' "[37]

Fully ensconced in its West Coast environs—which meant not only an embrace of its native San Francisco psychedelic scene but also some distancing from the kind of music and writing emerging on the East Coast—*Rolling Stone* not only thoughtfully engaged with the entirety of rock culture but also presided over determining its parameters. "Quite correctly, the employees of *Rolling Stone* saw themselves as leaders and tastemakers,"[38] noted chronicler Robert Draper, and because of this, the decisions made by *Rolling Stone* had significant impact on the music business and the artists within it. With a circulation that topped 100,000 in just two years, *Rolling Stone* also confirmed that publications centered around rock music could be not only useful promotional tools or smart sites for advertising but eventually lucrative as well.[39]

Like *Crawdaddy!*, *Rolling Stone* also made names of a number of its early contributors, including Greil Marcus, Hunter S. Thompson, and the aforementioned Landau, whose tenure at *Rolling Stone* elevated him into one of the country's most influential critics. *Rolling Stone* housed long-form journalism that allowed writers creative license, but unlike some of his more underground peers, Wenner wielded a much more forceful editorial hand. Ellen Willis later dubbed this the "San Francisco 'rock-as-art' orthodoxy,"[40] which played out not only in the magazine's prejudices but also in how freely writers could express their opinions. (An often recounted instance of this is when Lester Bangs, today one of the most lauded and imitated rock critics, was banned from the magazine in the early '70s for reviews that Wenner considered insolent.[41]) The magazine also marginalized women and people of color in both its staff and its coverage, though there are some notable exceptions, such as Chinese American editor Ben Fong-Torres and lesbian photographer Annie Liebovitz. In the first history of the magazine, published during the late 1980s, Robert Draper noted that *Rolling Stone*'s "reluctance to cover black music is infamous," it had never employed a black writer, and especially in its early years was dominated by a "male oligarchy."[42]

Another key later player in the rock writing scene was *Creem,* which began publishing in Detroit in 1969. Fans flocked to a magazine frequently characterized as irreverent, which was "more reckless"[43] than *Rolling Stone,* embodying the working-class, Detroit-based rock ethos from which it arose. The writers it propelled to stardom—Lester Bangs, Dave Marsh, and Nick Tosches being three of the most celebrated—explored rock with a bombast that was smart but anti-intellectual, "amateurist and faux lowbrow,"[44] positioning themselves between the studious class of New York writers and the deference that came out of San Francisco. But this irreverence often skidded into offense. Though they employed and published a few women writers, such as Robbie Cruger, Georgia Christgau, and Jaan Uhelszki, the magazine was often blatantly, if playfully, sexist; a brazen example was the *Creem* logo itself, known as Boy Howdy. Drawn by Robert Crumb and typical of his overtly sexualized style, Boy Howdy was an old-fashioned milk bottle that, in an iconic cover image, quite literally "*Creem*-ed" its white contents onto the face of a well-endowed, awestruck woman. (Jim DeRogatis dissatisfyingly called the men of *Creem* "no more sexist than their counterparts at other counterculture institutions."[45]) The magazine's racial politics were equally complex. The Detroit from which it emerged still roiled with the violent racial divisions that recent riots had made stark;[46] though the publication identified strongly with the city, publisher Barry Kramer relocated *Creem* to the suburbs in 1971, following the pattern of many white-owned businesses in retreating from the problems of the black inner city. The magazine aligned itself with the anti-racist radicalism of the White Panther Party, yet some of its writers displayed defiantly insensitive and racist attitudes, including flagrant use of racial epithets in their writing.[47] Cover images and staff pictures reveal a magazine that was tremendously white in content and composition and, likely, readership.

The critical style that developed in 1960s New York was decidedly different from those of the aforementioned publications. In a city where dedicated organs for rock criticism had not yet emerged, writers made names for themselves as individual personalities, publishing in the surfeit of local and national publications bent toward the arts and culture but with a wider readership than the rock audience. This lack of a natural habitat allowed a few publications to become places for rock writers to congregate, form communities, and foster relationships and critical approaches. *Cheetah,* a magazine affiliated with a disco of the same name, debuted in 1967 and lasted until 1968; despite its brief life, it published the writing of several figures who would become key persons in the New York rock writers' scene. Another publication was the *East Village Other,* the psychedelically bent underground newspaper Walter Bowart founded in 1965, which grew to be a vital resource for New York's hip community. But one publication arguably had the most long-standing influence for rock writing as an intellectual pursuit.

The Village Voice

Though a mainstay of the music critical community from the 1960s until the present day, the *Village Voice* was an unlikely place for rock criticism to flourish. The paper was far from overtly countercultural—its political leanings firmly democratic and its '50s sensibility, channeled through its beatnik ownership, deeply felt. For other reasons, though, these characteristics made the *Voice* an ideal home. As the country's most well-known alternative weekly and New York City's bohemian diary, the paper "changed the idea of what it was to be a journalist," to quote Louis Menand,[48] cultivating journalistic experimentation, participation, and intellectualism that proved uniquely conducive to the kind of learned rock criticism described in these pages. The paper also played a strong role in defining downtown culture, manifesting the post–World War II sense of "Villageness" not just for its denizens, but also for its readership nation- and worldwide. The *Voice* thus was also central, if only coincidentally so, in defining bohemia as a profitable demographic and serving as an outpost for its taste and beliefs; by the late 1960s its readers were "almost, a *New Yorker* audience in the making," making it "logical to infer that, within a few years, they would reach *New Yorker* status and *New Yorker* affluence."[49]

The *Village Voice* also paved the way for the underground press, a term that captures the upsurge of amateur newspapers that appeared in the mid-1960s to become one of the most noteworthy and influential manifestations of the New Left. As John McMillian writes, the *Voice* "helped to pioneer the kind of offbeat and subversive approaches that youthful journalists of the 1960s mimicked and amplified," while also proving inspirational through its investigative journalism and cultural reporting.[50] Over time, the paper's conventionally liberal politics would give way to news from the frontlines of the Village's (and nation's) culture wars, including landmark reporting on the Stonewall riots, feminism and sexual politics, and the intricacies of New York City government, with bylines from Susan Brownmiller, Pete Hammill, Jack Newfield, Howard Smith, Karen Durbin, and more.[51] But the *Voice,* even in its more radical content, was distinct from the underground press, too. First published about a decade before the hippie underground newspapers, the early *Voice* transmitted a polyglot alternativeness, dedicating itself to transgression in general rather than any ideology in particular. More important, it was financially solvent and was able to pay its writers, albeit meagerly. Though rock writers who contributed there might have felt snubbed at times by their counterparts at more underground or "Movement" publications, especially in the mid-to-late 1960s,[52] the *Voice* eventually came to transmit a sense of edgy legitimacy and earned its writers a prestigious national audience. These differences allowed the paper to emerge as a preeminent "writers'" paper; in an obituary of Ron Plotkin, one of the paper's longtime editors, one *Voice* writer explained, "The *Voice* has always prided itself on being a writers' paper, a place where those with something to say can give unadulterated and often fiery expression to their views without tailoring them to fit a set style or manner. But one of the paper's best-kept secrets is its stable of fine editors, savvy enablers who make sure those expressions are coherent, accurate, and at least roughly on point."[53]

That blend of strong writing and careful grooming came to manifest itself clearly in the paper's music journalism. In that area alone, the *Voice* can be credited with jumpstarting the career of the country's first newspaper rock scholar-critic and its most famous (Richard Goldstein and Robert Christgau respectively) as well as nurturing the development of many of the best known and esteemed music writers in the nation, an assertion that has been true for the majority of the paper's history. On nearly every viable genre of popular music since the mid-1960s—from rock to new classical, from jazz to punk—the *Voice* has been a leader, frequently on the cutting edge of the trend and if not that, at the very least exerting a powerful sense-making that defined, assessed, and in some cases encouraged nascent musical movements. The story of rock music will be recounted in these pages, but hip hop presents a more contemporary case of similar prominence. From prescient pieces about graffiti, B-Boys, and outer borough rappers in the early 1980s, writers for the *Voice* staked a claim to hip hop culture and, in the process, published the work and elevated the careers of some of its most astute observers, particularly black writers such as Joan Morgan, Nelson George, and Greg Tate.

The *Voice* has excelled in many other arenas of cultural criticism—as one anthology noted, "from almost the first issue, the *Voice*'s cultural 'back of the book' pages were strong" and the paper "virtually invented a new kind of cultural criticism."[54] Over the years, the paper cultivated leading critical voices in theater, film, dance, and more, as well as publishing notable poets and trailblazing comics. The full spectrum of the paper's cultural journalism holds numerous stories that await telling. In exploring one of them deeply, I hope to encourage other scholars to mine the depths of what is a surprisingly understudied newspaper.

That said, though the *Voice* itself is central to this story, it will play a supportive role to my main protagonists: Richard Goldstein and Robert Christgau, not only two of the most central and prolific music critics writing in the *Voice* in the mid-'60s and early '70s but also writers who have continued to exert influence on subsequent generations of music scribes. Several other contributors to the *Voice* through the long sixties period will help to demonstrate the paper's wider critical scope. Folk writers, often slighted or downright ignored in discussions of rock criticism, find a place here as trailblazers who helped to carve a niche in which rock criticism could gestate. This book also supplies the first academic treatment of the writing of Carman Moore, a classical and rock music critic who, in the spirit of Billboard Jackson, was a black writer working within an overwhelmingly white terrain.

That this book's primary subjects, Goldstein and Christgau, are both white, male, working-class college graduates reflects the historical circumstances as well as the norms that, ever since, have been deeply entrenched in the critical profession. As Left young adults of the 1960s, they had an awareness of and sensitivity to race, gender, and class politics that far surpassed the average, yet these identifying characteristics, and the discriminatory historical circumstances during which they began working, produced ways of seeing and modes of access that others simply could not have enjoyed. In a recent conversation with me, Goldstein relayed that much of the kinship he felt with artists stemmed from the similarities of their backgrounds, and this is a profoundly true observation; could rock criticism have emerged, in the manner that it did, were it not for the privileges these commonalities afforded? Yet as important as it is to bear these truths in mind, I find it equally important not to let them rule. Not only were factors other than gender, race, or class coloring their critical visions—for Goldstein, who later came out as gay, the repressive circumstances surrounding homosexuality are an obvious one—but also because letting them rule only takes us so far. Correcting the past is not possible, but learning from it is—not only what might not have been probable but also what they made possible.

Writing the Record

While the particularities that make rock criticism at the *Voice* a unique endeavor need to be named, this book contains much which can be generalized. The most important, and perhaps most obvious of these factors, is the simple fact that rock critics wrote about popular music. From a contemporary vantage, where respected writers parse cultural minutiae ad nauseam, it is difficult to imagine just how remarkable writing seriously about pop music could seem. For young people who were accustomed to hearing their music characterized as devilish, shoddy, stupid, and ephemeral, positive writing validated their experience: rock music excited their fandom *and* ignited their minds. Like the jazz critics before them, these budding rock writers situated their commentary within the social movements that surrounded them. Unlike jazz critics, they considered themselves to be foot soldiers, members of the very generation that played the music and called for social change. Their position as insiders, participants as well as observers, became an inextricable prism through which to view the music scene, as well as a kind of expertise. The tumult of the 1960s gave context as well as rise to these changes, signaling to rock writers that they were on the front lines of a revolution.

Rock writers, no matter where they wrote, found themselves confronted with the conflicts and contradictions of their era, too. What attracted them to music in the first place—its position as a potent cultural, political, economic, and social force—would also impinge on their understanding of music, and eventually on the practice of criticism itself. As criticism matured, both as an industry and as an intellectual activity, critics would be forced to grapple with their relationship to their publics, oftentimes through the prism of their own racial, gender, generational, and class identities. Moreover, to turn a love for music into a job would require a professionalization all its own that for some devalued the act of criticism itself—a dynamic that has repeated itself over and over in the genesis of many genres of new media in the last fifty years.

The title of this book, *Writing the Record,* is perhaps an obvious play on words, but it should signal two things. First, it is a reminder that rock critics wrote often, though not exclusively, about records, and we appreciate how the medium enabled thoughtful listening as it generated stockpiles of musical artifacts. Records, in this sense, *are* history, and rock critics acted, sometimes unknowingly, as custodians of that history. It follows, second, that rock criticism itself is a kind of record, evidence of a public conversation that helped to define the place of rock music in history as much as in its contemporary social life. When we laud the music of the '60s today, compare bands to their musical predecessors, or enjoy genre revivals, we are experiencing firsthand the resonances of early rock criticism in our own time. When we read commentary that dissects the political content of lyrics or that praises pop stars for coming out, we are not just coming to a better understanding of our own time—we are also participating in a tradition that early critics launched, when they insisted that this music needed to be part of a larger cultural conversation, and that their words could help it resonate beyond the confines of the music itself.

The next chapter begins to situate this intervention by examining the *Voice*'s early history and its first forays into popular music writing, on the folk revival. Within the context of New York's wider publishing market, where initially the *Voice* had to justify its existence, the paper's founders faced the challenge of melding bohemianism and capitalism into a publication that would be both viable and credible. I argue that in this effort, they produced a space for independent intellectual production in the midst of rampant journalistic professionalization—an environment that played an intimate role in determining what popular music writing would be, and why. The early music writing about folk shows how music played a crucial role in negotiating this equilibrium between the competing interests and audiences for the paper.

Chapter 2 examines the basic template for popular music writing that Richard Goldstein would establish in his music-focused column, Pop Eye. As the first pop critic in the United States with a regular column devoted to rock, he presented a theory as well as a practice of pop that took neo-Freudianism, New Journalism, and Pop Art as its referents. Goldstein's music criticism was an ongoing argument against the mass culture critique, highlighting how significant, revolutionary, and thoughtful writing about mass media could be. Yet the difficulties of pop-as-praxis would appear almost immediately, calling into question the possibilities of the ideal critical project Goldstein had set out to erect. Chapter 3 explores this quick and devastating disappointment, fueled by the rise of a full-fledged business around rock music and coinciding with the tragedies that overwhelmed progressive politics. This chapter argues that rock critics contended—sometimes naively—with the relationship between journalism and its subject matter, in the process developing a notion of "hype" that continues to influence how we think about cultural circulation, popularity, and authenticity.

Chapter 4 explores how critics reacted to the fundamental distrust of the music business that commercialization wrought. With Goldstein despondent over the state of criticism in the late 1960s, a more diverse cast of critics entered the ranks at the *Voice* and used their own identities as a solution to the problem of how to write about rock in a more commercialized landscape. I argue that in transitioning from a focus on the universal rock audience to one that addressed individual niches and consumers, critics helped to put to rest the myth of a solitary, unified rock audience, even as they frequently mourned the passage of that myth. The concluding chapter follows these concerns into the contemporary context, as new media, fragmentation, and a confluence of social dynamics threaten the social function as well as economic solvency of criticism, and reflects on both the challenges and the opportunities inherent in thinking about music criticism as a public intellectual project.

The writers at the *Voice* put forward a new iteration of the old concept of an intellectual. It was a concept wedded to transformative ideas and avant-garde culture, yet one also comfortable with capitalism and sympathetic to mass art. It was the voice of a young vanguard out to change the status quo, yet one also bringing established sensibilities into a new cultural terrain. It was one caught up in new media, in a way that threatened an older generation. Most important, it was one driven by a feverish love of music—a love that in the end would participate in fundamentally changing the object of its desire, and perhaps not entirely for good. For critics, regardless of medium or profession, of the past and our own time, it would seem that this is an inevitable fate, the taunting consequence with which engaged criticism of music must always cope.

A quick word about terminology: Though I often use the words "rock" and "pop" interchangeably in this work, there is a somewhat contentious debate among critics over what the use of one or another reflects about their critical perspective and identity; some of this can be traced back to the stance toward commercial culture laden in the notion of 1960s pop, which I discuss in depth in chapter 2. But rock, as both a word and a genre, often dominated critics' self-identification during the period under intense scrutiny here. It too was a term up for grabs, and it would be years before the exclusionary assumptions it now suggests—namely, guitar-driven music dominated by white men—would become inextricably lodged in it. While it is true that early rock critics are in some ways responsible for advancing this myopic view of rock (a theme I explore in chapter 4), my use of the term here is less a gauntlet in the name of rockism than an attempt at historical accuracy. I will use the conclusion to explore the ramifications of this accuracy in greater detail.

CHAPTER 1
Village

On October 30, 1955, the *New York Times* announced to the rest of the city word of a new downtown newspaper. Called the *Village Voice,* it printed its first issue on October 26 and sold for five cents every Wednesday at Lower Manhattan vendors. Editor Dan Wolf and publisher Ed Fancher intended to make their paper Village-centric not just in distribution. Localism also governed its choice of writers—as Wolf put it, the neighborhood teemed with "so many capable people who are ready and willing to contribute."[1]

Times columnist Harvey Breit used that day's installment of In and Out of Books to focus additional attention toward the renaissance afoot in Lower Manhattan, suggesting that "apparently things are beginning to stir again in Greenwich Village, that antique site of all sorts of creative experimentation."[2] Though things certainly had changed since the turn of the century when, Breit wistfully reminisced, "writers and painters and musicians somehow managed without jobs," the latter-day bohemia of the city's contemporary Village "has shown it isn't altogether moribund." Some evidence: a series at the New School dedicated to celebrating the Village's art scene; a new edited collection of writings from neo-bohemian writers; and the launch of the *Village Voice.*

That the Village already had a newspaper, however, tunes these laudations to a slightly different key. Siblings Walter and Isabel Bryan founded *The Villager* in 1933, and they served as publishers until their deaths in 1941 and 1957 respectively.[3] The weekly paper reported on neighborhood happenings and personalities, including event announcements, births, concerts, and recipes, and commanded a respectable circulation and advertising base. At the same time, *The Villager* was adamantly neither of nor for the eccentrics of the Village. Walter Bryan made this clear during his lifetime, when he proclaimed, "Many people . . . have the stubborn conviction that the Village is a Bohemian community. Well, it isn't."[4] The *New York Times* once described the paper as "small-townish," noting that its "star reporter and columnist" was a cat named Scoopy.[5] The paper not only boasted its unsophisticated leanings but likewise put forward a sanitized version of the Village, editing it both literally and figuratively. Noted the *Times*, "To the best of its ability, *The Villager* stays out of political squabbles, fastidiously skirts murder and scandalous doings, prints birthday wishes, Village booster stories and names, names, names"—thus staying true to its motto to reflect "the treasured traditions of this cherished community."[6]

Given this context, the *Voice* was not just a new community paper, another bud in a blooming cultural efflorescence. Nor was it simply a milestone in the "proto-underground"[7]—a concept some historians have used to situate the newspaper as a more moderate antecedent to the radical underground press that appeared during the next decade. Rather, the *Voice* both recognized and fostered the Village's emboldening bohemian community and in the process played a key role in enlarging the Village's conceptual borders. Along the way, the paper instantiated a vastly re-imagined vision of what journalism could be, and this new view would prove critical to the establishment of rock criticism and a wide range of freewheeling journalistic endeavors that would follow in its footsteps.

The *Voice* would need to earn and even create this position, however, rather than simply occupy it. This was a feat that would require not just balance, but a balancing act: of the Village's bohemian myth and its multicultural reality; of the paper's proletarian beginnings and capitalistic aspirations; of the time period's conservative veneer yet radical underbelly. Despite the paper's homegrown beginnings, the staff of the *Village Voice* would need to *enter* this terrain, making decisions on how to negotiate these and other forces that were often divergent, if not at odds. The paper's cultural journalism made these dynamics particularly evident, as a site where alternative cultural forms became standard topics for reportage and commentary—though not without contention, as revealed in its early forays into folk music, discussed at the end of this chapter. In this sense, the story I tell here is an insight into how media can go beyond representing or inspiring community to the fractious process of actually creating it.[8] This difficult work proved critical in the establishment of an intellectual, community-interested, radical cultural form such as rock criticism.

Bohemia and Its Discontents

During the late 1940s and early 1950s, New York City in general and Greenwich Village in particular held a special place in the imagination of America's dissident subculture. The repressions of the time, though often stereotyped, still are useful as an element of the explanation. But if certain confinements pushed people out of other spaces, the promise of freedom pulled them to this one. "New York had no real rival for youth who wanted to be at the creative—and creating—center of the American dream," wrote journalist and 1950s New York resident Dan Wakefield in a collective memoir about his youthful days in the city.[9] Such a statement is inextricable from wistful nostalgia, and that is precisely the point: it is the best evidence that New York City, both at the time and to a reflective gaze, was awash with intrigue and legend.

Much of this appeal took root in the Village, long one of the city's most storied neighborhoods. Beginning in the early twentieth century, Greenwich Village emerged into one of the main laboratories for American bohemianism, alive with literary radicalism, social progressivism, cultural experimentation, and intellectualism. Writing—and, more specifically, its mediation in print—provided a context for the articulation of these ideas and their broadcast to curious readers. In addition to plays, prose, and poems written in and about the Village, short-lived, small-circulation "little magazines" of literary and cultural criticism shaped the neighborhood's radical praxis and created communities of likeminded readers. Through these media, the Village became more than just a physical space; it had also developed into concept: an "imagined community," to borrow Benedict Anderson's oft-used phrase, bonded through a set of ideas as well as through geographic boundaries. In those pages, an alluring vision of the Village—as it was and, perhaps more important, as it could be—began to solidify, providing sustenance not only to the Village denizens seeking to establish an identity but also to those who would learn about the Village at a distance of space or time.[10]

Mid-century bohemians stressed over whether the Village still cultivated the kinds of creative dissonance so fundamental to its ken. This was an old worry: as early as 1916, residents lamented that the neighborhood was losing its freedom and charms. Yet as latter-day bohemian intellectuals saw stark contrast between the real and idealized Village, these concerns gained new traction. Writer Milton Klonsky's "Greenwich Village: Decline and Fall," originally published in 1948 and reprinted in the 1955 volume *The Scene Before You: A New Approach to American Culture*, resurrected the age-old bohemian grievance in this mid-century context. Klonsky surmised that while nearly everyone living in Greenwich Village came "to escape from the stunning heat and light and noise of the cultural mill grinding out the mass values of a commercial civilization," the truth was that "the good old days when nobody had a job and nobody cared were over."[11] Klonsky's writing resonated with the longtime fear of loss of the Village spirit, not to mention worries about conformism and technocracy that plagued the period in question—an obsession that existed on the coasts as well as in the heartland, among the middle class as well as the bohemians.[12]

The recurrent "death" of the Village cannot be extricated from anxieties about how the hegemony of mass culture and, in turn, the encroachment of the market in general would alter creative production. These too were long-standing concerns. Artists and writers stood in complex and versatile relationship to the economics of their activity, publicly damning the strangulating effects of rapid industrialization and mass culture while at the same time benefiting from the latter's tools, fashioning themselves into progressive cultural revisionists in ways that not only became the essence of early modernism but also secured their mythic celebrity.[13] Still, the romance of this period—to wit, Klonsky's "good old days"—remained (and remains) powerful, especially for the way creativity seemed to swell unencumbered by the stringencies of the economy and the banalities of everyday existence.

Yet the irony is that while these widespread charges of rampant conformity, soulless capitalism, and hollow culture darkened the mood of both oppositional politics and culture during the 1950s, they also gave rise to iconoclastic styles of dissent that exteriorized a sense of possibility for those seeking an alternative to the mainstream. Perhaps no group exemplified this more than the Beats, a literary movement beginning to take root in New York City that would find allies in the Village. Though it would take an additional decade for their writing to reach the height of its popularity, authors such as Jack Kerouac, Allen Ginsberg, William Burroughs, and Neal Cassaday began their quest for a "New Vision" in the late 1940s, when they congregated at and around Columbia University on New York's Upper West Side. These men and their circle of friends philosophized that society was rapidly in decline; the key to expanded consciousness under such dire circumstances was uber-realism that championed all experience, even the most base, and unfiltered artistic expression.[14] While their circle was small, they saw their malaise as widespread, affecting everyone who was their age—and from this generalization comes the phrase "beat generation." A November 1952 *New York Times* article by Clellon Holmes sought to rationalize, if not promote, their credo:

[Beats] have an instinctive individuality, needing no bohemianism or imposed eccentricity to express it. Brought up during the collective bad circumstances of a dreary depression, weaned during the collective uprooting of a global war, they distrust collectivity . . . Their own lust for freedom, and their ability to live at a pace that kills, to which war had adjusted them, lead to black markets, bebop, narcotics, sexual promiscuity, hucksterism and Jean-Paul Sartre.[15]

Besides Harlem, the Village was the neighborhood in New York most welcoming of these transgressions. The movement's main players actually lived in the Village only intermittently throughout the 1950s; however, its fiery life force made the neighborhood a home away from home.[16] According to historian Barry Miles, central Beat figures frequently traveled from uptown down to the Village for "the same artistic and tolerant atmosphere they imagined had existed on the Left Bank before the war."[17] To the many who eventually took up the manifesto's charge, Beatness was as confrontational as it was descriptive; not only had youth changed their views on their peers and society in general but they also modified what corridors of life were relevant stores of inspiration, meaning, and spirit. As proof of their success or perhaps a warning about it, Beat sensibilities held wide appeal especially to younger people, with the movement's main figures becoming noteworthy to the wider culture precisely because of their damnation of it.

The Beats loom large to a retrospective gaze on Village life focusing on writing, but they are significant also because their doomsday renaissance fit within a wider swath of cultural experimentation happening in the Village at the time. As among the Beats, many of the era's artists participated in movements that questioned how to exist, create, and rebel given the perils of modern society, as well as how to profit from art while maintaining integrity. The Village-based movement of Abstract Expressionist painting, for instance, fits a pattern exhibited in many other arts. Neighborhood artists such as Jackson Pollock, Willem de Kooning, and Mark Rothko began to receive attention and acclaim over the course of World War II and after for their rabidly individualistic artworks that defied conventional representational codes. It was also during this time that interrelated domains of galleries, museums, dealers and buyers, and critics known collectively as the "art world" came into existence—a development that would place New York clearly at the center of the global art trade. As artists tried to fight absorption into the conformist stresses of the 1950s, a new system evolved to accommodate and even praise their disobedience.[18] This came to include even the mainstream organs such as *Life* magazine, which approvingly covered Abstract Expressionism.[19]

Jazz and classical musicians also wanted to break free of artistic containments. In the late 1940s, progressive jazz instrumentalists such as Charlie

Parker and Thelonious Monk evolved the bop style and played it in jazz clubs in the Village, Harlem, and Midtown.[20] This turn away from swing, popular music, and dancing and toward contemplative listening was an effort on the part of jazz musicians to render their music high culture, an act closely entwined with their identities as black musicians.[21] Critics writing about jazz during this time also joined the modernist bandwagon, writing in the interest of institutionalizing jazz as uniquely American. Jazz was also becoming a global export at this time, which some observers considered especially effective American propaganda.[22] Jazz thus offered a critique of American culture at the same time that it was being institutionalized as one of its preeminent art forms.

Theater performance also rapidly advanced while facing worries about shrinking creative opportunity. While non-Broadway productions of plays had existed in various forms since earlier in the century, the nature and pace of production markedly changed beginning in 1947 and became known as Off-Broadway in 1952.[23] In this incarnation, new playwrights flocked to theaters in the Village as well as other locations in order to put on their productions for less money.[24] Many of the plays directly grappled with controversial issues of the day, making homosexuality, Puerto Rican migration, and other "impolite" topics fodder for public entertainment. Yet the circumstances which birthed this flowering passed almost as soon as they manifested themselves. In 1949, equity actors were allowed to perform Off-Broadway, which generally improved the acting in the productions. Next, the audiences and critics came, and with them, higher costs. By the mid-1950s, many lamented the disappearance of Off-Broadway's original intention as a place where aspiring playwrights cheaply put on their plays.[25] Off-Off Broadway was started in the late 1950s, by those who felt even Off-Broadway had become too safe.

Finally, publishing itself was a key component of the artistic rebellion. The usual suspects of this media rebellion include *Mad* magazine, the non-commercial comic book cum periodical lauded to this day for planting the seeds of irreverence in the minds of its young readership; *I. F. Stone's Weekly,* a small-circulation but highly influential newsletter of muckraking political journalism that began publication in 1953; and Paul Krassner's satirical *Realist,* begun in 1958. These publications and their kin are often pointed to as harbingers of the radical publishing of the 1960s, whether through their actual challenges to authority or simply the saucy, pro-amateur ethos they helped to engender. The publications also importantly championed an anti-commercial spirit that contextualized and nurtured the New Left of the subsequent decade.[26]

These and other revolutionary cultural movements symbolized the continuing significance of radical creativity and its potency as an instrument of social and political change. In sum, they suggested that the Village's renaissance was real, and worth documenting and celebrating. Yet the aforementioned artist movements struggled with precisely how to keep ahead of the constant threat of stagnancy, whether commercial, cultural, or otherwise. The neighborhood's consistent Janus face—alive *and* moribund, hip *and* square, an impoverishment of its former self *and* raging in a way it never had before—hinted that the *Voice* held the potential both to strengthen and to pervert the Village's culture. Thought of this way, the *Voice* belongs on this list of bold, unconventional, and risky creative ventures emerging out of 1950s New York even if, and precisely because, there was no simple path to respect, success, or legitimacy. As members of the Village scene for years before beginning their venture, founders Dan Wolf and Ed Fancher were both enamored of the local renaissance and thoroughly entrenched in these correlated yet conflicting narratives. The paper they started—an intervention in content and form, discourse and spatiality—tested and testified to these obdurate paradoxes even as it hatched something fresh and novel.

Wolf and Fancher, who hailed from the city's outer orbits, found that the Village lured them as if by gravity. Wolf was born in 1915 on New York City's Upper West Side, the child of a small businessman; after his father's death, his mother raised him and his siblings in moderate poverty.[27] He attended George Washington High School in Manhattan's northernmost neighborhood of Washington Heights and, after graduating, served in the army during World War II. Wolf returned to New York following his tour of duty and began taking classes at the New School under the GI Bill. It was there that he met Edwin Fancher—born in 1925 in Middletown, New York, the son of a man who owned a portion of the town's telephone company. Fancher was studying psychology and was also a veteran, and the two men became fast friends.[28]

Norman Mailer returned to the Village in 1951 in the midst of divorcing his first wife, at which point he reconnected with Dan Wolf, whom he had met in the late 1940s.[29] Mailer had achieved considerable celebrity and wealth thanks to the warm reception of his first novel, 1948's *The Naked and the Dead*, but during the previous spring had published *Barbary Shore*, a critical disaster.[30] During this tumultuous time, Wolf introduced Mailer to the woman who would become his second wife, a Spanish-Peruvian painter named Adele Morales, who coincidentally had been the girlfriend of Ed Fancher in the late 1940s.[31] Wolf quickly became a regular fixture in the life of the new couple; for a time, they even lived next door to one another in the East Village.[32] Wolf also ran in intellectual circles with Mailer, participating in a Sunday salon at the White Horse Tavern that included a number of rising stars in the literary world.[33] So when Wolf and Fancher sought backers for their newspaper venture, their wealthy associate was both a natural and savvy choice. The *Voice* began with a $10,000 investment, $5,000 each from Fancher and Mailer, with Wolf's donation in sweat rather than dollars.[34] From their base in a shabby two-room apartment at 22 Greenwich Avenue, they hired a small staff and went to work.[35]

The *Voice* set its sights on the neighborhood's bohemian occupants and its cultural blooming, simultaneously recognizing and challenging the local mythology. "A lot of people think the Village died 50 years ago," declared Fancher, near the paper's inception. "We don't. Those are the great days, this is the Golden Age."[36] His bold declaration not only named the budding renaissance but also tied the *Voice* to it as its raconteur and champion. An important mission of the new paper would be to highlight the region's unique cultural endeavors and transmit them to their rightful audience—in effect, creating a link between the two and identifying one as the market for the other.[37]

The *Voice* would face questions, though, about how it carried out this mission, particularly in terms of its journalism. Early on, the founders established an open-ended newspaper whose libertarianism struck some readers as confusing. "The editorial policy of *The Village Voice*—or the lack of such a policy—has been a source of some discussion among our friends, and even more so among our enemies," stated the column, entitled "Our Policy (?)" that appeared on November 30, 1955, six issues into the new endeavor. Yet the editors held strongly to the notion that "the *Voice* is not primarily interested in establishing a single journalistic or political program and hewing to it" due to reasons philosophical and even moral. Situated in one of the most diverse neighborhoods of a cosmopolitan city in a multifaceted nation, instead of toeing a party line the editors "believe our real function is to present every divergent view which is ready to use our pages."[38]

This position actively defied mainstream journalistic ideologies as well as the prototypical attitude of the dissident press such as the archetypal left-leaning journal, *Partisan Review*. Opposing "the Columbia School of Journalism rules and regulations" omnipresent during the period, those at the *Voice* believed that their mission was to allow "writers to express themselves" airing "young, new ideas."[39] In turn, the paper established itself as standing against the status quo while fostering a new way of connecting with and speaking to a bohemian audience. To do this, the founders experimented, taking liberties with language, content, and practices that at the time were rare, if not alien, within the journalistic profession. "We told writers to go out and see what's out there, and come back and tell us," Fancher has noted—a simple directive that is more illuminating for what it does not say than for what it says. At the *Voice,* it was often absence—of formal instruction, of rules, of censorship, of editorial "voice"—which conveyed the most powerful sense of what they wanted to bring into being.

The inexperience of both Fancher and Wolf at the paper's inception is the most glaring, most important absence of all. Though both men had worked as writers prior to starting the paper, neither knew much about either running a paper or journalism as a business; only Jerry Tallmer—the associate editor who came on board shortly after the paper began—actually understood what was necessary in terms of day-to-day operations, having worked on his college publication.[40] To establish a paper with so little know-how certainly presented difficulties, but it also gave the new enterprise an edgy credibility. Both feelings are exhibited in the first editorial statement printed in the paper on October 26, 1955:

> A new newspaper is here—and it's a painful business for an editor to write his first editorial. The sense of power that comes with the anonymity of the editorial "we" has not yet taken root. The omniscience, the firm point of view, and the certainty that is so integral a part of the editorial writer's armory is yet to be acquired. But as each must function according to his role, "we" will proceed in the forthcoming issues of the *Village Voice* to tell you what we are learning in this new experience.[41]

In openly displaying their inexperience and calling the editorial "we" a "luxury" it was "painful" to be without, the *Voice* editors advocated transparency, disintegrating the boundary between themselves and their readership. The editorial noted that readers would be let in on "what we are learning in this new experience," which includes the inner workings of the paper as well as the people producing it. Despite their blatancy regarding their inexperience, the editors exhibited a keen understanding of the construction of an editorial vision, and an acuity and openness about their own psychology—not surprising considering that Fancher was a licensed therapist.

Not heeding set standards bolstered the *Voice*'s unprofessionalism, and the editors increasingly wore it as a badge of honor. Writing in the first edited collection of *Voice* pieces in 1962, Dan Wolf proclaimed "The *Village Voice* was originally conceived as a living, breathing attempt to demolish the notion that one needs to be a professional to accomplish something in a field as purportedly technical as journalism." Doing this, he continued, was "a philosophical position" intended to "jam the gears of creeping automatism."[42] Fancher, in an interview, explained to me that in the mid-1950s he and Wolf were "bored to death with professionalism," and believed that "anybody who's been to journalism school [was] already ruined."[43] The founders clearly had come to understand their endeavor as a thoughtful re-imagining of the state of journalism—and through it, society at large—rather than a recreational attempt at creating a successful paper. Yet at the same time, they created this "jamming of gears" through selectively stepping away from traditional standards rather than expressing alternatives in every case. In this fertile soil, new ideas and critical interventions first sprouted, then thrived.

Though financial difficulties continued to dog the paper until the early 1960s, on April 18, 1956, a confident editorial memorialized their early successes. "Wisdom should have made us cautious six months ago," they wrote, "But we wanted to know if there was room for individual enterprise in a field where it was disappearing fast." Here, they declared the *Voice* a "ruggedly individualistic journal unhampered by surveys and statistics, a paper where people could speak to people in a community that is one of the most vital and knowledgeable in the world." In creating such a paper, what the editors "really sought to find out six months ago was if there was any room for the freest of free enterprise, or if caution was the only watchword of the day," and "With 26 issues behind us we have our answer."[44]

Despite these allowances and transgressions, however, the *Voice* at best displayed a qualified radicalism whose systems of checks and balances kept it from straying too far into radical terrain. Chief among these were its commercial aspirations. Whereas past radical journalism in the Village had often at least loosely associated itself with communism, the *Village Voice* followed a capitalistic business model, dependent upon circulation and advertising from local businesses in order to stay afloat. Though it took years to reach financial stability, this characteristic nonetheless resembled traditional newspapers more than it did alternative publications. Another feature that helped to temper the *Voice* was its advocacy of the exchange of ideas rather than the adoption of any one of them. For the writers who would find the *Voice* to be a platform willing to publish their work on their terms, such noncommittal politics—or in some cases, conflicting politics—could be deeply unsatisfying.

The parameters of this qualified radicalism can be clearly seen in the very public break Wolf and Fancher made with Norman Mailer in 1956. Beginning in January, Mailer wrote a column that was the paper's most noted, if controversial, feature, variously called Quickly: A Column for Slow Readers and The Hip and the Square. He used the column for antagonistic ruminations, often generating more letters, and more negative responses, than any other article in the paper. After one of his columns featured a typo, Mailer got into a heated argument with Dan Wolf and claimed the mistake was intentional. On May 2, 1956, in a column that announced itself as his last, Mailer wrote that the root cause of the break between him and the editors was not the typo itself, but the divergent visions he and the other founders held. "They wish this newspaper to be more conservative, more Square—I wish it to be more Hip," Mailer wrote, after explaining the week previously that hip encompassed the mode of existence found "in the Negro and the soldier, in the criminal sociopath and the dope addict and jazz musician, in the prostitute, in the actor, in the marriage of the call-girl and the psychoanalyst."[45] Although many years later Fancher would claim that he and Wolf had no problem with Mailer's cantankerous tendencies and disagreed that their vision of the paper was ultimately a conservative one, he did note that the fundamental break came because Mailer "wanted the paper to be absolutely outrageous and go out in a burst of glory and go down the tubes . . . and Dan and I wanted to save the paper."[46] Even in its most contrarian posture, the *Voice* aimed to be a commercial success; the editors would clearly make some compromises in order to achieve this, speaking once again to the mottle of binaries that beset the Village and the *Voice* within it.

The editorial statements showed the philosophical and intellectual motivations for what would actually appear in print in the paper. The last crucial point on which the *Voice* stood apart from journalistic conventions, then, was the content of the paper itself and its mode of presentation. Though in many ways the paper resembled a conventional tabloid, including front page news with large pictures, the layouts would often vary from week to week and the criteria that determined front page news varied. As often as not, an announcement or cultural story—about a lecture series at the New School or a notable play—would grace the front page as prominently as a straight "news" story, such as the long-running campaign in the late 1950s and early 1960s against Robert Moses's plan to run a road through Washington Square Park. Additionally, because the editors generally did not abridge their writers' contributions, the physical layout of the paper was considerably more haphazard than a mainstream publication's. For instance, stories often jumped once or even twice between pages, only to continue on the new page for a few lines.

The writing style and the content, as outgrowth of its neighborhood context, documented the paper's open, experimental philosophy. The *Voice* encouraged its writers to observe and create, allowing stories and beats to emerge rather than be imposed from above. Dan Wolf quickly earned a reputation as a deft, idiosyncratic editor-in-chief, more bent on editing "consciousness and character than . . . copy."[47] This technique aspired to shift writers' attitudes rather than change their writing, assuming the former was a better method of getting reporting that was both good and honest. According to Richard Goldstein, "they would kind of psychoanalyze you . . . they would say these cryptic things, and you would go 'whoa!' like it was really an insight into you."[48] From there, the copy itself went unchanged into the paper, even if typesetters had to accommodate copious length. In allowing its writers to write as they wished with the trust that their words would go into print as they had submitted them, the *Voice* gained a reputation as a preeminent writer's paper. Beats, Abstract Expressionists, and bop musicians had pushed the boundaries of their respective forms, and the *Village Voice* was the journalistic counterpart, allowing freer, more participatory expression. Journalistic openness of this ilk was not yet named New Journalism, but the *Voice* quickly became an important ground for its growth.

To be sure, "new" stylistic shifts in journalism were taking place in other publications around the city. An early harbinger was the *New Yorker,* founded in 1925, which in 1946 published John Hersey's now legendary "Hiroshima." Spanning an entire issue, the wrenching narrative of the effects of the atom bomb used literary tools such as novel-like characterization and visceral descriptive language to capture the cataclysm that mankind had witnessed.[49] Stories like this helped the *New Yorker* raise its profile, making it the upper crust reader's go-to publication for quality writing. In a similar vein, the men's magazine *Esquire,* launched in 1933, built a large and influential male audience during its first twenty years and, in the mid to late 1950s, entered a period of particular creativity.[50] It too would open doors for journalistic innovations, allowing writers the space and province to write at greater length, more creatively, and differently than they might in more traditional newspapers and magazines. In the realm of newspapers, a peer to the *Voice* was *New York,* the Sunday supplement of the *New York Herald Tribune* started 1963 and eventually spun off into its own magazine in 1968. In years to come, these publications would jockey for New York and national influence as well as for writers, with *New York,* the *New York Times,* and other publications well known for poaching writers from their downtown rival.[51]

Yet unlike its uptown competitors, the *Voice* placed capital on creative journalistic license that actively fostered a participatory relationship between reporter and subject matter. Less detached analysts than participant observers, *Voice* reporters wrote from a place of knowledge and insight that located them in the thick of their subject matter. As Villagers writing in and about their Village, they had an investment in neighborhood struggles that often shone through their stories. The aforementioned *Voice* campaign to help defend Washington Square Park from traffic is a case in point; as Aurora Wallace argues, through it "the *Village Voice* proved that it could rally its readers and prevail, even when fighting City Hall."[52] This is one way that this kind of journalism was more than just a shift in style; it also embodied politics, changing the meaning of objectivity, information, reporting, and truth.[53]

Cultural reporting was no exception. The unique culture of the Village, and the *Voice*'s close relationship with it, became one of the key wedges that the *Voice* would leverage within the constellation of publications with which it was competing and conversing. Early editorial statements also foreground the importance of culture to its goals; the *Voice* editors would bring to light the Village's indigenous culture, at the time underreported within the mainstream press and sometimes chastised from more niche publications. From its earliest days, the paper covered a wide mix of arts, including books, theater, dance, film, visual art, and music, which often accounted for more than half of the publication's total pages. Cultural reporting was generally reserved to the "back of the book" section, usually in the form of reviews or criticism, though such coverage sometimes made it to the earlier news pages as well. For many readers, it was here that the paper truly came to life.[54]

Gilbert Seldes, famed cultural critic and pop culture enthusiast was recruited in 1956 to write a column called "The Lively Arts," echoing his famous 1927 book, *The Seven Lively Arts*. His column focused mainly on theater and cabaret, but also sometimes discussed television and music. Leighton Kerner, who held a master's in journalism, wrote the classical music section, freelancing for the paper from 1957 before joining the staff in 1961.[55] But alongside these pedigreed writers were younger critics whose credibility arose from their participation in the scenes they covered. Jonas Mekas, who joined the paper in 1958 as a film critic, was a lauded filmmaker and cineaste prior to coming to the *Voice*, starting *Film Culture* magazine in 1955 as well as writing for *Movie Journal*; in addition to being a critic, over the years he worked to establish film cooperatives and movie houses in the city.[56] Mekas's strong penchant for the avant-garde found its ballast in the writer he recruited, Andrew Sarris, who covered more mainstream movies using a learned writing style that influenced film world notables from Roger Ebert to Martin Scorsese.[57] Drama critic Michael Smith also produced experimental theater productions, and Jerry Tallmer, who paid particularly close attention to Off-Broadway, founded the Obie Awards in 1956.[58] Jill Johnston came aboard in 1959 to write about dance, and for a number of years was a highly influential member of the Village dance community.[59] Carman Moore was a composer who turned to writing in order to bring more coverage of the new classical scene into the paper, and eventually he would shift from classical to rock criticism.

These critics not only extended conversations about their topics but also forged relationships between commercial, alternative journalism and underground scenes. In this fertile space, where editors encouraged reporters to test boundaries, new ways of writing emerged that challenged journalistic codes in myriad ways. The work these critics did amounted to more than criticism—it also made possible the serious discussion of undervalued culture in a journalistic environment that was primed for experimentation, novelty, and transgression. Taking a cue from its neighborhood environments, the *Voice* institutionalized Villageness to establish a place for this kind of writing to prosper.

The Village's Folk

A quote from Andy Warhol articulates well what the *Village Voice* stood for in those days:

> South of 14th Street, things were always informal. The *Village Voice* was a community newspaper, then, with a distinct community to cover—a certain number of square blocks in Greenwich Village plus the entire liberal thinking world, from flower boxes on MacDougal Street to pornography in Denmark. The combination of extremely local news with international news worked well for the *Voice* because the Village intellectuals were as interested in what was happening in the world as in what was going on around the corner, and the liberals all over the world were interested in the Village as if it were a second home.[60]

For bohemians living, working, and writing in the Village at this time, the parameters of where true Villageness resided were both in retreat and expanding. With the actual space of the Village under continual threat, bohemianism increasingly evolved into a state of mind that could be transported anywhere, a community that lived out its links metaphysically through mediated connections such as newspapers. Whereas the print culture of the Village once helped to bind those seeking alternative ways of living intimately to the immediate vicinity, the *Village Voice* participated in the full-on broadcast of that space and its ways of being to all corners of the city (and eventually, the nation and the world), while also bringing Villageness from the outside in.

The elasticity of Villageness was not boundless, however; the *Village Voice* had to contend with the history of the Village as a space as well as all the historical and contemporary contradictions that helped to shape it. Though they wanted, as Fancher would state many years later, to be a newspaper "for anybody who was intelligent," those who labored in the name of the *Voice* at the same time magnified a particular way of being. The *Village Voice* would come to represent the values of openness, creative expression, and experimentation that encapsulated what it meant to be a Village bohemian in the 1950s, but it would do this at a cost of truly attending to the Village in all its diversity. Its coverage of culture, and what it meant to deal with that culture seriously, would not be entirely benign.

One realm where this proved particularly acute was folk music. Folk music emerged as an important preamble to the rock music and criticism with which the remainder of this book is concerned; it is also an illustration of how the development of a language for cultural criticism also came to define the neighborhood, its readers, and the paper itself. In its fitful yet ultimately embracing response to folk, the *Voice* likewise demonstrated that being at heart of a new cultural movement does not always translate into being able to readily feel its pulse.

Alongside the other cultural innovations detailed earlier in this chapter, the 1950s also put the country in the midst of a folk revival, as traditional folk music began to dominate college campuses. Over the course of the decade, cities such as New York, Boston/Cambridge, Los Angeles, and San Francisco rapidly gained coffeehouses, clubs, outdoor concerts, and festivals which appealed to students, intellectuals, and others.[61] The first Newport Folk Festival took place in Rhode Island in July 1959, building on the already successful jazz festival established five years earlier. Folk continued to expand into the early 1960s, becoming a major component of the burgeoning student activist movements, especially that of civil rights.[62]

Though folk music had an unmistakable tie to rural and black communities, the music grew hearty roots in New York City and especially in Greenwich Village among white, urban singers; Pete Seeger and Woody Guthrie, two of folk music's best known personalities, called New York home. By the early 1950s, the folk revival came to occupy Washington Square, and Sunday hootenannies, or freeform jam sessions, enlivened the park for hours during much of the year. Later in the decade, clubs and record stores devoted to folk opened in the neighboring streets.[63]

Though a wide range of mainstream publications took an interest in folk music and helped to publicize the scene,[64] as the neighborhood's indigenous newspaper, the *Voice* was in a matchless position to adjudicate folk's impact on its community and potentially to transform it from a mere trend into something more lasting. Folk may be understood as a kind of litmus test, through which the paper would be making a statement about whose paper it was, and to what it would be devoted. Yet from the paper's very first issue, folk music was contentious and tangled, imbricated as much in local politics as local taste.

In a front page story in the paper's first issue, entitled "Music Makers Quit the Square (But Only For the Wintertime)," news editor John Wilcock explored the controversy surrounding the Sunday Washington Square Park hootenannies, which tended to go beyond their permitted time frame and whose crowds and noise had begun to annoy both city officials and the neighborhood's longtime ethnic residents, especially Italians. After an entanglement during which more than a hundred revelers descended upon the Square, the musicians lost their permit to play in the park for the winter season; yet this did little to dampen the presence of folk in the Square as well as in greater Greenwich Village.[65] A full-grown battle was under way as of 1960, with the firmly established folk revival camp regularly testing neighborhood relations and local politics. This was Mailer's hip and square transmogrified, and the controversy would prevent the *Voice* from simply being a neutral observer.

The drawn-out quarrel regarding the impact of folk on the Village's quality of life received heavy coverage in the *Voice* during the paper's first ten years, and among other things it documents the paper's precarious position and shifting allegiances. In the early 1960s, articles exploring the sundry of neighborhood issues—noise complaints, crowd control, license violations by the coffeehouses—were a regular part of the paper, as were reports that detailed how folk fans were responding through protests and demonstrations. The *Voice* thus became the public forum where folk fans and residents alike turned to air their views. But where folkies tended to use the paper to complain to the powers that be,[66] neighborhood Italians were as likely to be disenchanted with the stories themselves as they were the neighborhood happenings. For example, a 1965 article describing the scene on MacDougal Street at night prompted one resident to complain to the paper that, "for a long time you've been taking pot shots at a certain ethnic group because these people were loudest in criticizing the freaks who masquerade as artists and who have disturbed and disrupted their community . . . if the Italo-Americans were as militant and organized as other minority groups, you'd have pickets around your office day and night."[67] The portrayal of neighborhood Italians as the main obstacle to the folk-infused renaissance struck at least some *Voice* readers as patently unfair.

However, in other research on this controversy, I have argued that New York City experienced a moral panic around folk music, though unlike rock and roll it was not because the music itself was deemed immoral; instead, the culture around folk supposedly destroyed civic life.[68] I mention that here because, even though the *Voice* itself did not explicitly side with folk's detractors, that coverage of it appeared in the news portion of the paper for several years before it made the cultural "back of the book" arts section is telling, and indicates the *Voice*'s own attempt at balancing its position in the neighborhood. Unlike film or theater, which clearly counted as "culture" before they counted as "news," folk music had to earn its cultural relevance, mired deeply in neighborhood politicking. This means that while on the one hand, the *Voice* may have angered Village Italians, on the other hand its view of folk as news emphasized folk fans' deviance.

The paper's lack of cultural acceptance of folk is not surprising given the on-again, off-again presence of music generally in its pages. Unlike film and theater reviews, the *Voice*'s music reviews came and went; the music column, which focused on reviews of live performances, would disappear for weeks at a time and then appear regularly for a period only to vanish again. Yet as the '50s drew to a close, the *Village Voice* generally became more infused with music. Advertisements for record shops, turntables, and hi-fis were more numerous in the latter 1950s, and the listings section noted live music events. In those same years, jazz had earned its own regular review column alongside classical music; the *Voice* even sponsored a highly attended jazz concert in February 1957.

But the difficulties of understanding folk as worthwhile culture remained. As folk's impact on local life was ablaze in other portions of the paper, some began to denounce it as an affront to good taste. In February 1960, an article called "The Menace of Folk" allowed music contributor Bob Reisner to vent about the music. "The menace of folk music lies in Gresham's Law, which states that bad money drives out good," he wrote. "The humble, monotonous, skimmed-milk folk song is pushing classical and jazz albums out of homes . . . There are no standards of wit or intelligence or financial income. All you need are some dirty clothes."[69] None of the *Voice*'s own came to folk's defense, but an impassioned letter did arrive from uptown from Bob Shelton, notable *New York Times* critic and folk buff.[70] "There is no more menace of folk music's 'driving classical and jazz albums out of homes' than there is a menace that do-it-yourself carpentry will put an end to Chippendale or Swedish modern," Shelton countered. "For a host of wholesome reasons, people are re-discovering and communicating pleasure in making music for themselves."[71]

It took another full year after this spat for the paper to print neutral or favorable coverage on the aesthetics of folk music, suggesting that the context in which to think about this music as culture, including having an appropriate reporter, had not yet emerged. Folk reviews did not appear regularly until 1962, and J. R. Goddard, the paper's resident folk fan, usually authored them. Initially, Goddard applied the formula used for discussing classical music, heavily interested in the music's technical expertise and with little by way of advocacy one way or another. For instance, the premiere album review noted that Dave Van Ronk performed "powerful, gravelly voiced interpretations of Southern ballads and blues";[72] in the September 14 issue of the same year, a review of *Ewan MacColl Sings British Industrial Ballads* gave a nod to the album's political content by noting that the album offered "a realistic view of 19th century working class life" and told "stories of strike and strife."[73] Reviewing folk may have been a forward-thinking move for the *Voice,* but it still discussed it using methods left over from previous musical genres.

The debut of Bob Dylan's eponymous first record brought about an instant change to this tepid, matter-of-fact approach to writing. "Right off the bat, this reviewer has to say that the record seems to be one of the best to come from the boiling folk pot in a long, long time," Goddard wrote in his April 26, 1962 review, which was also considerably longer than his usual offerings. He continued to say that "Dylan is blessed with a gift of style—individual, dynamic STYLE!" (emphasis in original) and dubbed the record a "collector's item already."[74] Though it is of note that such passion emerged in reference to Dylan, more monumental is the shift toward writing about music using individual observation, taste, and advocacy, rather than standards of proficiency and musical execution. The terms for evaluating Dylan were new, subjective, enthusiastic, personal: in short, they were participatory, and emerged from a particular sensibility rather than any attempt at an objective cultural stance. The consecration of Dylan also implies that the *Voice* had begun to side more assertively with the hip community that was wild over folk and, in turn, aggravating their neighbors. This warming to folk as music, rather than as local politics, happened at the same time that the problem of folk remained unresolved elsewhere in the paper. Yet the paper's deep involvement in the minutia of folk's presence within the community was a step it needed to endure in order to accept and advocate for folk in less overtly political ways. Still, at the same time, this acceptance was a political choice that erased any semblance of neutrality from the news stories centering on the local politics of folk. Dylan in this sense was an opportunity to crystallize folk fans as a taste community and a key *Voice* demographic—but even this proved contentious as the genre's commercial turn and its subsequent move toward rock compromised many fans' understandings of what folk music was and could be.

The *Voice* loudly celebrated Dylan as his celebrity magnified, and other writers felt galvanized to comment on him. "Folk music is one of the battlegrounds where the hegemony of tho [*sic*] established canons and values is being challenged by a creative cadre of insurgents," mused Jack Newfield, more often than not a political writer; he called Dylan "the mumbling, ragamuffin genius" leader of the folk movement and "the rebel of a dozen causes."[75] A few months later, Goddard interviewed Dylan and his story further amped up the worship. "Four years ago a thin, aquiline-faced boy of 19 got off the subway from Hibbing, Minnesota, to come up for air in the Village, bearing with him no more than a battered guitar and an offhand way of singing that reminded some people of Woody Guthrie . . . American folk music has never been the same since," Goddard wrote. "Three of his Columbia LP records have made the charts. His songs have made him synonymous with the whole new topical folk-song movement. Kids try to tear his clothes off at Carnegie or Philharmonic concerts . . . All of which makes Bob Dylan, as the folks down home might say, one of your living legends."[76]

In remarking on Dylan's role as a "living legend," Goddard's piece also helped to create that status, and edged folk away from amateurs and community and toward celebrity and commerce. Celebrity was a contentious issue in the folk community, representing a shift away from a musician singing as a part of a greater whole to a musician seeking individual fame and glory.[77] Dylan in many ways became a vector for this debate, as well as for other changes that were beginning to fracture the folk community as it popularized.

It is no surprise, then, that *Voice* writers used his immediately infamous electrified performance at the Newport Folk Festival in 1965 as an opportunity to consider some of the emerging problems in the folk community and the nascent rock one.[78] Arthur Kretchmer reported that "10,000 folk purists" booed Dylan for playing "Like a Rolling Stone." At a concert in Forest Hills, Queens, a few weeks later, the *Voice* reported the divisiveness of the battle more emphatically. "The teenage throng was bitterly divided between New York equivalents of Mods and Rockers," wrote the article's author, Jack Newfield. "The Mods—folk purists, new leftists, and sensitive collegians—came to hear Dylan's macabre surrealist poems like 'Gates of Eden' and 'A Hard Rain is Gonna Fall.' But the Rockers—and East Village potheads—came to stomp their feet to Dylan's more recent explorations of electronic 'rock folk.'"[79]

This battle, which Newfield called "as fierce as that between Social Democrats and Stalinists" sent ripples through the folk community as it refigured the popular landscape beyond folk. The evolution of folk rock that Bob Dylan catalyzed most visibly enabled rock and rollers to experiment with folk style and add protest lyrics to their amplified melodies, while concurrently allowing folk musicians to electrify their poetic verse. Pop performers like Sonny and Cher also jumped on the trend, making folk-infused sounds no longer the province of rebelling outsiders.[80]

The changing character of folk also presented the final step the *Voice* needed to complete in order to embrace rock, and eventually print rock criticism. Not only did the emergence of folk rock provide a musical segue between the two movements; it also marked the first time the *Voice* identified diversity—taste communities—within a popular musical landscape. This was proof that folk music was no longer news, but it had assured its existence as culture. It also heralded the importance of celebrity and mass culture to the most powerful musical movements, which rock music would exemplify. Still, the *Voice* had not yet gotten to the point of evaluating this controversy aesthetically, i.e., what determined "good" and "bad" folk. The completion of this act, then—not only recognizing the social and cultural implications of music but giving it a thumbs up or down in the same stroke—would be left to be completed in the birth of rock criticism. And rock criticism would continue to wrestle with the community dynamics the paper faced in reference to folk.

CHAPTER 2
Pop

Over the course of Goldstein's polemic, his tone grew more urgent—one might even say incensed. "We learn to tell Dostoevski from Spillane, but we know nothing about the flicks," he wrote. "We learn to tell Rembrandt from Keane, but we know nothing about advertising." Here, in the fourth edition of his new *Village Voice* column Pop Eye, Goldstein's argument crescendoed toward the neglect of music. After outlining the sonic and stylistic differences between genres within the new popular music, the author charged:

> We learn to deal with classical music and legitimate theatre but we know nothing about the sights and sounds which bombard us perpetually in the name of pop. And pop is not mere entertainment; it is anything but passive and conventional. Television, radio, advertising, and cinema have radically changed the perceptions of every man on any street. The question now is how to deal with pop—how do we screen the fallout from Madison Avenue? How do we evaluate our responses to the electronic waves racing through our living room? How do we tell what is noise and what is good, even artistic, rock 'n' roll?[1]

Goldstein's column mounted a sharp rebuttal to the critical stance on popular culture that prevailed in intellectual circles for much of the post–World War II period. Using the *Voice* as a platform from which to intervene in the mass culture debates, Pop Eye pioneered "pop criticism": writing that aimed to engage seriously yet accessibly with mass culture on its own terms. In this gesture, his writing resonated with, responded to, and extended arguments of his contemporaries such as Susan Sontag, Marshall McLuhan, and Herbert Marcuse, as well as the companion movements in Pop Art, new media, participatory democracy, neo-Freudianism, and postmodernism which enthralled and included them. In devoting itself primarily to rock music, Pop Eye ensured not only that the new music received serious treatment, but also that music was the lynchpin of a new critical ethos.

Yet the difficulties of this endeavor revealed themselves almost immediately, delimited by the contradictions of the age, of rock music, and of Goldstein himself. As he railed against the educational establishment's neglect of his generational culture, it was that same education on which he built his own critical lexicon and praxis. His arguments fell in line with critical and popular movements that championed appreciation of popular/populist culture, while at the same time they reproduced old hierarchies and erected new ones in this uncharted terrain. Moreover, to the degree that popular culture was rapidly changing in form, content, and industry, criticism itself became not only a commentary on trends, but a tool that increasingly could, and would, be utilized to manage them.

As the critical perspective of Goldstein's Pop Eye column developed during its first months, it redirected the discourse about popular culture in journalistic, intellectual, and political terms. Pop Eye became more than a celebration of the popular: it was a space that tackled and laid open larger questions about the substance and use value of popular culture and the critic's role within it. The initial installments were also experiments, displays of the difficulties involved in maintaining a robust criticism without altering the thing criticized for the worse. In time, these difficulties manifested a striking change in Goldstein's attitude toward popular culture, whereupon enthusiasm for its revolutionary power quickly transformed into shrewd, even cynical expositions on its machinations.

Developments within the music business factored heavily into the environment on which Goldstein was commenting, though I will for the moment table an in-depth discussion of those points. It is not my intent to artificially separate economic components from cultural ones, but rather to give the intricacies of this situation their proper weight. Together, this chapter and the next will illuminate how rock critics began to negotiate the paradoxes that were becoming visible within the music industry, the music itself, and their own profession during second half of the 1960s.

Mass Culture and Critique

The questions Goldstein's writing confronted locate him within centuries-old deliberations about the social worth of popular entertainment. The pastimes of "the people" occupied the minds of commentators in the ancient civilizations of Greece and Rome as much as they did those of intellectuals of early twentieth-century America and at many points in between, though with different contexts, manifestations, emphases, and results.[2] These perennial conversations highlighted, and often tried to police, shifting notions surrounding the idea of culture—metamorphoses that, as Raymond Williams usefully reminds us, mark "a general reaction to a general and major change in the conditions of our common life."[3] Culture has been the name we give not only to the deeply engrained common sense that guides our everyday interactions, but also to the art and creative work that we deem most worthy of praise and preservation, and this duality reveals once again the kernel of this congenital unease. Among its many other duties, culture supplies an analogue to democracy, a way to think about as well as a way to observe the politics of freedom and constraint, access and censure, equality, inequality, and difference that are the hallmarks of any heterogeneous society.

Goldstein's intervention arrived shortly after intellectuals had unleashed "the full flower of the attacks" on mass culture, an apex that built upon several decades of amplifying critique.[4] For much of the period since the early twentieth century, the burgeoning and emboldening critical professions such as education and journalism had been sounding concerns in response to the massive demographic and geographical changes in the American population; these changes arrived alongside the invention, development, and proliferation of a number of media technologies—phonograph recordings, cinema, popular magazines, newspapers, radio broadcasting—over the course of just a few decades. This class of intellectuals, located somewhat surprisingly on the Left, not only challenged a rapidly advancing consumer society but also, in turn, instantiated themselves as arbiters of public taste and the health of American cultural life.[5] It would be wrong to say, though, that their critiques were uniform in either purpose or tenor—an observation a number of scholars, notably Paul Gorman, James Gilbert, James Carey, and Michael Denning, have made clear in their work. That the variability of intellectual responses to mass culture culminated and is largely remembered though the prism of the mid-twentieth-century mass culture critique should instruct us, however, as to how deeply the fate of mass culture and intellectual life came to be aligned.

The Progressives and other reformers of the early twentieth century took a strong interest in the advancements in mass media, under a number of different guises. The most moral wing of Progressivism railed against the amusements of urban life that, they believed, enticed the white middle class as well as victimized its patrons, especially the working class, immigrants, and minority populations.[6] Their strong moralism often belied deep prejudices against these populations, bordering on the idea that they were subhuman.[7] Among other Progressives, especially those affiliated with the social sciences, observers found reason to both cheer the technologies of mass communications for their ability to unite a bigger and more diverse polis and jeer them for the impersonality the same technologies made possible. John Dewey and Walter Lippmann, though often caricatured in their positions, loom large in this discussion about the degree to which media could generate an active democratic community; joining them in conversation are founding figures of American sociology such as Charles Cooley and Robert Park.[8] Progressive ideals also inflected the regulation that emerged in relation to telecommunications media; the Radio Act of 1927, the basis for the Communications Act of 1934 as well as much later telecommunications legislation in the United States, defines Progressive ideals such as the public interest and the monitoring of who had access to the public.[9]

A reform mindset, a desire to oversee what the public could consume, and the empiricism of the social sciences came together as early twentieth-century researchers developed an interest in measuring the impact of mass media on audiences. The Payne Fund Studies, published in 1933, was a series of twelve research papers that explored how children reacted to movies, and it remains a telling document of how social scientists, intellectuals, and religious leaders began to make sense of the vast implications of mass mediated entertainment.[10] In 1936, the Office of Radio Research began at Princeton University, charged first with developing a rationale for educational radio. Under the leadership of Paul Lazarsfeld, the office moved to Columbia University in 1939 and assumed the name the Bureau of Applied Research.[11] By the 1950s, Lazarsfeld had conducted groundbreaking research into voting behavior and had started his government-funded work to develop effective anti-Nazi propaganda.[12] These endeavors would form the backbone of the discipline of communication, especially informing its tradition of research into media effects.

The above recounts in broad strokes the basis for public policy and social scientific interest in mass media, which despite growing secularism never strayed very far from religious interests. For Greenwich Village bohemians, advocates and progenitors of modernism, the interest in mass media derives from more humanist considerations, as they sought new terms for American cultural production. As mentioned in chapter 1, these modernists fostered an intellectual culture within specialized literary magazines and monographs, and through these publications denounced the strictures of Victorianism in the attempt to espouse a uniquely American taste culture. One way in which this project aligned with that of progressive critics was in their relationship to the system of "brows" of culture. In 1915, writer and intellectual Van Wyck Brooks noted in his essay " 'Highbrow' and 'Low-brow' " that there was arguably no distinction that was "more central or more illuminating" to American life;[13] though Brooks was a critic of both absolutes, the novelists, poets, and editors who were his contemporaries and sometimes sympathizers produced difficult works that appealed to elite audiences or those who aspired to be among them. Later, these works would encompass the very essence of high art, everything that mass culture was not.

Communists' shifting attitudes toward mass culture show another aspect of intellectuals' attitudes during this period. Following the directives of the Soviet Union, early American Communists first sought to establish prole-tarian culture that would reflect working-class experience, and as such took a hard line against commercial mass entertainments. That changed with the birth of the Popular Front in the early 1930s, as the desire to build alli-ances with the West softened Communist attitudes toward Western culture, including mass culture.[14] In what historian Michael Denning has called the "laboring" of popular culture, the loosening of Communist attitudes during this period had a specific demographic catalyst, as members of the working class became employees of the culture industries as well as its "pri-mary audience."[15] Despite the lasting influence of this change both on the cultural industries and on the population writ large, its forgiving attitudes toward popular culture lost charm after the end of the Popular Front, es-pecially among the anti-Stalinist Left into the 1940s.[16] These neo-Marxists, including the class of New York Intellectuals and German émigrés from the Frankfurt School, blended anti-Fascism with radicalism to produce pas-sionate denunciations of mass culture, which today have become almost synonymous with the mass culture critique.[17]

Jazz provides a useful example to chart these variegated dynamics at work. As jazz emerged as a distinctly African American musical genre around the turn of the century, the most traditional white cultural critics lambasted it "not only for returning civilized people to the jungles of barbarism but also for expressing the mechanistic sterility of modern urban life."[18] Jazz also enflamed Progressive piety; it was music for dancing, making sin a probable adjunct. In these two moves jazz existed as the very converse of culture, an embodiment of everything that culture was not.[19] Among bohemian and communist intellectuals, though, jazz was harder to classify. For instance, experimental combinations of jazz and socialist theater and the communist allegiances of black musicians such as Duke Ellington and Billie Holiday in the '30s and '40s contrasted sharply with attitudes, held by many white intellectuals, that jazz was a debased music; Adorno, a vehement critic of jazz, called it "fine for dancing but dreadful for listening" and indicative of "ecstasy without content."[20] In the thought of modernist sympathizer toward popular culture Gilbert Seldes, jazz was "the normal development of our resources, the expected, and wonderful, arrival of America at a point of creative intensity," yet this was at best a half-hearted endorsement. He also contended that "it is possible that [jazz] will divide into and follow two strains—the negro and the intellectual" and that "the negro is more intense than we are, and we surpass him when we combine a more varied and more intelligent life with his instinctive qualities."[21] His questions as to whether expressions of African Americans were of the same genus as those of whites existed even as some of his counterparts developed into ardent advocates of black creativity, romanticizing and patronizing—in all senses of the word—jazz and other aspects of the Harlem Renaissance.[22]

Distinctions within intellectual criticism over the first decades of the twentieth century evidenced that the role of intellectuals in defining, debating, and often opining against popular culture had precious little to do with the accuracy of their prescriptions. Nor did being wrong—about jazz, or movies, or dance halls, or much of anything else—stave their bluster or stature. By the 1950s, a range of attempts to utilize, reform, or replace mass entertainment had failed, but what had succeeded was the legitimizing of the critical act itself. In the wake of this, "intellectual" connoted opposition to mass culture.

During the 1950s, intellectuals regularly convened to discuss, debate, and criticize popular culture. In 1952, a symposium held in *Partisan Review,* called "Our Country and Culture," brought together prominent thinkers such as Leslie Fielder, Reinhold Niebuhr, David Riesman, and Lionel Trilling not only to praise the increased role of intellectuals in American society, but also to bemoan mass media—a task that most of the participants, with the notable exception of Norman Mailer, took up with great enthusiasm. The first issue of the three-part series proclaimed, in an editorial statement by William Phillips and Philip Rahv, that "mass culture not only weakens the position of the artist and the intellectual profoundly by separating him from his natural audience, but it also removes the mass of people from the kind of art which might express their human and aesthetic needs."[23]

Similar views prevailed a few years later in Ben Rosenberg and David Manning White's volume, *Mass Culture: The Popular Arts in America.* "There can be no doubt that the mass media present a major threat to man's autonomy," noted Rosenberg in his introductory piece. "To know that they might also contain some small seeds of freedom only makes a bad situation nearly desperate. No art form, no body of knowledge, no system of ethics is strong enough to withstand vulgarization."[24] Striking in the Rosenberg and White work is the inclusion of both social science and humanistic approaches to criticizing mass culture—these modes were methodologically and ideologically distinct, but they blended and empowered each other. The concordance was also on view at the summer 1959 conference held in Tamiment in the Poconos which Paul Lazarsfeld hosted, where the question of mass culture was posed to a distinguished interdisciplinary group of commenters: sociologists Melvin Tumin, Leo Lowenthal, Daniel Bell, Ben Rosenberg, and Nathan Glazer; philosophers Hannah Arendt, Sidney Hook, and Charles Frankel; historian Arthur Schlesinger, Jr.; novelist James Baldwin; and editors ranging from William Phillips of *Partisan Review* to Leo Rosten of *Look*. The desire Rosenberg raised to develop more "empirical studies of the effects of the mass media" thus sat alongside Hook's "revulsion against too much trash on radio and television,"[25] as both perspectives grappled with how mass culture might take on a more desirable form. In the introduction to the compendium of speeches published afterward, Lazarsfeld spoke for the majority of the conference participants when he noted:

> The liberals of today feel terribly gypped. For decades they and their intellectual ancestors fought to attain certain basic goals—more leisure time, more education, higher wages. They were motivated by the idealistic hope that when these goals were reached, the "masses" would develop into fine human beings. But what happened? After the liberals had won their victories, the people spent their newly acquired time and money on movies, radio, magazines . . . The situation of the liberals is much like that of the high school boy who, after weeks of saving, accumulates enough money to buy a bracelet for a girl, and who then learns that the girl has gone out with another boy to show off her nice new trinket.[26]

The important takeaway is that various kinds of intellectuals thought mass media was a problem. As evidenced in the Lazarsfeld meeting, "gypped" liberals left it to the actual employees of the culture industry, some of whom also attended, to offer what amounted to an outnumbered and sometimes meek defense.[27] Yet despite their empowerment in the seminar, these critics acknowledged that they were the underdogs going up against a most powerful enemy. Their adversaries were not just the industry personnel who made this culture, though—it was also the consumers, especially youth, who according to Ed Shils had "become a major consumer of the special variants of mediocre and brutal culture that are produced for transmission through mass media."[28]

Demographics supplied additional reason to worry: birthrates that had been declining for decades rose during the first years of World War II, and again, by bounds, in 1947. This increase continued well into the 1950s and early 1960s, paralleling a historically unprecedented period of affluence and suburbanization.[29] This "baby boom" forced the whole country to adjust to it—by building more schools and housing, increasing the production of food and consumer goods, and, eventually, allotting university educations, jobs, and political power. Youth were thus a major consideration in the media boom that also flourished post-war. Spurred by the massive growth in population, the widespread adoption of mass media was something not even the most compelling critic could curtail.

Television offers one illustration of this point. The medium's penetration widened after World War II; though there were just 60,000 TV sets in the U.S. in 1947, 86 percent of households had at least one by 1960.[30] Though TV was clearly aimed at the whole family, television took on a special meaning for boomer children, who would scarcely recall a world without it, making them key to television's development and collateral in debates over its social ramifications. Children's television programming took off during the 1950s, with kid-friendly shows such as *The Mickey Mouse Club* and *Howdy Doody* and adventures like *The Lone Ranger* and *Davy Crockett,* not to mention memorable commercials that often gave birth to fads.[31] Television was a playmate, a teacher, and a babysitter rolled into one—making the stakes high for those who wanted to appeal to this new market, but possibly higher for those wanting to squelch its march.

Critics obsessed over television's ubiquity, force, and potentially malignant effects to a degree that outstripped concerns with previous forms. In stark contrast to film, which at least sometimes captivated critical imaginations,[32] television was reviled most of all; it was the "colossus in the mass entertainment field" whose astronomical growth promised, in the eyes of some, to "hasten the transformation of autonomous individuals into mass man."[33] The situation was especially dire for its youngest viewers. Television threatened to create children who knew too much about the adult world too soon, who sassed their mothers and disobeyed their fathers, yet whose indulgent parents spoiled them because advertisers manipulated Mom and Dad, too.[34]

In the minds of critics, the youngsters who grew up on television promised to be different. A similar perspective, though differently valued, existed among members of this generation, as television became an instrument of self-definition. For those who would form the counterculture especially, television served many purposes: the technology that determined their rejection of the status quo, the institution that presented them with the society they came to revolt against, and the generational glue that bound all people under a certain age together, in some cases more viscerally than any other.[35] The rise of youth culture built upon the spread of media, with magazines, motion pictures, and comic books joining television to form a major artery keeping the heart of postwar American consumer culture alive.[36]

Music also defined boomer youth. By 1950, two new record formats had entered the market, with the long-play (33RPM) serving for classical music and its portable sibling the single (45RPM) dominating in pop.[37] These technologies were then sold to different populations based upon consumer age, segmenting teenage consumption from that of adults.[38] Also in the early years of the 1950s, the retail apparatus selling these new technologies gradually turned from full-service to self-service, giving purchasers more control over their musical selections.[39]

Increased agency and motility for young music consumers in particular accompanied significant developments in the radio environment. By this time, television was displacing radio as the primary medium in the American household.[40] Live music had declined as the standard heard on the airwaves, which resulted in radio becoming a vital promotional vehicle for records, which made up the bulk of the on-air schedule.[41] In response to these shifts, the radio industry restructured itself as a local rather than national medium, attempting to draw in niches television did not serve well and thus secure untapped revenue streams. Young listeners were one critical growth demographic—and this change in radio facilitated what Susan Douglas has called a unique social space for young listeners.[42] Transistor technology buoyed this youthful listening environment even further, enabling the radio to drastically shrink in size and become more amenable to the lifestyles of younger consumers; by 1965, 12 million of these smaller devices were being sold annually.[43] Radios also became standard in automobiles, with 60 percent penetration by 1963. Young people could thereby take their music anywhere, turning any space into a youth zone simply by cranking up the volume.[44]

Rock and roll was born of, capitalized on, and furthered these evolutions. By the early 1950s, the black music previously identified as rhythm and blues began to attract the interest of an expanding segment of white listeners, whose fandom compelled enterprising disc jockeys to introduce the music to the mainstream of white youth culture.[45] As black musicians found success among the lucrative mainstream audience, white musicians across a range of regional and popular musical styles experimented with black vocal expressions, language, and rhythms.[46] Around the same time, country or "hillbilly" music—another previously marginal genre, primarily the province of rural populations—began to attract mainstream attention, blurring regional, class, and race boundaries as well as those of genre. This was especially the case as some country artists—most iconically, early Elvis Presley—took influences from rhythm and blues to craft the explosively popular genre of "rockabilly."[47] Though it would take time for these various strands to consolidate, the emergent music reconfigured the rules by which the popular music industry operated, particularly the relationship between major and independent labels and the importance of the young demographic.

Independent labels readily embraced the growing trend of rock, but even as record sales for independents skyrocketed,[48] the music's racial and sexual content remained distasteful to major labels. Hoping that rock and roll was a fad, many of the major labels sat back and awaited the trend's passing, while others took an active role in expediting its demise. During the latter 1950s and early 1960s, a core faction of music industry insiders was "prepared to use all their resources to destroy rocknroll [sic]."[49] This was well illustrated in the 1959–1960 ASCAP crusade against its competitor BMI, the primary licensing group for rock and roll music that came into existence in 1939, after ASCAP and the stations had a contractual dispute.[50] At the Congressional hearings held to air testimony on a bill outlawing monopoly activity by broadcasters and music publishers/manufacturers, leading voices from the professoriate, arts, and non-profits excoriated rock music as the deplorable result of flagrant "selective exposure" of BMI music by NBC and CBS. According to one authority who spoke at the hearings, "If the broadcasting interests are allowed to continue their dominance and manipulation of America's musical taste, they will shortly strangle all true creative effort, and consequently jeopardize the future development of our culture."[51]

Over the course of the '50s and early '60s, the mixture of blackness, sexual energy, and unapologetic commercialism would dismay conservative and liberal white America in equal measure. The miscegenation of the airwaves indicated more integration at live performances.[52] Southern whites in particular loathed this trend, with groups accusing rock and roll of being an NAACP conspiracy and attacking certain black performers who were on tour in the region.[53] Elvis conjured a backlash in a range of media outlets: the *New York Times* to *Time, Downbeat* to *Look,* where writers accused him and other rock and rollers of contributing to juvenile delinquency, teen violence, and sexual promiscuity.[54] Gennari notes that among liberals, the Cold War period "remained largely blind and tone-deaf to developments in African American cultural expression" despite an eagerness, at least in terms of rhetoric, to confront the country's racism.[55] Even Adorno's afore-mentioned polemic against popular music, at the time aimed toward jazz, harbored subtle racism—a point worth raising when considering the influence Adorno would have on American critics on the Left.[56] The scandals that rocked the musical establishment in the latter 1950s—the arrest of Chuck Berry, the shaming of Jerry Lee Lewis, and the payola scandals—were less obvious, though no less effective, ways of signaling the corrupting force that rock could bring.[57]

Ultimately, rock's popularity spread in spite of campaigns against it, and radio and records expedited not only the upswing of rock as mainstream American culture but also its global spread. By the late 1950s, rock and roll had "swept the world," becoming a phenomenon in many places world-wide.[58] The international boom also echoed back in the United States. After the music industry tried to push other trends in the late 1950s, the American rock market triumphed once again with an infusion of talent from Great Britain.[59] It almost goes without saying that the most successful of these acts were the Beatles, who earned a spot on the British charts in 1962 with their single "Love Me Do," and subsequently were heavily marketed stateside.[60] The $50,000 publicity barrage dubbed Beatlemania was an unmitigated success. Just a few weeks after the Beatles had their first U.S. number-one single, "I Want to Hold Your Hand," the band caused riot-like conditions as thousands of screaming fans received them at New York's Kennedy Airport on February 7, 1964. Later that week, the band appeared on the Ed Sullivan show for a record 73 million American viewers.[61] In April, the Beatles became the first musical group in history to command the top five slots on the Billboard Hot 100 charts.[62]

The Beatles were the first foreign act to reach massive success among American youth, and in subsequent months their popularity mingled with record company greed to produce the British Invasion. As companies jumped at the chance to find their own Fab Four, groups such as the Rolling Stones, the Yardbirds, Herman's Hermits, the Who, and the Hollies began to take over the American pop charts. Mainstream Americans grew to accept, and even crave, their homegrown music as translated to them by largely working-class British youth.

These developments serve to highlight how the rapid change in technology and popular culture created an aesthetic gulf to which older critics could not and, for the most part, would not attend. The divisions go beyond a simple difference in what young and older people did or did not appreciate. They corresponded to fundamentally different definitions of culture and ways of consuming. To appeal to younger audiences operating under such different assumptions, pop music criticism would need to do away with these outmoded ways of thinking, performing the radical gesture of asserting that this culture would be good not just to listen to, but to think with.

Postmodernism and the Making of Pop Criticism

The world of art first produced an identifiable movement with the goal of articulating a new conception of mass culture through both aesthetics and criticism. Eventually known as Pop, the U.S. incarnation of the movement was centered in New York City and focused on creating art that celebrated and played with mass cultural forms.[63] Pop Art includes now well-known artists such as Roy Lichtenstein, Claes Oldenburg, and Andy Warhol, whose work often consisted of large, multicolored interpretations of popular forms such as comics, celebrity images, and industrial design.

Pop was a controversial addition to the artistic world that challenged conventional hierarchies between high and low, shocking many in its embrace of what had long been disparaged as middling mass culture.[64] Dwight Macdonald, for one, saw it as yet another example of the crisis of "midcult," the unsavory melding of high and low culture in American life. His faith that the avant-garde might save high culture (articulated in essays such as his 1957 "A Theory of Mass Culture") had, upon the start of the 1960s, faded into overall pessimism that even the avant-garde had been supplanted by the drivel of kitsch. Pop Art, to critics of Macdonald's predilection, doubtlessly proved that this horror had come to pass.[65]

Curiously, despite the views of critics such as Macdonald, Pop Art held much in common with the avant-garde as it was traditionally known. Not unlike Dada or surrealism, Pop begged its connoisseurs to find artistic expression in unlikely locales. Moreover, Pop was not only an artistic style but also a posture toward creation, implying a knowingness that could see sophistication in the glossy pages of a magazine and cunning in a colorful detergent box. In kind, it inspired a new critical approach. English art critic Lawrence Alloway, who has been credited with coining the term "Pop Art" in reference to the related though distinct movement within British art, named the popular arts as one of the most notable features of modern society, stressing that their democratic tenor made prototypical critical reflexes inadequate. According to Alloway, "it is no good giving a literary critic modern science fiction to review, no good sending the theatre critic to the movies, and no good asking the music critic for an opinion on Elvis Presley."[66] Such an act would simply be allowing minority taste to dictate mass taste. Instead, the new aesthetics created through massification required their own values, approaches, and attitudes.[67]

Despite Pop's initial gestures toward populism, the movement quickly became intertwined with a brand of elitism articulated most emphatically in the work of Susan Sontag. As a high-profile spokesperson whose work appeared in both academic and popular publications, Sontag not only praised Pop as a meaningful expression in the age of mass culture but also located it within an emerging "new sensibility" that could see mass culture with fresh, accepting eyes, yet still find meaningful ways of discriminating among its artifacts. Between 1964 and 1965, Sontag published several influential essays to fulfill these purposes. "One Culture and the New Sensibility," published initially in *Mademoiselle*, served to name this ideology and locate its rightful place. "The new sensibility understands art as the extension of life—this being understood as the representation of (new) modes of vivacity," she wrote in the expanded version, published in the 1966 anthology *Against Interpretation*. Rather than oppose judgment altogether, Sontag argued for a new paradigm of appreciation. The new way of seeing art "does not mean the renunciation of all standards: there is plenty of stupid popular music, as well as inferior and pretentious 'avant-garde' paintings, films, and music. The point is that there are new standards, new standards of beauty and style and taste."[68] Under this vision, the traditional lines that demarcated high and low culture had begun to dissolve, but the ability to exercise good taste had not.

Suggested within this sensibility is the idea of camp, explained in her essay "Notes on Camp," which appeared in *Partisan Review* in 1964, one year prior to "One Culture." Camp, a perspective available only to "societies or circles capable of experiencing the psychopathology of affluence," allowed for the appreciation of artifice and style on its own terms, even going so far as to laud culture which would otherwise be considered terrible for the excesses it displays. According to Sontag, "Camp introduces a new standard: artifice as an ideal, theatricality."[69] Camp furthermore emerged from homosexual culture, and so Sontag found gays at its leading edge.

This notion of camp became central to Pop Art's reception, especially as the concept entered popular discourse following the essay's publication.[70] Yet, for my purposes here, the Pop expression of these ideas warrants remark for its specifically *undemocratic* tone: the culture might be accessible, but the terms on which to appreciate it were not. Sontag's work had an incredible influence on altering the conversation about the meaning and use of mass culture, moving it to a place where it could be discussed at least in neutral terms, if not in positive ones.[71] But if her views on popular culture were liberating in the sense that it could be discussed without knee-jerk condemnation, they were confining in the sense that true understanding was an exclusive ability.

"Against Interpretation," published in 1964 and again in the aforementioned volume, was Sontag's account of what this all meant for critics. In her estimation, interpretative criticism killed the sensual appreciation of art. Blaming this stranglehold on the reflexive act of critics to first wrest the content of art away from its form and then explain it, Sontag advocated that critics "cut back on content so that we can see the thing at all." She charged critics with a very different purpose—"to show *how it is what it is,* even *that it is what it is,* rather than to show what it *means.*"[72] For those who would write amid this emergent critical territory, "Against Interpretation" urged approaching culture not just with new eyes, but with a whole new lexicon and method. Sontag's wholesale abandonment of detachment in favor of recovering "the sharpness of our sensory experience"[73] aimed to recuperate the art object itself, and in the process produce a rigorous, robust, and ultimately erotic criticism.

Adjoined to the innovative modes of artistic production, Sontag's outlook signaled the opening of a new chapter of cultural life—the deterioration of now sedate modernism in favor of something more carnal and evocative, more playful and electric, more embodied and socially relevant. Written at a moment where artists working in a variety of media had used their creativity "in order to produce a commitment or at least a response from the viewing audience,"[74] Sontag's criticism exposed but also played a part in ushering in the demise of modernism and the ascendance of what would come to be known as postmodernism. As a wide-ranging and hotly contested cultural movement and moment, postmodernism will factor into many of the subsequent conversations in this book, particularly the discussions of economics and politics that take precedence in chapters 3 and 4. I mention postmodernism now to emphasize it as an "avant-garde revival"[75] that named and drew out commonalities among neorealist fiction, psychedelic music, theater "Happenings," Pop Art, experiments in video and mixed media, and other creative endeavors of the mid-to-late '60s period, and as such excited new critical and intellectual impulses.

One of the most sweeping of these assessments came from Marshall McLuhan, a Canadian English professor who published two groundbreaking books, *The Gutenberg Galaxy* and *Understanding Media,* in 1962 and 1964 respectively. Read together, the books detail the changes electric media promised contemporary society, conceiving of the new technologies as catalysts for the retribalization of humankind. Though in past work McLuhan had focused primarily on the negative unintended consequences of media technologies, this time he eyed media's possibilities, imagining an electric media revolution that would amalgamate utopian futurism and idyllic antimodernism.[76] He commented as media integrated themselves ever more fully into our everyday lives. "All media are active metaphors in their power to translate experience into new forms," he wrote in *Understanding Media*. "In the electric age we see ourselves being translated more and more into the form of information, moving toward the technological extension of consciousness."[77] McLuhan's esoteric, even trippy, proclamations were sufficiently malleable to endear him to disparate groups of followers, including Pop artists, cyber-pioneers, and corporate executives.[78] For young people who encountered McLuhan as college students and twentysomethings, his ideas had endless applications, explicating the appeal of hippie communes,[79] the righteousness of new intellectualism and New Journalism, or, as we shall see in Goldstein's case, the use value of rock criticism.

Herbert Marcuse provided fodder for the re-assessment of new culture and the logic that guided new critical approaches. A well-loved and charismatic professor at Brandeis who would become "the idol of American leftists,[80] Marcuse published his influential *One-Dimensional Man* in the spring of 1964. The book brought together his ideas on the increasing strangulation of individualism and independent thinking by one-dimensional society and helped fuel student movements that, like him, sought "to liberate the imagination so that it can be given all its means of expression."[81] For Marcuse, the threat was not just domination but also the shiny surface it wore, one of mass consumer goods that served to placate the public into willing submission. This resonated with those among the younger generation—notably, members of the SDS—who saw their own privilege as an alienating burden. Moreover, he placed his faith in those communities most marginalized, among them, minorities and (in their own view) youth, who "[hit] the system from without" to bring the transformation to fruition.[82]

Marcuse's expression of both utopian and dystopian themes carried youth's immense fears of social oppression and gross systemization toward hopefulness for all-encompassing revolution.[83] It also offered comment on how culture might suit revolutionary ends. Taking inspiration from the student protests and rioting of African Americans in inner cities,[84] the highly influential 1969 *Essay on Liberation* pivotally understood what Julie Stephens termed "aesthetic radicalism" as capable of undermining the capitalist order.[85] "The aesthetic dimension can serve as a sort of gauge for a free society," Marcuse wrote. He continued:

> A universe of human relationships no longer mediated by the market, no longer based on competitive exploitation or terror, demands a sensitivity freed from the repressive satisfactions of the unfree societies; a sensitivity receptive to forms and modes of reality which thus far have been projected only by the

aesthetic imagination. For the aesthetic needs have their own social content: they are the claims of the human organism, mind and body, for a dimension of fulfillment which can be created only in the struggle against the institutions which, by their very functioning, deny and violate these claims.[86]

Guerrilla theater, rock music, dance, flower power: each was a gateway toward the possibility of a society governed by an evolved sense of pleasure and the radical transformation of the civilized Ego. Such neo-Freudian ideas connected Marcuse to Norman O. Brown, another widely read 1960s critic who was involved in the reintroduction and reinterpretation of Freud, especially in its mystical expression in his 1966 *Love's Body,*[87] and call to mind McLuhan's notices about the retribalization of man, where technology actually created the means for its own rebuke (or, at least, primitive use).[88]

These thinkers—and the movements they touch in new media studies, critical theory, and neo-Freudianism—each shaped the thinking of Richard Goldstein as he set out to write about the music he believed could help restructure society. In calling his column Pop Eye, he annexed himself to the burgeoning Pop movement and extended its purview as well as its possibilities. In his writing, music was not only a new art valid for discussion; it also required a whole new vocabulary emanating from a whole new, younger class. Not only did it have the power to reach the masses as a cultural pandemic, but like a pandemic, it could wipe out the existing culture and provide something entirely new. And, importantly, critics had the duty to experience this culture for itself, to mire themselves in the thick of it and see what happened, rather than view it from a safe, sterilized distance.

His column would also make him part of a small but formidable New York City community of writers devoted to the expansion of these ideas. Writers Ellen Willis and Robert Christgau befriended Goldstein in the early part of 1966[89] and worked with him at *Cheetah,* a magazine that existed from 1967 to 1968. Willis later went on to become the pop music critic at the *New Yorker* magazine; Christgau, at the time Willis's partner, began writing Secular Music for *Esquire* in 1967 before taking over the position of chief music writer at the *Voice.* Richard Meltzer, another music writer, started his career at Paul Williams's *Crawdaddy!* magazine and also floated around the circle of New York–based writers, as did figures such as Lillian Roxon, Ellen Sander, and Sandy Pearlman. But with Goldstein's column as an anchor and the paper's reputation as a stable home base for writers, the *Voice* began to evolve into a nucleus for pop writing and a rite of passage for many music scribes.

Importantly, the foundations of pop criticism specifically and rock criticism more generally mark a renaissance of generational criticism. As it had near the turn of the twentieth century, generationalism strongly informed how young people of the 1960s thought about themselves and their role in the world, and framed both the wealth of creative expressions and the critical responses to them. The relationship between the most celebrated creators of popular culture and its most vociferous critic-fans was essentially a peer one and could go further than that, too; Goldstein later put it to me that he was "the same class as these people," meaning they often also shared similar economic, educational, and—though it often went unmentioned—racial backgrounds.[90] Adding to this the sheer dominance of youth in demographic terms, it makes sense that these critics might well have viewed themselves as tastemakers of the up-and-coming army of pop enthusiasts. In the context of a Pop critical movement, Goldstein was an early and prominent example of how critics of his generation purposely conceived of themselves as radical cultural intellectuals.

Though generationalism prevailed as a prism through which Goldstein and his ilk understood their contribution, they did take pages from the work of older critics, some of whom predated them and others who were contemporaneous. One of these was Pauline Kael, film critic for the *New Yorker* from 1968 until 1991 and a model for how cultural criticism might adopt intelligent pathos. Kael was born to Jewish parents in Petaluma, California, in 1919. A precocious youngster with a voracious appetite for books, Kael also enjoyed moviegoing from an early age, and she regularly visited her town's Mystic Movie Theater. She attended the University of California at Berkeley but dropped out during her senior year, in 1940. After giving birth to a daughter in 1948, Kael spent much of her adult years in a struggle to support the two of them, moving among odd jobs before landing beloved but unprofitable movie reviewing work in obscure publications as well as on a local radio program in the Bay Area.[91] Her passionate defense of the movies she adored—as well as her mordant critiques of those with which she disagreed—earned her respect and admiration. In 1965, Atlantic Monthly Press collected her writings in a volume entitled *I Lost It at the Movies*, which coincided with a growing public enthusiasm for movie reviews and would become a rousing favorite with many first-generation rock critics.[92] The book's celebrated reception eventually led to the *New Yorker* offering her an appointment as a film reviewer.[93]

Kael's writing has a magnetic quality; she pulls in the reader with unadorned yet exacting description, where she is as much on view as the films and scenarios she describes. Writing about *The Bride of Frankenstein*, for instance, Kael intones "It's a horror film that takes itself very seriously, and even though I thought its intellectual pretensions silly, I couldn't shake off the exquisite, dread images."[94] Later in the same piece, she gives the following rationale about moviegoing:

> People go to the movies for the various ways they express the experiences of our lives, and as a means of avoiding and postponing the pressures we feel. This latter function of art—generally referred to disparagingly as escapism—may also be considered as refreshment, and in terms of modern big city life and small town boredom, it may be a major factor in keeping us sane.[95]

For rock critics, Kael was an exemplar in at least two ways. Her unrepentant love of "intelligent trash" heartened rock critics who at times enjoyed mass culture precisely for its kitsch.[96] Second, her fierce, independent intellect expressed in highly readable fashion provided a goal that many cultural critics since have tried to achieve.

Television, often seen as the basest of media, nonetheless also found an early and ardent supporter in the career of Jack Gould, born in 1914 to a well-to-do New York family. His first job in the newspaper business started in 1932 at the *New York Tribune*.[97] He initially worked as a copy boy and was shortly promoted to a staff reporter, a position he held until 1937, when the *New York Times* hired him away from the *Tribune* to work their theater beat. In 1944, Gould transitioned to the radio department and, from there, commenced reporting on the budding television broadcast business as it emerged from radio.

Gould's work included reviewing programs, interviewing prominent figures in the television industry, and commenting on the present and future of the evolving medium.[98] From his perch at the nation's most prestigious newspaper, Gould enjoyed privileged access to television insiders and commented authoritatively on some of the most notable television events of the period—from the rise of Edward Murrow to the quiz show scandals and the public's ardor for *I Love Lucy*.[99] He was never arrogant, though, about the ultimate influence of his criticism. Quoted in a collection of his writing edited by his son, Gould stated in 1972 that "most criticism is useless and wasteful in a mass medium distributed for free."[100] Despite this, he strove to be an even-handed critic who believed television warranted consideration rather than knee-jerk denunciation. "A medium which daily pre-empts the attention of millions of adults and children surely cannot be ignored," he wrote. Taking a position exceptional for the time among critics of his standing, he continued:

> Television is not a static or passive force. It can either elevate or lower national tastes and standards; it cannot operate and leave them entirely untouched . . . Television can not be judged only by the rules and mores of its own making; it

also must be weighed in light of contemporary life as a whole, just as theater, movies and books are. Television quite properly should be hailed in many ways for widening the horizons of the public. But it also must be mindful of the reality of its narcotic ability to deaden the national awareness of important standards and serious issues.[101]

Gould and Kael did for visual media what Jane Scott would begin to do for pop music. Born in 1919 in Cleveland, Scott began working for the *Cleveland Plain Dealer* in 1952, assigned to the society beat.[102] She later assumed editorship of the newspaper's teen page, and in 1964 decided to attend the local concert of the Beatles—an event which marked the auspicious start of her fifty-year run as a rock journalist for the paper.[103] Scott's efforts forged the new youth music as a topic worthy of column inches and public awareness, leading the way for the (mostly) men who took up the pursuit she initiated. It is important to acknowledge, however, that although Scott and the generational critics on whom I am focusing shared the objective of legitimating the new music, their techniques as well as outcomes were very different. Unlike the analytical, occasionally snarky, and culturally politicized writings of younger rock critics, Scott maintained an encouraging, positive outlook on the music, cultivating and coaxing rather than pushing and sharp dissection.

Sixties rock critics owed a debt to jazz writers as well, though there were meaningful distinctions. I draw heavily here from the work of John Gennari, thus far the most eloquent and comprehensive historian of jazz criticism, who has called the jazz critic "crucial to the history of jazz, to the lives and careers of jazz musicians, and to the shaping of ideas about jazz's significance in American culture."[104] Gennari traces this seminal role for jazz writers back to the 1930s, when figures such as John Hammond and Leonard Feather took a strong interest in the music. For white writers delving into a black musical genre, jazz writing necessarily had to confront the racial politics of their practice, as well as how important it would be for jazz to be considered legitimate, rather than popular, culture. By the mid-twentieth century, jazz had begun to be accepted as an American art form suitable among segments of the elite, counterpoised to debased mass culture such as rock music. Put another way, the objectives of jazz critics were often expressly modernist rather than postmodernist.[105]

Of course, there were jazz critics who also wrote about rock or had direct relationships with rock writers and their publications of choice, and whose perspectives on jazz heralded things to come as rock criticism established itself. Ralph J. Gleason, for instance, began writing about jazz as a college student in the 1930s and spent the bulk of his career as a jazz critic, but by the 1960s became enamored of rock and roll and helped Jann Wenner start *Rolling Stone* in 1967.[106] As would prove important in rock criticism, Nat Hentoff, of *Downbeat* and later the *Village Voice,* used jazz as a way to explore social and political issues; his gradual transition from music critic to political commentator indicates the potential fluidity between the pursuits.[107] Hentoff also wrote an early, notable profile of Bob Dylan for the *New Yorker,* indicating that newer forms of popular music merited extended, serious discussion.

To the degree that pop criticism took advantage of these expansions of the journalistic form, it also warrants consideration as a subset of New Journalism. New Journalism had antecedents in writing that appeared in publications such as the *New Yorker* and the *New York Herald Tribune* as early as the late 1940s and shared spirit as well as practitioners with the Beat writing of the 1940s and 1950s; as I mentioned in the previous chapter, the early writing in the *Voice* also bears these markings. But New Journalism gained a high-profile and outspoken advocate in Tom Wolfe, whose 1965 publication of *The Kandy-Kolored Tangerine-Flake Streamline Baby* helped catapult the journalism Wolfe had been writing for *Esquire* and *New York* (then a supplement of the *New York Herald Tribune*) into the limelight, especially among college students.[108] Wolfe's journalism was unique in the way it employed devices usually reserved for novels, such as dialogue, deep characterization, and point-of-view. Wolfe also advocated "staying with the people they were writing about for days at a time, weeks in some cases," thereby more deeply accessing the "subjective or emotional life of the characters."[109]

Goldstein's writing took much inspiration and influence from Wolfe, and the challenge Wolfe waged against journalistic convention also inspired Willis and Christgau as well as other young intellectuals, many of whom were located in New York. Yet in the end, Wolfe was a writer, not an activist or an advocate; his goal was to join the pantheon of great writers via journalism rather than to effect social change or necessarily advocate for fresh perspectives on mass culture.[110] In contrast, though Goldstein and his peers certainly wanted to be good writers, they staged both a creative and a political intervention into journalistic practice, growing in tandem with it and best expressing the political and cultural changes becoming manifest at the time. New Journalism, for these writers, would be both a politics of style and a style of politics. Here, I am building upon the ideas of John J. Pauly, who calls New Journalism of this era "a politics of cultural style" that "spoke for a social movement that aimed to transform not just the styles of nonfiction writing, but the very institutions through which society produced and consumed stories about itself."[111] As a *politics of style,* New Journalism was a way to rebel against journalistic conventions of objectivity, balance, and order; establishing participation and investment on the part of the journalist as a more honest posture, a dynamic form as a reflection of dynamic content. As a *style of politics*, Goldstein put it best when, years later, he recalled the belief that he was "a cultural worker" who was "helping to build something called the revolution, which was going to transform society along democratic socialist lines, and create a new kind of socialism in which desire was front and center."[112] Participating in what Aronowitz describes as New Journalism's "definition of politics in which pleasure would radically replace the old Victorianism,"[113] Goldstein found his method of passionate political intervention in rock criticism.

The efforts of rock critics further evidence the abandonment of objectivity and the increasingly situational view of knowledge and knowledge production that typified the 1960s. Across a range of subject matter and spaces, intellectuals of the day began to discard notions of "disinterested" knowledge in favor of considering ideas as "social artifacts having a definite utility."[114] Yet this act would raise as many questions as it could answer, especially as rock critics began to think about the effects of their work. To what sorts of uses could rock criticism be put? Could cultural politics—listening to good music with good messages, using and advocating new technologies—translate into the kind of politics that could liberate minds, bodies, and souls? Was the deluge of new culture a moment of reckoning or just one of marketing? These quandaries would come to define Goldstein's practice, played out in the pages of the *Voice* as he strived to explain and celebrate, dig and dig into, music.

Goldstein Pops

Richard Goldstein was born in 1944 and grew up in the housing projects of the Lower East Side and the Bronx in a working class Jewish family. Self-described as a "very alienated kid," he was deeply stirred by the music which was a vital part of his neighborhood, and as a child his main focus, other than reading, was tuning into the do-wop he heard on street corners. "It was a strange combination of being a hermetic proto-intellectual and also loving rock music at the same time," Goldstein explained recently. He was also a fan of folk music, and began in the mid-1960s to hear sonic meldings that for him "represented a significant change in my generation." When a cover of Bob Dylan's song "Blowin' in the Wind" topped the *Billboard* charts, "I thought 'wow, this is a change,'" Goldstein has noted, leagues apart from "trekking downtown to see Bob Dylan in these small village clubs."[115]

Around this time, he enrolled at Hunter College—an increasingly common decision for young adults at a time when the university system and its social stature were vastly expanding.[116] Once there, he began praising acts like the Beatles and Bob Dylan in a column called "The Second Jazz Age" for *The Uptowner,* an upstart newspaper at the college. He continued to write about this music after entering journalism school, much to the dismay of his professors. "One of my professors gave me a paper back saying 'I don't know what this is but you owe me a story,'" he said.[117]

Nineteen sixty-six was an important year in Goldstein's life. He published his first book, *1 in 7,* which chronicled the rise of drug culture among students at colleges and universities around the country. He also completed his graduate degree at Columbia, after which he approached the *Voice* to inquire if he could write a column on rock.[118] In characteristic *Voice* manner, editor Dan Wolf was a tad incredulous, but agreed anyway. As a result, Pop Eye would become the latest major development in the nascent world of critical writing about rock music. A few months before Goldstein established Pop Eye, a Boston-based college freshman, Paul Williams, had begun to publish *Crawdaddy!,* hailed by one of its early contributors as the first community of rock writers.[119] Like Williams, Goldstein based his assessments less on the technical qualities of the music itself than on its general gestalt, which included its sound, politics, emotional, and sexual elements. Unlike Williams, Goldstein demonstrated an intrinsic interest in rock as an element of a systemic change in culture more generally.

The June debut of Goldstein's column announced a marked change in the way that music would be reported on in the *Voice.* Until that point, there had been two places to look for regular critical music coverage. The most regular feature was a column called Music that either Carman Moore or Leighton Kerner wrote, which generally covered chamber music, classical, and opera. Michael Zwerin penned Jazz Journal, a regular column devoted to reviews of both live and recorded jazz music. Zwerin occasionally ventured into the intersections between jazz music and classical, though his column was by and large focused on the former and written with a deep technical knowledge, paying attention to things like pitch, sound quality, and rhythm over persona and politics. J. R. Goddard still occasionally wrote columns on folk music, with unpredictable frequency; a few other *Voice* writers intermittently pondered music. However, with Goldstein, the new music for the first time had a dedicated place for discussion in the pages of the *Voice.* The paper in turn gained a foothold in the growing critical conversation about rock.

The *Village Voice* had enjoyed positive publicity, growing circulation, and good luck for a number of years at this point. In 1962, a 114-day strike of New York City Typographical Union No. 6 shut down many of the city's newspapers, but the *Voice* continued to print, bringing it many more readers. The uptick during the strike partially remained after the strike's conclusion and jumped again, in 1965, with another month-long strike during a critical mayoral election season.[120] More readers meant more advertising, more pages for stories, and more attention. "No longer a rebel flaunting the ways of Greenwich Village in the face of the Philistines uptown, the *Voice* has become something of an establishment of the Left," a November 1966 *Time* magazine article on the paper proclaimed.[121] As of early 1967, the *Village Voice* was the nation's top selling weekly newspaper, with a third of its readership outside the city limits.[122]

The *Time* article, "Voice of the Partially Alienated," pointed to another trend that boosted, but also changed, the position of the paper: the growth of the underground press. Starting with the *L.A. Weekly* in 1964, a number of radical newssheets began to emerge in cities around the country, emulating the *Voice*'s bold amateurism and freewheeling writing, but often minus its capitalist ambitions and with a more revolutionary political thrust in its place. Alternative press historian John McMillian has noted that alternative weeklies were a crucial "counterinstitution" of the New Left, harnessing many of their objectives of participatory democracy. This is an important point, but it should not obscure the fact that many youth who identified with the counterculture read and participated in many kinds of culture, from reading mass market magazines and listening to rock music, to keeping tabs on alternative weeklies, underground publications, and guerrilla video. Moreover, for those who were cultural workers, there were some clear economic, political, and professional advantages to disseminating their work widely. Despite what would be Goldstein's clear sympathies with the counterculture and youth movements, his decision to write for the *Voice* is a meaningful choice and yet another example of his pop politics.

His second column was a case in point. Departing from "Soundblast 66," his piece a week earlier on a concert featuring the Beach Boys, Ray Charles, the Byrds, and Little Stevie Wonder, "The Soul Sound from Sheepshead Bay" melded concert reportage with an artist profile of Queens natives the Shangri-Las, who were well known for their 1964 chart-topping hit "The Leader of the Pack." The Shangri-Las had moved on from the innocent personas that characterized their early careers as well as those of most girl groups of the period, and their music spun melodramatic stories of girldom that flirted with danger, often spectacularly. Their unique edge has since attracted substantial academic interest, and it likewise intrigued Goldstein, who used his piece to explore the larger implications of "soul" emanating from this unlikely source.

"To speak of soul as a synonym for Negritude is a narrow, limited definition," he wrote. "Soul is what separates artistry from the koobs in an echo chamber. A soul singer talks about real experience . . . soul is intimately tied to suffering, and sorrow is not exclusively a racial experience."[123] Goldstein's attention to the changing racial politics of music speaks to two important themes that would become crucial in his writing. The first was that music should not be separated from the environment in which it was produced. Noting that "their look and their sound is New York"—down to their dress, accents, and the ambient noises that surged through their music—Goldstein suggested that the social environment which produced them and attached certain racial expectations to different kinds of music must factor into how to respond to them as musicians. His view of the concept of "soul" at the time reflected a guileless optimism about the possibilities of racial openness and harmony—a view that would, as I will discuss in chapter 4, be challenged in response to the inexorable change in tenor of race relations. Second, the enthusiasm Goldstein exhibited over this boundary-shifting music spoke more generally to the level of respect, attention, and assessment that he felt pop deserved. Before him, a girl group such as the Shangri-Las might have been written about as hit-producing fluff, and while Goldstein may not have had as much artistic appreciation for this act as he did for the Beatles or Bob Dylan, he found a way to highlight their most appealing characteristics and depict them in a way that crystallized what they were trying to accomplish. This effort displayed the possibilities but also the difficulties that were inherent to understanding pop on its own terms.

"Sheepshead Bay" was still a warm-up to columns where Goldstein more fully realized his pop ethos. In his estimation, rock music could not be considered anything less than a meaningful change in the culture that could portend or resonate with other changes. The music Goldstein wrote about was vital not just for its sound or energy, but also because of its cultural politics; his critical responsibility was to articulate this.

The July 14, 1966 column mentioned at the opening of this chapter is an excellent example of this belief. Its title, "Evaluating Media," alludes to McLuhan's book *Understanding Media,* and right off the bat Goldstein grapples with the book's implications. "The most disturbing thing about Marshall McLuhan's 'Understanding Media' to most readers of this column will be its insistence that those who attempt to impose standards upon the 'cool' electronic media based upon their aesthetic experiences with the printed word are cultural illiterates." Yet citing McLuhan's prescriptions that form and content should not be separated, Goldstein contended that the new media required an entirely different critical perspective, which he dubbed "pop aestheticism." This stance was a natural one for youthful critics, he argued, because of their long-standing intimacy with media. But additionally, it showed how the cultural hierarchies traditionally championed by more learned (or aged) critics must fall away in the face of new culture. Goldstein wrote:

> The dichotomy between classic and pop, between hot and cool, between high and low art forms, is especially apparent in the area of popular music. Adult intellectuals may never be able to comprehend why Bob Dylan is worshipped by legions of pubescent 'teeny-boppers' and, at the same time, considered a major American poet by many serious students. These parochial critics face a practically insurmountable obstacle in their unwillingness to accept the fact that a poet can work in a medium such as rock n roll—that this is an age of electronic troubadours.[124]

Goldstein's argument that Bob Dylan exemplified the union of mass appeal and seriousness echoes the points I've made earlier in this work about the major role the folksinger/rock star played in transforming critics' thinking about the possibilities for rock culture. More than this, however, it highlights the centrality of a new kind of criticism that was obligated to bypass traditional modernism. Goldstein's advocacy of the revolutionary power of electric media—toppling once rigid boundaries, befuddling dominant critical voices—substantiated the view that this work was, indeed, a type of cultural politics. He thus positioned himself as a mouthpiece for his generation, best attuned to describe and champion the cultural changes.

"A pop critic needs his eyes, his ears, a typewriter, and an impressive German vocabulary," he wrote near the end of this particular column, apparently referencing German critics of vogue such as Marcuse and Marx and also signaling the function of education to his critical practice. More important than those factors, however, was that a critic "needs his youth. Understanding media is hardly enough; we must learn to evaluate as well. And, in rock 'n' roll at least, the child may be father to the man."[125] Clearly, his generational identity became his best asset for establishing authority and credibility. It was also the prism through which new standards of evaluation would be refracted; rather than banishing standards all together, youth would be the arbiters of this new sensibility.

From this point, Goldstein's column would flesh out a method for what he called pop aestheticism and I am calling pop criticism. With his keen, youthful eye, Goldstein began to take on music and music-related issues with a critical perspective that banked upon not just his social location, but also his fervent adoration. "I was in love with what I was hearing, and I did think that what was going on in the music represented a significant change in my generation," Goldstein later explained. In the early days, his column was that of a fan blessed with the surreal opportunity to write about, and even meet, the celebrities he adored. "It was like a dream come true for me, it was totally an enthusiasm," Goldstein has remarked since, noting that he loved his work even though he made just 20 dollars a week. "I was always in awe of the stars that I met."[126]

As an ardent fan, Goldstein assembled narratives about the music and celebrities he encountered, and his column began to grapple regularly with the construction of pop celebrity. In writing he based on classic short story form, articles about the Fugs, the Rolling Stones, and others that followed over the next several months depicted the stars he encountered as characters, then carried the reader, along with the subject, toward some type of epiphany. Additionally, though restricted by the rather traditional layout of the *Village Voice*, Pop Eye still took liberties within the form of his column, often breaking it into multiple fragments with subheadings, utilizing a highly conversational style that bordered on stream-of-consciousness, and cursing or inventing neologisms. "Every now and then, the editor Dan Wolf would call me into his office and say something like, 'Do you have to use all these four-letter words?'" Goldstein has said, "And I would say, 'Yes!' and he said, 'Okay.'"[127] Within this stretched-out journalistic space, Goldstein placed the triumvirate of the music, the musician, and the mediation of both—which included his own commentary—into a necessary dialogue.

To illustrate, his July 21, 1966 article about the Fugs, entitled "The Fugs Go Pro," considered how the band, formed a year earlier, dealt with their skills which were the inevitable outgrowth of experience. With the smoothing of their unrefined style, Goldstein noted that "the Fugs have become an act—alas," who were best described as "pop, pop, POP!" But a more pressing wonder was what this meant for their music and artistry. "The question is whether [the musicians] are still poets or whether they have become performers, or whether poets and performers aren't the same thing after all?" Goldstein quickly refuted this useless binary, though, pointing out that audiences who worried about these concerns might be missing the main point of the music. "The true Bohemia on Saint Mark's Place will be bitterly disappointed at what has happened to its favored sons. Every ballad, every bit of counterpoint, will seem to cry 'sell out,'" Goldstein wrote, alluding to one of the main drags of the New York counterculture scene. "But for scores of fans who do not subscribe to so rigid an image of hip, this 'Evening with the Fugs' will be an enjoyable and effective rock concert," he concluded.[128]

In a context where intellectualism melded with pleasure, being entertaining remained the foremost concern for Goldstein, and how a band achieved it was secondary. Goldstein had yet to object uniformly to the effects that commercialization and popularity could have on musicians; so long as they continued to produce superior music, the experience of listening to them was worthwhile. Still, it is telling that already there was awareness of an argument that had been circulating at least since Dylan went electric: whether the effects of commercialism were ultimately adverse. In this case, mass popularity remained overwhelmingly a positive: the thing that ensured lots of people would be privy to messages that would thrill them, ignite them, and sate their desires.

In spite of his largely pro-Fugs argument in this column, he voiced a modicum of skepticism. Goldstein wrote near the article's conclusion that "the question—the big one—is whether one must lament for the Fugs and their thunder from the East: 'I saw the best minds of my generation . . .' "[129] The quotation referenced a song on the Fugs' first album, itself pulled from Allen Ginsberg's "Howl," wherein the words precede the line "destroyed by madness." The Fugs might not go mad, he suggested, but their own success might destroy them.

Although the same slick professionalism which had made its way into the music of the Fugs might corrupt the "best minds of his generation," Goldstein had yet to blame the music industry itself for it. This particular column ignored arguments that commerce could be a corrupting force in a global sense, and in fact was somewhat incredulous that "True Bohemia" would react poorly to market infiltration. Rather, at this point the trouble seemed to be one of how individual artists reacted to the experience of joining the business, rather than how business in and of itself co-opted unsuspecting musicians. Market forces remained benevolent, or at least neutral.

Additionally, this article about the Fugs was one of the earliest examples of a theme that would become more prevalent in Goldstein's work: how to determine when a trend had passed its prime. The serial nature of the column gave Goldstein a voracious appetite for the new, paralleling in many ways the market forces that were continually churning out new bands for public consumption. Becoming hypersensitive to these ebbs was the job of a critic, but it also introduced a contradiction into what, ultimately, the function of his criticism was. Was his job to champion what was popular, or spot what would be popular? Did "evaluating media" also include turning against artists when they stopped being effective, even if that lack of effectiveness was simply the product of how they were treated in the marketplace? In turning his attention to trends, Goldstein made all the more clear that he participated in their success or failure. Through this channel, Goldstein became a critic in a literal sense—and began to bring more negative writing into the music pages.

The British Invasion was one of the first trends he determined dead-on-arrival, mourned in his August 4, 1966 column. Noting the difficulty that accompanied witnessing a trend's demise, "Even in pop, when the only blood shed is in profits, and the only decay in reputation," Goldstein declared that the British Invasion had reached a tragic low.[130] He closely attended to chart activity as proof of his point—noting his acquiescence, at least on some level, in the mechanisms of the industry—making much of the fact that Frank Sinatra was enjoying the number one single in the country, and that for the first time in many months American musicians were proving competitive with their British counterparts.[131] In this context, Goldstein noted for the first time that pop music appeared to have nothing new to offer the listener. "What's new in pop music is that there is nothing new," he wrote, lamenting that adults seem to have taken to purchasing 45 records, once a format consigned almost totally to youth. The connection between flailing pop and ho-hum British bands affirmed that what was once a youth-driven trend had not only lost its potency, but, worse, had been tainted by adults. Within the context of Goldstein's previous discussion of McLuhan, the ramifications proved immense. If the new music, delivered in a new format, inherently signaled some level of social change, was this all there was? Perhaps instead of full-blown revolution, it simply meant that adults could now put Sinatra on the charts.

The Beatles redeemed themselves at least somewhat later that month, when Pop Eye featured its first full-blown record review of the band's latest offering, *Revolver*. Until this point, Goldstein had mostly written think pieces about popular culture, focusing on stars, trends, and live performances. His review of *Revolver* brought a new function to this mix. Whereas before he had occasionally written with the tacit intent of advocating for a particular concert or artist, the *Revolver* review brought the commercial potential of his criticism that much closer to the surface. Goldstein wrote, " 'Revolver' is a revolutionary record, as important to the expansion of pop territory as was 'Rubber Soul.' It was apparent last year that the 12 songs in 'Rubber Soul' represented an important advance. 'Revolver' is the great leap forward. Hear it once and you know it's important. Hear it twice, it makes sense. Third time around, it's fun. Fourth time, it's subtle. On the fifth hearing, 'Revolver' becomes profound."[132]

Given the increasing regard in which the column was held by both readers and other writers over this period, such direct advocacy of music was noteworthy. Moreover, it couched the notions of pop aestheticism in a new way—seeking to further publicize that which would "expand pop territory," and, maybe therein, expand the minds and souls of its listeners. Here Goldstein's role as a tastemaker was clarified significantly. He went further by announcing the historic importance of this work, thereby recognizing its importance not only for the contemporary moment, but also for posterity.

Elsewhere in the paper, however, the Beatles were being flogged for their diminishing popularity. Jules Siegel, writing a week later, noted that the band had only nine girls greet them for the start of their 1966 American tour, insignificant when compared to the Beatlemania of just two years earlier. This change, morbid as it may have been, also heralded great potential; for Siegel, a sign that "history is not with the kids but with the intellectuals who write it."[133] The same *Voice* that contained Goldstein's review also included reporter James Kempton's tongue-in-cheek account of one of their press conferences.[134] Amid such a backlash, Goldstein's praise became evidence that perhaps the Beatles should not be given up on so quickly. "If nothing else," Goldstein wrote, " 'Revolver' must reduce the number of cynics where the future of pop music is concerned"—apparently, a self-conscious statement addressed to himself as much as to his journalistic peers.[135] Yet we must wonder whether the band could have achieved such a pinnacle of artistry if they remained firmly seated in truly mass appeal. The fact that they were no longer the mass culture icons of previous years facilitated and was facilitated by critical belief in their artistic genius.

As the fall of 1966 led into the winter of 1967, doubts about the power of pop that were a subtext of his writing about the Beatles gained ground. A growing theme in the columns of this period was the dominance of fabrication over organics, of artificial trends over natural ones. Mass culture had held mammoth possibility just a few months earlier, but Goldstein now carped to his readers of its confinements, warning against the infiltration of base commercialism at every turn. For several weeks in late 1966 and early 1967, for instance, he railed against the radio industry and censorship in pop radio. "The entire process of hit-making is an inside operation into which your consumer preference has only incidental effect," Goldstein wrote in a column entitled "69 with a Bullet" on November 24.[136] His column also began to periodically feature a mini-section called "Warnings of the Week" which were intended to caution consumers against the most treacherous developments in the new music, as well as to lob insults against artists whose sales capability was only a sign of their fakeness, nothing more. One target of his derisive new perspective was the Monkees, about whom Goldstein fumed that "record execs think it's the Beatles all over again. But the influence of this pre-fabricated foursome on teen style is nil. They imitate, never innovate, and their emergence becomes submergence at the flick of a dial."[137]

What is clear in examining these columns is that while originality still lingered in the musical realm, the drives of the record business had made those places harder and harder to locate. Where before the business went almost unmentioned—simply the delivery system that channeled the music to youthful consumers who themselves were the real locus of power—that pipeline was having an increasingly negative effect on what it transmitted. "There are signs of merger between Madison Avenue and Tin Pan Alley," wrote Goldstein in February 1967, noting that a group called the Fabulous Fakes had started a line of cosmetics and half-joking that the next corporation seeking sponsorship from the music business might be General Motors.[138] He had already lamented the "MacDougalization" of drug culture,[139] hinting that this march of commerce wasn't just affecting music, but instead colonized multiple mechanisms of youth rebellion. Coincidentally, Goldstein's column was as often short vignettes and mini-ruminations as it was the longer think pieces that were characteristic of his earliest editions. As the culture he wrote about had become more digestible, so too, in a sense, had his writing—and himself.

John Wayne and Richard Goldstein look every bit the odd couple in a photograph of them together that appears in a December 1966 *Newsweek* profile called "Pops and Boppers." Wayne, all rugged and rangy in his cowboy attire, towers over the mop-topped, cherubic Goldstein, who at 5'4" is a full foot shorter than his companion. It was Goldstein's growing stature, though, that the article sought to detail. "Goldstein has created his own journalistic discipline—the 'pop' beat," mused the report, and thanks to it, he was free to roam the wild terrain of "miniskirts, underground filmmakers, LSD cultists and rock 'n' roll musicians."[140] The *Newsweek* piece marvels at Goldstein's "adventure" of a column, by that time also being reprinted in *New York* magazine. Its top concern, flying above the rest, was Goldstein's "musical Esperanto" of rock music.

What makes the article precious is its open display of wonder, even disbelief, that such a column existed. This alone makes plain just how successful Goldstein was in his endeavor, for these days it is hard to imagine what kind of pop cultural criticism would actually warrant remark. But the article is also a prescient example of how hard it would be for pop criticism to achieve the lofty and varied goals it established for itself. *Newsweek* portrays Goldstein not as the vigilante of a threatening politico-cultural front, but as a media darling setting a trend, one that might easily nose its way into mainstream press sensibilities. More than this, Goldstein had raised the profile of pop—and of himself—so that both might be recognized, named, catalogued. Recognition absolutely marked a change in values—the mainstream finally giving this culture the serious attention it deserved—but it also meant more attention, period—an eventuality that would come with costs.

The anointing of pop coincided with Goldstein's increasing retreat to something he dubbed "the underground." He first found this underground in the San Francisco music scene of early 1967. But why had this underground emerged?—or, maybe better said, why had good music stayed under wraps? If underground culture harbored the seeds of revolutionary change, how could it be disseminated to the masses without losing its poignancy? How had the music business become so good so quickly at selling this culture, when once it was better understood as its unwitting vendors? And was popularity something that musicians—and music critics—should seek and seek to create, or something they should shy away from?

Goldstein could no longer naively proclaim that popular culture was a revolutionizing force in the world, because the media that had "radically changed the perceptions of every man on any street"[141] had also radically changed the process of peddling it. Though his style and techniques for evaluating media did not alter much over this period, his mission did. "The public is only incidentally responsible for bland popular art," he explained. "The men who keep music sterile are the trendmakers themselves—the ones who play the hits play the hits play the hits. What they are really doing is creating a pop underground. What the journalist must do is bring this underground to the surface."[142]

CHAPTER 3
Hype

In college, they showed us an anthropology film about a tribe in Africa some-where, in the middle of a ferocious famine, and the men had to go out hunting giraffes, with water slung over their shoulders, and singing, walking for arid days, trying to smell giraffe dung in the clouds, until finally, over a distant ridge, they saw just the neck of an enormous giraffe with spots like brown eyes. As it smelled them its feet churned and its neck waved panicky in the wind—glorious in color—but the men whooped, shook their singing bolos overhead, and ran after the animal; it leaping, careening, and the men toss-ing their weapons at the animal's legs—legs spread apart for distance—until, hit once, again, it fell straight on its head like the log of the century . . . fell on its face, waiting, and as the men slashed with their knives, the animal's eyes closed slowly, heavily, lids quivering . . . Rock 'n' roll is the giraffe. Public rela-tions men, disc jockeys, emcees, executives, socko boffo copy boys, fabulous blondes, prophets, frauds, fakes, connect-the-dots copies, and under-assistant West Coast promo men hunt with their snares and bolos, cut, castrate, slice up the meat, and hang shaggy heads in trophy.[1]

The above is an excerpt from Richard Goldstein's "Giraffe Hunters," a piece he wrote toward the end of 1966. Its graphic imagery portended what would be the overwhelming theme of his writing as his tenure at the *Voice* came to a close: the industry's violent, dramatic capture of the spirit of rock. Com-ing just months after his column's enthusiastic beginning, "Giraffe Hunters" heaves with both resignation and fear. With little to hope for, Goldstein watched in disgust as hungering ravagers devoured the music he loved.

The hunters sought more than just music; Goldstein himself had become prey. As the quality of mainstream rock deteriorated, Goldstein began a tactical retreat to the underground, a zone he imagined would nurture his continuing faith in the possibility of cultural radicalism. Yet as underground music exploded in popularity, it too ran the risk of exploitation, and this reality struck the young writer with a deep and highly personalized blow.[2] He quickly recognized that the process of unearthing music was far from simple—it was thorny, and potentially even wrong.

Goldstein's transitioning attitudes regarding the power and perils of media exposure contained new truths about mass culture and critical practice that clashed angrily with his one-time fantasies of mediated revolution. Moreover, though Goldstein did not damn criticism in his rant, journalism in general and rock criticism in particular played an explicit role in the very situation he was lamenting. As the industrial production of music changed over the course of 1966 and beyond, the press around it developed into an established business that intertwined with the industry it covered. At the same time, mainstream journalism, unevenly hipping itself to new cultural trends, spread awareness of the new music beyond the reach of the alternative press that generally housed rock criticism, and began to mimic the types of coverage found in the below-radar publications.

The emerging collusion between the music industry and the mass media would earn a name: hype. Coming into common parlance during the middle 1960s, hype in the most straightforward definition is public relations, usually of the type that borders on stunt. But for Goldstein, hype had both literal and metaphorical implications that would deeply impact his practice. Hype was the antithesis of authenticity—the poison pill that threatened to contaminate his beloved underground culture and choke the spaces where good rock music could flourish. Hype defiled mass media, turning what was once the powerhouse behind popular culture into just another mechanism for selling it. Hype was an indiscriminate and stealthy traveler, coming variously in the form of a psychedelically tinged advertisement or over the lips of a long-haired music executive, on the cover of a major market magazine, or even from the pen of a fellow rock critic. And hype threatened, and perhaps even made impossible, the profession that Goldstein held dear and the kind of intellectual work that had come to define him.

The previous chapter concerned how Goldstein's pop criticism intentionally de-territorialized the categories of high and low; this chapter explores what it did unawares to reshape the relationship between culture's mainstream and its margins. In the mire of intensifying music industry and media interest in countercultural rock music, rock critics starkly confronted the pitfalls of commercialism and the promotionalism of their own practice. Unable to completely forsake the commercial, they honed intellectual and professional strategies, such as the rhetoric of hype, that helped them come to terms with their role in the "socioeconomic circulation of popular music,"[3] and allowed them to construe rock in terms of the period's most treasured values: community, authenticity, and social change. This chapter presents both the calculated and the ad hoc solutions that critics utilized in an attempt to make sense of rock's contradictions. These tactics likewise served to legitimate critics' power, with lasting though not entirely positive consequences for how we think about popular music and commercialization.

Authenticity, Community, and Folk Ideals in Rock Music

To proponents of pop criticism, rock exploded existing boundaries between mass culture and art, creating a space in which it was possible to think of the two in tandem. As a result, it had tremendous effects on the conception of taste. But beyond, and somewhat in contrast with these tastemaking impulses, rock music also represented collectivist, democratic ideals that resonated with the era's communitarian revival. Like grassroots organizing, urban renewal, and the articulation of fraternity along lines of subculture, race, and gender, rock music advanced community as a goal as well as a moral imperative, and "appealed to a desire for place . . . and for fellowship, posing an alternative to alienation."[4]

For rock critics and the fans they sought to represent, rock music was an auditory as well as a tangible space in which these ideals could come to fruition. In his book *The Hippies and American Values*, Timothy Miller notes that "rock was an essential in the rise of communalism"—it provided the impetus for people to gather together to dance and listen, alternative models for work and familial arrangements, and a tie that bound fans together for the common purpose of liberation. Rock revealed its communalism along two different axes. The first, described in the last chapter, had to do with rock's existence as media: "a totality . . . infused with power" that impelled retribalization.[5] Second, rock was a watershed generational moment that, ideally, aligned all young people and articulated a unified struggle against the status quo. Together, these features made rock into a species of folk music,[6] with different potential than more traditional forms, as well as a unique palette of problems.

To understand the problems inherent in rock critics' imagining of rock as folk music, it is worth spending a few moments clarifying what folk music typically entails. In a useful definition, Roy Shuker contends that folk is a historical musical form that often "is reserved for music passed from person to person or generation to generation without being written down." His definition draws a bright line between recorded, commercially distributed music and music without those features, and explains the generic conventions of folk musics such as acoustic instruments and vernacular singing styles. For this reason, scholars often call folk the music of the people, though how they define "the people" varies considerably. Shuker further notes that folk music is tied "to forms of culture which are tightly linked to particular social groups and which are not subject to mass production." Many genres of music thus qualify as folk, including the blues, early reggae, "hillbilly"-era country, work songs, and protest songs.[7]

Folk music often signals ethnic, working-class, rural and black or indigenous communities in ways that can essentialize as well as celebrate the genealogies of popular music, highlight them as well as efface them. Bob Dylan, an early trailblazer in the folk-rock category, became a symbol of the contrasts between the folk and the rock community around issues such as electrification and celebrity. Dylan and his peers also borrowed themes, performing styles, and songs from rural, black, and working-class musicians in ways that critics have since called theft or even minstrelsy, making the interpenetration of folk and rock bound up in the histories of racism and classism. For these reasons as well as the major differences between rock and folk along lines of technology, economics, and modes of distribution, rock music could not be "folk" as easily as it could be "pop."

Despite and in some ways because of these frictions, key figures of early rock criticism trumpeted the music's folk credentials. Jon Landau, a writer for *Crawdaddy!* and *Rolling Stone* who later helped launch Bruce Springsteen, called rock music "unmistakably a folk form" and contended "there existed a strong bond between performer and audience, a natural kinship, a sense that stars weren't being imposed from above but had sprung up from out of our ranks."[8] Landau's use of the word "our" is critical; it allows him to claim alignment not only between the audience and the performer but also between both and himself as a critic. Goldstein similarly invoked the spirit of folk in observing that rock unnerved "adult intellectuals" and that the budding rock critic would "[need] his youth" in order to be successful.[9] Rock critics spoke to and for other young people, the folklorists of a rebel youth community.

The folk ideals of rock critics presented a major quandary, though: How could something that depended on its mass appeal also maintain ties to a bona fide community? The concept of authenticity helped resolve this serious dilemma. In the years after World War II, Americans grew preoccupied with finding and achieving authenticity, a quest that took hold in the upper class alongside industrialization.[10] In general terms, to be authentic meant to be real, nobly dedicated to one's core self, beliefs, and goals. Among white youth of the New Left, this pursuit frequently took on political dimensions, their revolutionary aims a pathway toward undoing their own alienation.[11] For rock music, the political goals of authenticity existed but could be muted; more important, authenticity added "an ethical dimension to the aesthetic experience" of rock music.[12] Lawrence Grossberg argues that authenticity "depends on [rock music's] ability to articulate private but common desires, feelings and experiences into a shared public language" and asks that "the performer have a real relation to his or her audience."[13] Authenticity therefore became the most significant discourse through which to evaluate rock's relevance, where music had to be good as well as index a rock community.

It is at the nexus of these ideas—rock as communitarian and ideally authentic yet also intrinsically a business—that we must understand the developments in rock criticism concerning rock's commercial expansion over the late 1960s. Much of the scholarship on popular music and commercialization relies on simplified understandings of how rock commercialized in the 1960s, and overemphasizes the role of economics while not paying enough attention to the idea of community. For instance, Simon Frith, in an influential characterization, argues that "the problematic issue that runs . . . through the history of all forms of popular music since the development of industrial capitalism is the relationship between music as a means of popular expression and music as a means of making money"[14]—a statement which I endorse. Yet, this point too often has been treated to mean that commercialism hampers popular expression in an automatic fashion. On the contrary, rock critics obsessed as much about the power of mediation as they did about the gross impact money might have on rock music. The music business became problematic only when it began to impinge upon and threaten the rock community, and that impact related directly to its level of media exposure.

In the previous chapter, I noted that intellectuals began to take an interest in the possibilities of mass media to both make and unmake community in the early twentieth century, forming one plank in the foundation of the mass culture critique. Rock critics shared this interest and like earlier intellectuals started to doubt the quality of the connectivity mass media engendered. But where mass culture critics traditionally turned against pop cultural forms in favor of an isolated, "outside" avant-garde, rock critics imported favored popular music and lesser known music that excited them into their own "inside," a delicate ecology that too much mainstream attention would unbalance (and that, as it turned out, their own work could injure). Though nascent in the early 1960s, the emerging rock underground and its cagey relationship to media set the stage for later "indie" music cultures that would also rely on, yet vehemently resent media coverage.[15] From the British Invasion to the psychedelic sounds of San Francisco, questioning media, marketing, promotion, and segmentation became a shorthand for discussing rock's devotion to its folk community, the gymnastics it would need to perform in order to stay authentic and—only lastly, if at all—the unintended consequences of the criticism itself.

Media and the Commercialization of Rock

With money pouring in during the mid-1960s and the importance of popular music to growing youthful audiences undeniable, the end of the decade was a time of incredible consolidation in the music business. Warner-Reprise bought out Atlantic Records, a successful independent label since the late 1940s, in 1967—just one of a number of examples of domestic and international horizontal integration in the business.[16] Major labels also moved to integrate vertically, purchasing distribution and rack-jobbing companies as well as enterprises such as music equipment and record stores. Framing all of this was the widespread merger movement of the decade, at the time the largest corporate concentration the nation had ever seen. Companies seeking to diversify, inflate stock prices, and boost profit margins gravitated toward music companies, which not only were highly profitable but also attracted the coveted youthful demographic.[17]

Consolidation and growth led inevitably to an expanding promotional structure for rock music, within music labels as well as outside them. The fever to better understand the new youth market moved labels to look to their own personnel for guidance. One example was the appearance of positions known as "company freaks" or "house hippies," an informal, flippant name given to the rock fans who worked in label publicity and promotion departments after 1966. With loosely defined job roles and little supervision, company freaks helped labels to authenticate rock, mediating between business executives and the bands and alternative news outlets they desired as clients and contacts. These men and others like them were often the chief liaisons for rock critics, providing them with tips on bands in unfamiliar cities, concert tickets, places to stay when traveling, and sometimes drugs.[18]

Many of the new acts flourished in a live setting, making the rock concert business a lucrative venture and yet another example of the spread of rock and roll marketing. By the middle 1960s venues began to crop up in metropolitan areas; often these were repurposed or refurbished theaters or else music clubs whose owners tolerated rock music on some nights. The most famed of them was San Francisco's Fillmore, which Bill Graham opened in 1965.[19] Graham, an immigrant from Germany, was a cunning businessman in a context where many people, including artists, willfully evaded commercial matters.[20] Soon, the Fillmore became the home base to the city's psychedelic music scene, making Graham quite wealthy. By 1968, he expanded his franchise to New York, where he opened the Fillmore East in Manhattan's East Village. Like-minded entrepreneurs in other cities helped to create the beginnings of a nationwide rock circuit, making it much easier for bands to tour. In Los Angeles, Whiskey A-Go-Go morphed into a rock venue in 1965 and transformed the Sunset Strip into a hub for rock fans, while in Boston, an older club christened the Boston Tea Party in 1967 began showcasing rock acts such as the Velvet Underground.[21] Other comparable clubs opened in cities such as Philadelphia, Detroit, and Chicago.[22]

The establishment of rock festivals exploded the concert scene even further. An offspring of folk and jazz festivals, the first rock festival was the Monterey Pop Festival, held in Monterey, California, during June 1967 and drawing a crowd of at least 50,000.[23] Monterey was a joint effort of concert promoter Ben Shapiro, businessman Alan Pariser, and Derek Taylor, a "company freak" who had previously worked as a publicist for the Beatles.[24] While the original plan for the concert was to make money, protest from some of the hip community's most prominent advocates—including music critic Ralph J. Gleason of the *San Francisco Chronicle*—thwarted the profit motive and transformed the event into a benefit concert. Despite this change, the music labels were the real beneficiaries. Record companies tested their acquisitions in front of their potential consumers and collected new acts. For example, Warner/Reprise showcased the Grateful Dead, whom they'd signed just a few months before, and CBS Records offered a contract to San Francisco–based Big Brother and the Holding Company, featuring lead singer Janis Joplin, for the then-astronomical sum of $250,000.[25]

Radio likewise influenced and answered to the expanding commercial potential of rock. The Top 40 format, initiated in the 1950s on the AM dial, became endemic to youth culture by the early 1960s, serving as the perfect counterpart to an industry focused on promoting the charts.[26] During these years, when radio-friendly British Invasion artists dominated, shortened playlists, syndicated shows, clipped DJ remarks, and various automated features restricted the format even further.[27] Newer rock music, with longer songs and more controversial material, did not work well in this highly con-

fined environment. A 1964 modification to FCC policy changed this, allowing independently programmed FM stations to innovate programming that
was favorable to the new music.[28] By the late 1960s, these stations would
prove highly useful as promotional tools both for music and for music-
related services such as concert halls.[29]

Rock writing and its companion alternative press presented the vastly expanded music business with new entry points to shape the music's
meaning and reception. *Rolling Stone's* launch in late 1967 added another
dedicated publication for rock music to the growing number of alternative weeklies, mainstream magazines, and daily newspapers that covered
this music. From its first issue, the magazine mingled coverage of rock with
politics and culture of interest to the rock audience; editor Jann Wenner
tried to produce engaging content while distancing the magazine from the
headier approaches to rock that dominated out East.[30] Wenner was also an
unabashed capitalist, and believed rock journalism could be profitable if it
attracted an audience that youth-targeted businesses wanted to reach. The
Voice, now the financially solvent elder statesman of a sizeable field of alternative publications, abided by the same principle and began to regularly
print ads from record companies. Other publications, often harder up for
cash than the *Voice,* were even more reliant on the music business to support them.[31] For music labels, these publications were excellent venues for
ads and prized publicity tools that could boost or dampen sales and concert
attendance through their editorial content.[32]

Over time, labels came to identify rock journalists as a constituency
worth wooing, and their writing as a desirable form of publicity. "Publicists
just had to hold on for dear life," noted Robert Christgau, in speaking of the
shift. "I mean there was suddenly this new avenue and they just had to go
down that avenue."[33] One measure of critics' growing importance to labels
was the increasing ease at which critics obtained the materials and access
they needed to do their jobs. "Fewer than a dozen copies of *Sergeant Pepper's
Lonely Hearts Club Band* were sent to the press in 1967," explains Jim DeRogatis in his biography of early rock critic Lester Bangs, "but two years later,
things were changing."[34] Thanks at least in part to the presence of company
freaks, labels of the late 1960s would regularly foot the bill to fly a writer to
cover a show in another city, invite him to press junkets or a concert, and
shower him with more records than he could conceivably listen to.[35] Labels
did not relinquish control entirely to the whim of rock critics, who at this
point rarely felt pressured to cover a band or album in a particular way,
and even sometimes blatantly disrespected their hosts.[36] (As Christgau has
admitted, "There are a few things I shouldn't have written about because I

went to the recording session which I thought was such a cool thing to do . . . but very quickly my attitude always was, I'll take anything you'll send me in the mail and it will not get you anything"—a philosophy Goldstein echoed.)[37] Nonetheless, a relationship developed between rock journalism and the rock music industry that had not previously existed and thus had no established precedent—economic, ethical, or otherwise.

Any border between rock criticism and the industry it covered grew increasingly porous or, perhaps more accurately, failed to materialize in any significant way. In fact, as rock criticism matured, its practitioners often cultivated their industry ties rather than rejected them. Goldstein has described company freaks as "really great people [who] would take me to see bands that were unknown but that they believed in"—an unsurprising assessment considering that company freaks often had much in common with rock critics.[38] Some company freaks worked as critics before, after, or even during their jobs in publicity, and critics who left writing at times took jobs in the industry, as *Rolling Stone*'s Jon Landau famously did when he began to manage Bruce Springsteen.[39] This imbrication especially proliferated in the 1970s, but the trend seeded during this late 1960s period. If rock critics had a debt to their authentic community, that community existed within music labels as well as outside of them.

Critics were not the lone rock fans or hip community members growing more at ease with business. As the music industry sought to forge organic connections with the counterculture, some members turned to it for job opportunities, while others joined different industries or started companies that catered to alternative markets. By the late '60s and early '70s, these dynamics acquired the name "hip capitalism," a term applied to a wide range of companies with a "counterculture business philosophy"[40]—from head shop owners to camping goods retailers, vegetarian restaurateurs to rock radio DJs. "The enemy is the machine-like Corporate State," explained Marilyn Bender, who devoted a *New York Times* article to the trend in 1971. Rather than rejecting commercialism outright, hip capitalists wanted to humanize the commercial relationship.[41]

Detractors of hip capitalism stridently questioned its motives. Craig Karpel's 1970 *Esquire* article "Das Hip Kapital" identified hip capitalists as those "who coin their gold from a system their customers would like to destroy" and reserved particularly harsh criticism for anyone who used music to do so. "The bedrock value of hip capitalism is black ink on the bottom line," Karpel opined. "Long hair, dope and rock music have become means to that end. The hair is a way of identifying the market. Smoking dope sensitized the consumer to the product. And rock music is what is sold."[42] Citing examples where young people refused to pay concert entry fees or tickets for rock documentaries, Karpel viewed rock music as politicized content that, when properly created and channeled, necessarily opposed the will of the market. Many shrewd music-focused hip capitalists "sell underground radio . . . without being called to account for their political or moral or existential position,"[43] which inevitably problematized their actions. Karpel was equally skeptical of anyone who wished to challenge the music business from the inside. "The hip capitalist who attempts to work from within soon finds himself within a metaphorical recording studio," Karpel noted. "The men in the booth—the straight executives—dote on him and humor him and send coffee and sandwiches in to him, as much as he wants and more. But they are not about to change the way the board is set up just because he asks them to, let alone invite him to try his hand at the controls."[44]

Karpel's anti–hip capitalist manifesto also harbors a deep ambivalence that evokes the larger paradoxes within the hip community about capitalist practices, particularly when they pertain to music. Near the article's conclusion, Karpel writes that "[hip] capitalists are increasingly finding that their market is becoming antagonistic because the kids who consume their product do not want to be consumers"—a telling word choice, given that these antagonistic young people are still "consumers," never mind their desires.[45] Moreover, an undercurrent of the piece is that businesspeople who provide "vital services to Woodstock Nation" are, in fact, vital; the major sin of business is that "it has gulled 'the people' into thinking that the culture is *their property,* susceptible to larceny, rather than their community, which is inalienable."[46] For Karpel, true community and its attendant culture were impervious to marketing tactics, even if at the same time they provided ample fodder for them. With sincere intentions, business could help as much as hinder that community.

The best example of the mutable relationship among capitalism, music, and the "hip community" is Woodstock. Occurring over three days in mid-August 1969, the concert was the joint venture of two "young men with unlimited capital," John Roberts and Joel Rosenbaum, and two stereotypical "long-hairs," Artie Kornfeld and Mike Lang.[47] Though the men often clashed about their differences of perspective as they planned the event, and would-be participants bristled about the presence of two entrepreneurial "straights," in its aftermath Woodstock was interpreted as a peaceful if somewhat chaotic expression of hippie values.[48] A number of attendees did not pay, and though many considered that action a triumph of counterculture over capitalism, it does not change the fact that a significant portion of the crowd did pay, that many people spent money while at the concert, that the musicians who performed were paid, or that the originators of the event still intended to turn a profit even if they were unsuccessful in doing so.[49] Why, then, was the communitarian vibe of the festival enough to underplay its capitalist intentions—so much so that, to this day, the original Woodstock stands as a sacrosanct emblem of the way things could have been?[50]

This last question lays bare the ambivalent status of the consumer culture of the late 1960s, conflicted not just among countercultural youth at the time but also in reflection. Over the years, we have learned that this period was a crucible for changing capitalist tactics, as hip sense found admirers within the stodgiest of businesses, and marketing executives moved segmentation from the periphery to the center of their practice.[51] Too often, however, observers blame the counterculture, especially its hippie contingent, for yielding to the market's embrace of their ethos or naively envisioning their lifestyle as resistant to commercial threats. The landmark study to articulate this point remains Thomas Frank's *The Conquest of Cool,* an examination of how industries of the mid- to late 1960s adopted the discourse and imagery of the counterculture to promote consumerism and usurp cultural dissent. While I find much of Frank's work insightful, his orientation is toward industry and producers who attempted to take on the signifiers of alternative culture, rather than the reactions and activities of consumers themselves. Likewise, despite his sincere attempt to complicate what are often blunt understandings of the process of cooptation, Frank is deeply skeptical that consumption could potentially be a space of resistance, suggesting that the battles to be fought lie in the realm of production rather than that of culture—a particularly problematic stance considering that his own study focuses on cultural industries such as advertising and men's fashion, and his methodology depends upon discourse.

Hip communities and capitalist industries frequently worked together, knowingly cross-pollinating one another, although not without friction. Frank is correct that media industries assumed a youthful perspective, but we must not forget that youth started their own businesses and defined themselves both through and against mass media such as television and radio from the earliest onset of teenage culture. As a counterculture developed, there was never a clean divide between it and the mainstream and not always a belief that there should be. Assessments such as Frank's grant both too much power to capitalism and not enough to consuming audiences. They likewise do not acknowledge that certain cultural forms, such as rock music, could not mean what they have culturally without being commercial mass media. Yet at the same time, consumerism is not inherently resistant, and I am wary of perspectives that suggest this. Somewhere between these poles, a muddier yet more faithful depiction exists. Plainly, it is this: the music business, music consumers, and music journalists confronted novel cultural situations through which initially it could be hard to see the big picture or know exactly what to do. In these situations, they made do with the culture that was around them, made choices dependent upon their own instincts as well as the insights of their peers and media, tried more often than not to act in their own best interests, and only in retrospect developed a narrative to explain what they did.

Over the course of the late 1960s, the music business was becoming more lucrative and more immense. Rock critics *did* complain about these changes, as we shall see. Yet the brunt of their objections to the music business's increasingly phony output underscored their desires for authentic community, which suffered less at the hands of capitalist industry than it did in the unremitting gape of mediated spectacle. Like many of his peers, Goldstein searched for an explanation for the changes he witnessed, and media—the very apparatus he was using to highlight this culture—again and again emerged as an instrument with potentially fatal consequences for everything it touched.

Hype = Death

At sunrise on October 6, 1967, mourners gathered in San Francisco's Buena Vista Park to observe a widely felt loss. They carried candles and raised bells, graciously welcoming the rising sun, then set a fire upon which they tossed what was now refuse of the dead: "shaven hair, copies of *The Chronicle* and the *Berkeley Barb,* and even a matchbox of marijuana."[52] The grieving mass then walked through the streets of Haight Ashbury, following a casket that had been loaded with ashes from the blaze.[53] Some passed out a flyer to those who passed, and it read:

MEDIA CREATED THE HIPPIE WITH YOUR HUNGRY CONSENT. BE SOMEBODY. CAREERS ARE TO BE HAD FOR THE ENTERPRISING HIPPIE. DEATH OF HIPPIE END. FINISHED HIPPYEE GONE GOODBYE HEHPPEEE DEATH DEATH HHIP-PEE. EXORCISE HAIGHT ASHBURY. CIRCLE THE ASHBURY. FREE THE BOUND-ARIES. OPEN EXORCISE. YOU ARE FREE. WE ARE FREE. DO NOT BE RE-CREATED. BELIEVE ONLY IN YOUR OWN INCARNATE SPIRIT. BIRTH OF FREE MAN. FREE SAN FRANCISCO. INDEPENDENCE. FREE AMERICANS. BIRTH. DO NOT BE BOUGHT WITH A PICTURE, A PHRASE. DO NOT BE CAPTURED IN WORDS. THE CITY IS OURS. YOU ARE ARE ARE. TAKE WHAT IS YOURS. THE BOUNDARIES ARE DOWN. SAN FRANCISCO IS FREE NOW FREE THE TRUTH IS OUT OUT OUT.[54]

Almost exactly a year after Richard Goldstein claimed that rock music was being hunted, an ardent fan of the music died: a coincidence that suggests an ecological relationship between the two, as if one were the victuals and the other the creature dependent on it. This proclaimed hippie extinction followed the Summer of Love, a period when media outlets descended upon San Francisco and declared it the hotbed for all things countercultural. The hippie community of San Francisco, unready for this attention, buckled beneath it, so overwhelmed that metaphoric death seemed the only escape.

These two eulogies can be considered hallmarks in the history of the counterculture as well as evidence of the emerging belief that media promotion could extinguish underground culture. The phenomenon of hype, then the word itself, became an important part of Goldstein's work at the *Voice* as he evolved to protect his readers from it. I focus on three events in the following examination of hype in Goldstein's writing: the rise of San Francisco, the release of the Beatles' *Sergeant Pepper's Lonely Hearts Club Band,* and the Monterey Pop Festival.

Though Goldstein had been talking about inauthenticity in music almost since his column began, it took several months before he identified its presence as part of a larger trend. Prior to that moment, he classified phoniness in performance or personality in individual terms: a band that reacted poorly to pressure or lost its raw energy by practicing too frequently on the road to recognition. Goldstein was as likely to come to the defense of artists as he was to disparage them. As often as not, at issue was not the musician him/herself but the crowd's unreasonable expectations. Ultimately, for Goldstein, experience overrode commerciality and capitalism was a funnel that fed culture to its patrons, if it was of concern at all; the audience's obligation, simply, was to dig.

Yet an early 1967 profile of a club promoter named Steve Paul shows Goldstein's growing concern that promotion threatened authenticity. Paul was the owner of a club in midtown Manhattan known as The Scene, which was swiftly becoming a lodestar in the constellation of New York's musical venues. While the club itself was "good—sometimes great," the owner exuded a level of slickness that disgusted the journalist. "He is never bathtub naked clean, he can't be," Goldstein wrote in his depiction. "He wears veils. Even under his flesh."[55] Sinking his belief in the power of the music, its listeners, and the experience however, Goldstein viewed Paul as incidental to his club's success. The Scene thrived "not because he stands onstage sobbing solipsistic epiphanies to an audience that gobs on his soul, but despite it. It's got good acts, not because Steve Paul can move mountains with the thumping sound of his ego but because he knows how to use money wisely and well. It will probably succeed, not because a man can will a movement but because the underground needs a springboard in midtown." His pronouncements suggest that the power of the underground community at this point remained more than that of any opportunistic force that might exploit it. Hype had not yet prevailed.

The psychedelic music of San Francisco presented the first test of how tenacious an underground culture could be in the face of mounting industry and media attention. The city arose as an epicenter of new rock and roll sounds in 1965 and 1966,[56] and Goldstein began writing about this music in early 1967, when he covered Jefferson Airplane at their first industry showcase in New York City. "Bay Area rock, with its spaced-out sense of the exotic, is making waves," he reported. "The music is simple, zestful, melodic . . . The sound makes it." Though the crowd watching this show "is not so sure it cares," with many of the more strait-laced types leaving early or otherwise showing consternation, Goldstein himself was taken and even found the industry reaction amusing. "Discarded buttons [reading 'Jefferson Airplane Loves You'] clatter on the staircase. And a giant ice sculpture which spells out RCA over the buffet table, is melting into all that kinetic heat. All of which means that Jefferson Airplane has arrived. Or something."[57] The article's tongue-in-cheek close pointed out how hopelessly clueless he still believed the music industry to be, perhaps so much that they would not be able to fully exploit the band.

Just two months later, on March 2, the music that had produced such an ambivalent response by the industry (and such hopeful promise to Goldstein) had already reached a level of overexposure. "The Bay Shore area is the Liverpool of the West," Goldstein wrote, comparing the northern California region to the famous cradle of the British Invasion just a few years before. Evidence for this claim appeared in media outlets of every kind: "*Newsweek* says so. *Ramparts* says so. *Crawdaddy* says so." The presence of *Newsweek* in this list is significant. On one level, the mainstream press paying attention was absurd—after all, the culture it was elevating was one that had begun to recoil from mainstream acknowledgment. At the same time, however, this mainstream notice gave the city a credibility that was undeniable: San Francisco was so important, even the mainstream press knew it. "American culture is a store window which must be periodically spruced up and redressed," he intoned. Because of this, "Hip San Francisco is being carved into bits of business territory" and bands were "being wined and dined like the last available shikse in the promised land."

Media attention had become more than just exposure—it flirted with becoming overexposure, even self-fulfilling prophecy. And overexposure might destroy this culture that imagined itself as born outside of media frames and at least partially in opposition to mainstream values. No longer were inauthentic music or personalities cause for alarm—promotion through the media itself could foul its subjects. The underground that Goldstein desired to promote had been exposed to a bleaching spotlight. "The most fragile thing to maintain in our culture is an underground," he penned, noting, "No sooner does a new tribe of rebels slip out, flip out, trip out, and take its stand than photographers from *Life* magazine are on the scene doing a cover layout." Just a short while away from the time when the hip community's biggest worry was persecution from society's dominant strand, "The new bohemians needn't worry about opposition these days; just exploitation." Instead of offering a genuine alternative, the underground had become a petri dish that gestated new products, dress, and modes of behavior to mainstream culture—in a word, a storehouse of "style."[58]

"Style" was a dreaded word in Goldstein's vocabulary. It was the worst thing that could happen to any movement; years later, he noted that every "institution that began in those days is now a sort of stylized version of itself," with 1960s politics too often boiled down to a barrage of tie-dye and peace signs.[59] His pessimism was growing at this point in early 1967, yet he managed to exhibit continued passion and excitement for the music itself. The new sounds that emanated from San Francisco were "the most potentially vital in the pop world" and "shoot a cleansing wave over the rigid studiousness of folk rock." Though the threat of stylization loomed, San Francisco would prove a formidable opponent—its vital music, which refused "to add technological effect" and thus demanded liveness, transmitted a life force that Goldstein guessed would be difficult to exploit. "It will be interesting to see what happens to San Francisco when the money men move in," he prophetically wrote in closing the column. "It will be a stone gas to take a Greyhound tour of the Haight. But that's another story about another time. Right now, give or take a little self-righteousness, this city is full of new ideas, new faces, and new music."[60]

A review that followed weeks later on the Grateful Dead's eponymous album lends more weight to this emphasis Goldstein placed on liveness—and his belief that gripping music could still thrive. The key quality that made the Grateful Dead worth listening to was their dynamism, which they had managed to preserve on record. "A good album, like those long lasting cold remedies, is filled with tiny time capsules which burst open at their own speed." Because of this, it was an album whose meaning deepened upon repeated listening, and with each one the record "feels spontaneous, it sounds honest . . . the Grateful Dead are a musical community."[61] With music such as this, the critic could only hope to approximate the album as a sensory experience.

In response to this pressing cultural dilemma, Goldstein maintained his critical belief in the power of popular culture through a focus on the agency of the audience community over any outside structure that might corral it. His convictions about experience and the power of music implied that his journalism wanted to strike a balance between highlighting and exploiting. Clearly, there was a difference between what he did as a journalist writing for the *Voice* and what was happening beyond, but what was that difference? Some of it turned upon the ideas of critical consecration, authenticity, and hype. As a participant in the culture who himself found the sounds he heard deeply moving, he provided his subjects coverage, but also a certain kind of credibility. The assumption seemed to be that as a self-aware member of the community, he could only offer authentic reverence, pointed toward a likeminded readership. Yet two blind spots would prove this assumption to be flawed. The first was a failure to own up to the way in which authenticity itself had become promotional, a style that rock critics could and would use strategically to draw clear demarcations between what they favored and what they opposed. Second, Goldstein overestimated the communitarian aspect of his journalism. As the readership of the *Voice* grew and it became a paper of the nation and world,[62] his writing was also sanctioning music to a widening body of readers—including other journalists.

As adamantly as he might have tried to use his journalism as an instrument of veneration and even defense, San Francisco marked a clear turning point for Goldstein, where an underground that once could insulate itself from greedy attacks by media and industry instead became exploited—and even created—by it. "It was inevitable enough to actually happen," he wrote just a few months later. "With every slick magazine in God's domain proclaiming the rise of the San Francisco sound, it is risen."[63] Media of various stripes were culpable for turning what was once local culture into something far more widespread and artificial. "The surest, swiftest way to spread a sub-culture in America today is through advertising," Goldstein noted.[64] "The line between exploitation and proselytization is barely visible." But what was advertising—and when did criticism become a part of it? And how did criticism itself guard against slipping into exploitative territory?

To avoid becoming just another arm of promotion, Goldstein rapidly morphed into the polar opposite: a Cassandra who foretold the demise of the music and lamented its inability to deliver anything other than another demographic. Such a response had dual effects, simultaneously confirming the sold-out nature of most culture while making his praises, when given, that much more powerful. In a world where nearly everything was sullied, a pessimist's rare cheer carried a great deal of potency. This had the potential to distinguish his writing from other kinds of media coverage, to elevate his power, and to ensure that he was indeed maintaining his authenticity.

The negativity with which Goldstein regarded his once beloved culture at this point had become overwhelming. He described "hippy aesthetics" as "the most potent force in pop culture today"—an assessment that previously would have been filled with promise but here read as a resignation. It "took the 'industry' only a few weeks to discover flower music," and the nascent genre "is now being stretched and distorted to fit a dozen commercial possibilities." The frenzy over "flower children" and "love" also percolated over into the retail sphere: "No sooner do a band of peripatetic flower children decide to stage a non-specific gathering in the park, than every shoe store and music center is running something they call a Be-In." Indeed, with "love spurting freely" Goldstein wondered, "will no one perfect a workable contraceptive?" But the real trouble, in his view, was the potential this had to adulterate the music itself. He cited several examples where hippie sensibilities had been watered down to catch the wave—a radio station calling itself "The 50,000 Watt Flower Pot"; a singer "with San Fernando shmaltz" who sang a song about flower children; the composer of the apocalyptic anthem "Eve of Destruction" having a new, sunny work entitled "Sunflower." "If the hang-ups over structure and struggles for power don't kill the Hip Community, Tin Pan Alley will," Goldstein griped toward the column's end. "That pisses me off."[65]

Labels and their promotional apparatuses collapse upon one another in this passage, and this argument in its most crude form has remained a popular one that critics of all stripes use to explain commercialization. Yet its subtleties should not be mistaken. While Goldstein does gripe about "Tin Pan Alley" and the impact of wanton commercialism, it is the "stretch" and "distortion" of its true meaning that he chastises, which are at best externalities of commercialization and not strictly based on the fact that the popular music industry profited from rock. What goes unstated but is assumed here is that when a culture gets sold out, disconnected patrons can buy in—and what allows that to happen is indiscriminate advertising and promotion.

As the battle for the soul of San Francisco continued, the Beatles released *Sergeant Pepper's Lonely Hearts Club Band.* Coming ten months after *Revolver,* an album that was critically acclaimed but could not resurrect the moribund British Invasion,[66] the June 1967 release of the much-awaited sequel was met with effusive praise, which many viewed as a defining moment. The quintessence of the new studio technology as well as the first LP that could be termed a "concept album," *Sergeant Pepper's* was understood as a work of art and widely acclaimed as rock music that had taken on the best influences of art and classical.[67] On the day it was released, radio stations nationwide broadcast the album in its entirety, and many listeners as well as critics understood it as a call to change the world.[68] In the *Voice*'s own pages, guest writer Tom Phillips called *Pepper's* "the most ambitious and most successful album ever issued, and the most significant artistic event of 1967."[69]

Goldstein's *Voice* reaction—notably reserved until after this extolment from Phillips—saw the album much less sanguinely. His response was a reaction against both the media frenzy surrounding the album and the underground's wholesale acceptance of its transcendence. Though he did not yet use the word "hype," the situation he would describe constituted it emphatically, with expectations so overcoming music that they clouded its reception. He rose to be a voice of caution in a chorus of wild admiration. That he initially reviewed the record in the *New York Times* speaks to this even further in two ways. The *Times* was a stodgy, mainstream newspaper rather than an edgy, alternative one, and publishing the review there suggested a more measured response, aimed toward a less easily awed readership. Moreover, Goldstein's coverage in the *Times* exposed *Pepper's* to a much wider audience.

Goldstein's *Times* review was not so much scathing as it was frustrated. "Like an over-attended child, 'Sergeant Pepper' is spoiled," he lamented, after explaining the unprecedented investment in the record, in both studio time and money. The resulting "obsession with production, coupled with a surprising shoddiness in composition, permeates the entire album" and subsequently, "There is nothing beautiful on 'Sergeant Pepper.'" The blameworthy factor in this for Goldstein lay in how much the band had isolated themselves from their fanbase. "In substituting the studio conservatory for an audience, they have ceased being folk artists, and the change is what makes their new album a monologue," Goldstein concluded.[70] Without a true organic connection to their audience, not only did they create overblown music, but their listeners were also prone to exaggerated responses.

Goldstein extended his critique a few weeks later in *Voice* under the title "I Blew My Cool Thru the *New York Times*." "If being a critic were the same as being a listener, I could just enjoy 'Sgt. Pepper's Lonely Hearts Club Band,'" Goldstein wrote. "I find the album better than 80 percent of the music around today; it is the other 20 percent (including the best of the Beatles' past performances) which worries me as a critic."[71] In this passage, Goldstein's main grievance with the record focused on his belief that it was its moment, not its merit, that inspired such acclaim. Once the novelty of *Sgt. Pepper's* wore off, the album would be no better than "Beatles baroque—an elaboration without improvement."

Once again, the album's lack of authenticity was particularly dangerous both to music and to criticism, especially given that the musicians in question were the Beatles. "The Beatles are the creators of the rock ethic," he wrote. "Without them there could be no such discipline as 'rock criticism' " and, as such, people were right to "expect meaning and significance" from the band. However, *Pepper's* was not the album that delivered that meaning and significance. It was "an engaging curio and not more." "Too bad," he continued. "I have a sweet tooth for reality. I like my art drenched in it, and even from fantasy I expect authenticity. What I worship about the Beatles is their forging of rock into what is real. It made them artists; it made us all fans; and it made me think like a critic when I turned on my radio."[72] Here, spelled out in terms of the Beatles, are the reverberations of hype: not only does it elevate unworthy music, but that music can then crowd out what is more deserving and potentially fail to inspire the act of criticism. Dismissing the Beatles was a metaphor for dismissing this process of hype more generally—necessary in order to protect critical practice.

The Monterey Pop Festival, also during the summer of 1967, serves as a third example of how skeptical Goldstein had become of hype, even as hippie culture reached heights he could only have dreamed of a few months before. Despite the impressive turnout and good music, the festival sparked resentment from Goldstein. His "The Hip Homunculus," published after the festival on June 29, demonstrated disgust for hype and an apocalyptic vision manifesting in Goldstein's heightened attention to business practices in his own writing. Monterey was a feasting ground for "the business and p.r. men—not the Brill Building set, but younger, leaner faces" who came to the festival in order to "watch, to mix, and to sample the merchandise." The industry added to its malice by finding ways to buck previous stereotypes of uptight, clueless music executives. "The balding starmaker with a payola factor is a myth in rock today. People still bribe, but today's tycoon knows that good music has a sexuality of its own. Today's kids collect art on wax—and the pop entrepreneur must know the soul of the flower child. Without hipsense he is a relic."[73]

Goldstein still maintained a flicker of optimism, writing at the time that "we are witnessing something strangely dazzling in American youth culture . . . a new kind of hip homunculus."[74] Yet he guarded against proclaiming youth culture the ultimate winner of this turn. And a year later, smarting from what Monterey wrought, Goldstein devoted his July 18, 1968 column to "Autohype," reviewing in detail what truly went down that last summer:

> To the left of us, there stood a gaggle of men in double-breasted ecstasy, California breeze whistling through their razor-cuts—that scene. And these men

(who spend their days back in the city copulating with culture) were staring profoundly at the crowd (the way only promo men can stare), and the crowd gazed back. A vast chorus of "groovy, groovy, oh-wow groovy" arose from that arena, and these men heard the word. They knew then, that a man may speak in signs, but dig his symbols, and you've mastered his soul.[75]

This, Goldstein decreed, was the very definition of autohype. "All publicity . . . is aimed at getting you to convince yourself that the client in question should be canonized," he continued. "A scene makes judging easy for the rest of us. It creates myth and market, aura and audience, product and prophecy. It accomplishes all this without ever stopping to think how little the dynamics of pushing have changed over the years." The publicists, whom he referred to as "autohypnotists" were skilled at "[shielding] any work or dogma from the barbs of pragmatic criticism, which strives to consider each event in terms of its own expectations." Hype had in effect made such an act impossible—which presumably qualified how he viewed his own work.

That a year elapsed before this diatribe came out is telling; in retrospect, Monterey's symbolism as an emblem of a counterculture in decline became all the more clear. A particularly painful example of this for Goldstein was Janis Joplin, a symbol not only of the callous decadence of the rock industry but also of its cruelty toward women; the singer, for him, had become "a spectacle of need" for whom he has mourned deeply in years since.[76] In the late '60s, the ongoing tragedy of Joplin might have been among the more dramatic examples, but it had become clear, more generally, that criticism could offer no protection or relief. Critics had become "afraid to evaluate" in such an environment, and their criticism had become ineffectual because "publicity men seldom sweat their client's bad notices. They know it's the mention, not the verdict, that sells product." This existential crisis drew the article to a close:

> Two years ago, I remember writing here that rock needs a critic. Now I think it needs a shit-detector. Someone who can stand up to the grand inquisitor in his expense account mufti, and ask him why miracle, mystery, and authority are more important for a rock group than music . . . If we all lost our cool occasionally, we wouldn't need promo men. The scene would go out of the charisma business. And I could start writing about rock again.[77]

The Second Generation: Post-Hype Criticism

Such a declaration in July 1968 explains another notable trend in Goldstein's writing over this period: that there was a lot less of it. His columns became intermittent toward the end of 1967, and by 1968 what had once been a weekly contribution sometimes disappeared for more than a month. During early 1968, Goldstein also ran a reader poll and quantified his audience's taste for the first time, detailing the average age of the column's readership as well as their favorite albums, songs, and performers.[78] This irony highlights the great degree to which Goldstein himself was seeking out innovation in critiquing rock music, railing against not only personal and professional despondency, but also plain old boredom.

Goldstein's struggle with these issues created a vacancy in rock music writing at the paper, and by spring, a new column appeared to fill it. Riffs was primarily written by Annie Fisher, an editor first hired in 1962,[79] but it was founded as a multi-writer column, featuring many new writers as well as allowing established *Voice* critics to try their hand at rock. Riffs thus gave birth to the "second generation" of criticism being written at the *Voice*—a generation that would in some ways resemble Goldstein's, but would differ in critical ways.

Riffs diverged strongly from Pop Eye. First was the marked difference in energy. Fisher displayed enthusiastic and positive reactions to musical culture where Goldstein became increasingly negative and despondent. Fisher also took issue with what criticism had become in the *Voice* under Goldstein. A few weeks after beginning the column, she offered her own manifesto about critical practice. "I don't read 'underground' newspapers" she explained, nor did she "read publications dealing with pop music." Her explanation of her avoidance was that she didn't "want to write reactively— i.e. reactively to another writer. I want to hear pop music the way I've always heard it, unprofessionally, subjectively, and to report a direct confrontation with it." Her use of the word "professional" comes across as a particularly pointed dig against Goldstein—a writer who had clearly become a professional writer thanks to criticism—as well as staunchly anti-intellectual. Fisher followed the lead of an undated article from the *L.A. Free Press* by a writer named John Carpenter, whom she quoted at length: "Rock and roll music, any old way you read it, is being talked to death . . . I still LISTEN to pop music. Seldom do I feel the urge to rap or write about what I hear . . . Record reviews are just more verbal garbage about a nonverbal art, though, so why write about a boring album? Better to bomb their record company in the night."[80]

That Fisher filled the majority of one of her first columns with a diatribe *against* the practice she was embarking on is both ironic and consequential. On the one hand, it is hard to understand how or why she would want to write a column about rock music if she was so sincerely opposed to what writing had done to the act of listening to and enjoying music. Taking a page from Goldstein's philosophy that experience was king, Fisher, through her mouthpiece Carpenter, argued in effect that music criticism wasn't necessary. In this way, her invective was a direct critique of what Goldstein's column had become—too pessimistic, but also too slick, thereby worsening the disease rather than offering a cure. If Goldstein represented the quandary of what critical practice should be in an age when mediation risked killing the very culture he loved, Fisher provided an answer: return to pleasure and give up analysis (a stance that would be taken up, in a different way, by the journalists who helped to build *Creem*). But in a context where these questions implicated the future of a culture and of politics, this declaration was, in a way, already a type of defeat. Fisher's posture pronounced that the battle that Goldstein set for himself was a losing one by design.

Elsewhere, other crucial cultural battles were also being lost. The sum total of the dramatic, violent events of 1968—the assassinations of Martin Luther King Jr. and Robert F. Kennedy, the escalation of the Vietnam War, the riots at Columbia—shook Goldstein to the core, changing his belief in the possibilities of real systemic change.[81] But the most devastating of them all was the Democratic National Convention in Chicago, where abusive police greeted protestors with tear gas. Chicago symbolized the potential for revolution, making what was happening to the music more pertinent. When Goldstein considered the Chicago revolution, questions about the use value of music and criticism for business purposes paled in comparison to ones that engaged in the worth of music as a political device. Indeed, the apocalypse for him was driven by the fact that music was no longer in a position to do anything to advance the revolutionary cause.

A piece called "Homecoming," published in September 1968, wove together his political frustrations and the resulting pop cultural desert. "[This] is the most terrifying year anyone my age has ever had to endure," he wrote. How he continued is worth quoting at length:

> We still haven't come to terms with the public extinction of our heroes . . . This polarization is bound to have an immense effect on pop culture, since that scene is an immediate expression of emotional climate. Already the stylistic "rules" of pop are solidifying, and the innovative frenzy of mid (mod) '60s has become a predictable, rather sedate elaboration of existing forms . . . It is as though the entire rock establishment were pulling back to reassess its relevance—always the primary criterion for a pop artist. What must eventually suffer in this tightening of reins is that precious spontaneity which characterized the pop explosion . . .
>
> As America congeals into opposing masses, and the freedom to move among ideas becomes subservient to the necessity of commitment, pop culture

will function as a clenched fist. Already, the liaison between the underground and the middlebrow (which produced the most widely felt pop renaissance since the '20s) is beginning to fall apart . . . The underground will respond to this seizure by retreating into the protective isolation which it cultivated during the '50s . . . When that happens this column will probably cease to appear, not out of any ideological protest on my part, but because pop will no longer excite me.[82]

In this passage, Goldstein described the music's lack of inspiration, which previously had been described solely in terms of the actions of business, as an element of a political landscape in which progressive opportunities appeared increasingly dim. Music had been an aspect of cultural politics—in critics' beliefs that it could not be separated from the world around it—yet in the upheaval of the time, music felt increasingly disconnected. For a terrified young person, not even popular culture could offer solace. Though he continued to write Pop Eye for a few more months, clearly the buoyancy had left him, in part because the potential for political music had all but been erased. An interview with Country Joe and the Fish shortly thereafter is telling. "I had come to rap about the revolution. Since the Fish have come to represent the quintessence of commitment in a rock group," he explained, "I was searching for a few predictions, a reminiscence of life at the barricades, and perhaps a scenario or two. But Country Joe snickered. 'There isn't going to be any revolution. Let's be realistic,' he said, and went off to brush his teeth."[83] Deflated, Goldstein could only read this political apathy as having penetrated their music, writing "that sharp certainty has given way to something almost laconic. The Fish still push the same old stuff, but the deal is different now . . . only the symptoms of energy remain."[84]

Writing during that same time frame, Annie Fisher had none of the remorse. A John Lee Hooker concert during the week of September 26 elicited: "Without compunction, I will tell you that the first set was breathtaking and the second the most awesome performance of music I have ever heard or witnessed in my life—and that I'm not going to commit the obscenity of trying to review them."[85] On October 3, Fisher proclaimed that "anyone worried about the scene being moribund" should spend more time going out to shows.

Though Goldstein left criticism at the *Voice* shortly after this time, the questions raised in his column over this period lacked ready answers. Subsequent critics would be obliged to contend not only with Goldstein's legacy, but also with the historical moment that could have produced such a bleak outlook on the music and, in turn, their chosen career. Robert Christgau, Goldstein's successor, entitled one of his 1970 columns "Rock Is Obsolescent, but So Are You," and therein discussed the origins of the "rock is dead" movement. A "cycle of excitement and ennui" explained why fans turned on, then burned out on the music, but another dilemma factored in as well. "In the past, one aspect of the rock discovery had to do with a sense of unity with listeners who were often quite different from oneself: ghetto kids, hippies, bikers, pre-pubescents," Christgau wrote. "Now that communion has been sundered into sects, often friendly but always in some sort of competition."[86]

Eve of Destruction

Goldstein used his writing at the end of the 1960s as a pulpit from which to mourn the decade's passing and the whirlwind spectacle that would prove to be the New Left's last gasp. More than this, however, was that the commercialism of rock culture moved in tandem with the promotionalism of its criticism. As intellectual discussions of popular culture gained increasing turf in mass media publications, intellectuals became enmeshed in the systems of productions they critiqued, both tacitly and overtly. Because he was a journalistic critic and an advocate for the popular, Goldstein's dependence upon a mass mediated venue is not as fraught, but his reliance upon the commercial system of music (and its on him) was.

Rock critics like Goldstein thus initiated another version of the mass culture critique, and this twisted rendition—where mass culture is both friend and enemy, counterculture and sold-out—allowed rock critics to pronounce rock dead while still continuing to diagnosis its health. The confluence of economic changes in music and the dashed political expectations of thousands of youthful rebels had a lasting effect on rock criticism as a journalistic genre and practice; this journalism, in turn, is evidence of the problem that continues to crop up in our collective memory of music of the 1960s. The assumption that rock music listening should be a revolutionary experience politically, personally, emotionally, and intellectually has within it assumptions that were born in the experience of rock as a widespread, novel, collective experience—an experience that was mythic from its inauguration, and fleeting by its nature.

CHAPTER **4**
Identity

The *Voice* critics who wrote into 1969 and beyond continued to question the efficacy of a rock-fueled revolution—a debate deeply intertwined with concerns over whether rock culture was losing its momentum, cogency, and meaning. Christgau professed his ambivalence in his column Rock & Roll &, writing "Rock and roll . . . is going to revolutionize the world," before qualifying it with a glib "Well, not exactly."[1] Lucian Truscott IV, a regular writer for Riffs, explained that recent experiences had been "leading me in one direction: away from rock," but allowed that perhaps "rock has left me," in part because it "has become a subculture." He continued, lamenting that "within the realm of rock remains a *memory* of the excitement of days and music long past, even though the excitement is today no longer there" (emphasis in original).[2] Another occasional Riffs contributor, Sandy Pearlman, hypothesized that "rock 'n' roll's no political instrument" and that any sway it might wield in that realm will last "only momentarily . . . It can't be sustained."[3]

The changing contours of rock music culture baffled critics, causing them to question the nature of rock music as well as their role as its gatekeepers. Saying that the music lacked "excitement" did more than indict the output of musicians. It also implicated the audience, which included critics as the consummate consumers. Was it wrongheaded, the critics wondered, to believe that music might politicize listeners—and, if so, should criticism be excused from any requirement to, say, champion the movement, stand against the Vietnam War, or instigate revolutionary sentiment? Rock music may have been "energy," but that energy increasingly directed itself toward a "revolution in style," as Christgau adroitly observed.[4] Should criticism take a stand against this trend, or go with it?

Rock music of the late 1960s and early 1970s was vital popular culture and thriving capitalist enterprise, but to many observers both inside and outside of music labels, its reign as the predominant music of young people was coming to an end. More acts, from a variety of musical genres and subgenres, attracted the attention of the majors of the music business; these labels, in turn, paid keen attention to audience demographics and poached profitable acts from weaker independents, fragmenting the audience even further.[5] These strategies reflected movement toward market segmentation, a practice that had become more sophisticated and widespread throughout the consumer landscape during the previous two decades. As Lizabeth Cohen writes in her authoritative history of American consumerism, it was during the late 1950s that market researchers began to emphasize segmentation in earnest, presuming consumer diversity rather than conformity and exploring distinct ways to market products to multiple populations.[6] As the technique became entrenched over the course of the 1960s and 1970s, it gave rise to ethnic marketing, which took off during the 1970s and played a fundamental role in the "demassification of American cultural identity" and Americans' morphing relationships to their immigrant heritage.[7]

Segmentation in the consumer market found something of an unlikely corollary in the political realm through the rise of identity politics. The landmark civil rights and voting legislation of 1964 and 1965 evidenced a pinnacle in the integrationist strides the Civil Rights movement inspired in American political and social life, but the movement would also recalibrate the form and tenor of grassroots politics. By the early 1960s, the New Left, the early stages of the feminist movement, protests against the Vietnam War, and the transgressions of the counterculture joined the Civil Rights movement to demand rights, reconfigure the relationship between public and private, significantly revise and in some cases reject core American values, and push ethnicity, race, gender, sexuality, and other categories of identity to the forefront of political participation. While these progressive movements overlapped significantly and shared a mission to redesign the status quo, they also pinpointed divisions that would magnify as the 1960s moved toward and into the 1970s.

The shift toward identity politics and other modes of granular political change reflect yet another aspect of postmodernity, which I have already discussed in earlier chapters in terms of its economic and cultural shifts. David Harvey's classic characterization, for instance, calls postmodernity a moment in which "The experience of time and space has changed, the confidence in the association between scientific and moral judgments has collapsed, aesthetics has triumphed over ethics as a prime focus of social and intellectual concern, images dominate narratives, ephemerality and fragmentation take precedence over eternal truths and unified politics, and explanations have shifted from the realm of material and political-economic groundings towards a consideration of autonomous cultural and political practices."[8] While Harvey's claim of a diminishment of "unified politics" is itself questionable given the historic, systematic exclusion of certain groups from political participation, his views do underscore that postmodernity produced a sharp contrast in how those groups articulated and justified their political demands. As DeKoven notes, postmodernism's emergence across the "long sixties" resulted in progressive political movements that tried, sometimes with great difficulty, to embrace both the "liberatory humanist universalism of modernity and the local, particularist subject politics of postmodernity."[9] Of feminism, for example, DeKoven argues that it "was at the heart of the emergence of the postmodern from within the ultimate, culminating modernity of the sixties"[10] because it attempted to dismantle patriarchy through offering an alternative metanarrative marked by subjectivity and "the personal." Paradoxes of this nature—proffering universalisms that in their very existence disposed of the possibility of universality—reverberated through the feminist, black power, gay liberation, Chicano rights, and American Indian movements. Postmodernism proves useful in coming to terms with not only how "difference"—in language as well as in representation and bodies—became endemic to cultural politics, but also the challenges the acknowledgment of difference presented to political commonsense.

The predicament critics confronted about rock music at this moment extended cultural conversations that intellectuals had been having for decades about politics and culture, but also had a distinctly contemporary cast. As the modernist ideals of unity began to give way to a postmodern recognition of the realities of continued inequality and inalienable difference, rock critics were forced to re-imagine their concept of music's power and forge another way of discussing the politics of music. In response, *Voice* rock criticism began to exhibit its own version of "identity politics" that dramatically revised the critical act. I will make this argument via two separate, though interrelated, interrogations. First, I will examine how race issues percolated through the discussion of music during the height of the black power movement. My second inquiry concerns how the identity of the critic himself became an oft-utilized entry point into a discussion about music and its wider outlines. These variegated connotations of the term "identity" reveal strategies rock critics employed once they could no longer assume that they were writing about a unified culture. Critics responded by mobilizing themselves as authoritative, authentic, yet limited individuals who were speaking to an increasingly piecemeal audience.

Because identity persists as a central strategy for analyzing popular culture, I find it helpful to preface the body of this chapter with some of the wider conclusions I plan to draw. It is my position that identity is a functional yet very narrow lens through which to view popular culture, and that overall, "identity centrism" in pop culture criticism has some complicated and not entirely positive consequences. This relates to some of the unintended effects of the preponderance of subjectivity that arose alongside New Journalism and, more broadly, the individual participation and experience that was a privileged characteristic of the 1960s more generally. The debates about identity politics that have ensnared the academy in countless fields in the social sciences and humanities since the 1980s appeared early on in the problems rock critics faced near the turn of the '70s. I do not mean to criticize the development of minority/area studies, or the important ways that identity has allowed for greater attention to diversity and multiculturalism in numerous social, political, and cultural arenas. Nor do I wish to follow the rationale of scholars such as Todd Gitlin, who argues that the fragmentation in the late 1960s spoiled "the movement" and festered into the latter twentieth-century culture wars.[11] I limit my critique in this chapter strictly to the epistemological ramifications of identity—that is, what identity allowed and continues to allow critics to claim as areas of understanding. At bottom, too much focus on identity limits what critics can know, and that in the worst case produces lax criticism.

Let me pause for a moment to offer some additional words of preface. First, the commercialization that played such an enormous role in Goldstein's departure from the paper also characterized the environment during which his successor, Robert Christgau, would begin his *Voice* career—one that, with the exception of a two-year hiatus in the early 1970s, lasted until 2006. His somewhat cheeky, self-proclaimed title, "Dean of American Rock Critics," gives a sense of his sardonic wit, but it is also a fairly accurate assessment of his influence on rock criticism over the vast majority of its existence, as both a writer and an editor of many well-regarded journalists. For those reasons, Christgau's response to these issues factors greatly in my analysis. At the same time, Christgau was but one of many voices who participated in a lively reckoning with the role of identity in their analyses. Arguably, his stature grows over the period currently under examination, and his greatest fame arrived in during the 1970s and '80s—a topic to which I will return in this book's conclusion.

Another point I would like to address is my intentional use of the male pronoun in the above references to the critical self. Though Riffs added a few female writers to the roster at the *Voice*, the most dominant voices during this time period were male; the outstanding exception to this rule in the late '60s is *New Yorker* columnist Ellen Willis, who in addition to being a pillar of rock criticism, was an initiating thinker in second wave radical feminism. Willis joined the New York Radical Feminists shortly before its 1968 dissolution, and subsequently helped to forge the New York City brand of radical feminism that formed around the Redstockings Collective, an organization she co-founded in early 1969 with Shulamith Firestone.[12] Understanding women as victims of both patriarchy and capitalism, the writing and activism of Willis and her peers articulated the concept of sexism, promoted the tactics of consciousness raising and speakouts, and modeled boldness that mobilized so many women in the late 1960s and early 1970s, in New York City and elsewhere. Willis's feminism also defined her rock writing; her central role in early rock criticism complicates the notion that the genre belonged entirely to men. Yet it would be a mistake to suggest that because of this, rock criticism was some kind of bastion of gender awareness—a telling point when considered alongside the frequent, though not always nimble, discussions of race.

In a city pulsating with feminism—among writers such as Willis as well as female *Voice* writers on other beats, not to mention the thousands of women who became active during this period[13]—male rock critics' consciousness of women's issues was erratic and at times inelegant. A piece that we might deem sensitive and forward-thinking by today's standards might also contain perplexing musings about women that negated raising the gender question in the first place; the issue might appear one week only to disappear for months or longer. One of the first articles to tackle gender and rock was Christgau's "Look at That Stupid Girl," published on June 11, 1970. In this sharp and energized piece denouncing the "male supremacist" aspects of rock music, Christgau remarked that he received his "sexism sensitivity training from a militant feminist who is almost as fervent about rock as I am"—doubtlessly an aside to Willis—and magnanimously declared that "women's oppression demands the most far-reaching analysis of social structures ever attempted."[14] Yet despite some reverberations from readers' letters in the weeks following Christgau's manifesto, this "far-reaching analysis of social structures" did not materialize in the paper's rock criticism. About a year later, Christgau charged that "the only theme in popular music as worthy of attention as rock and women is rock and race," noting that in most instances, "rock writers shun both." Later in the same piece, his attention to the issue produced the odd characterization that "basically, there are three kinds of female singers: the virgin, the sexpot, and her close relative, the sufferer."[15] More crudely, another music writer pondered in late 1971: "what does it feel like to be a female? . . . what does sex feel like when you're taking it rather than sending it out? . . . does your menstrual cycle affect your sense of aesthetic time?"[16]

Voice writers regularly struggled with the relationship of race, music, and themselves in ways that they simply did not do with gender—at least not at this point in the late 1960s and early 1970s. Though this chapter focuses on race, I mention this absence to remind us of the relative transparency of masculinity when compared to whiteness at this historical moment. Echols agrees, observing that race issues maintained traction among left-leaning thinkers in ways that gender simply did not as of this period, despite the gains earned through feminist activism.[17]

The Racial Politics of Rock in Black and Blues

In 1968, James Brown released one of his most (in)famous singles, "Say It Loud (I'm Black and I'm Proud)."[18] Brown became a force on R&B charts in the early 1960s, winning a Grammy in 1965 for "Papa's Got a Brand New Bag" and attracting a strong black fan base that also included some white listeners; rock stars such as Mick Jagger and later, Bruce Springsteen, imitated his highly energized performance style.[19] Yet "Say It Loud" was different. The single debuted in October; in light of the recent spate of violence, including the Chicago Democratic National Convention riots and the murder of Bobby Kennedy that summer, and especially the April slaying of Martin Luther King Jr. and ensuing riots, many feared the country's descent into chaos.[20] "Say It Loud" resolutely addressed its black listeners, and called on them to come together, support one another, and celebrate their heritage. It contained a message for whites, too. Directly and in echo, for its listeners and non-listeners alike, "Say It Loud" directed them to heed a purposeful distinction between the races, this time on African Americans' terms.[21]

To explain as well as complicate music as emblematic as Brown's requires considering the change in racial politics during the late 1960s period, as Civil Rights gave way to black power. This is a complex story recounted more thoroughly elsewhere, but for the present argument some broad outlines are in order. Most histories point to 1966, when Stokely Carmichael, then-president of SNCC, made a call for "black power" in response to an overflow of frustration with the continuing abuses of white power structures.[22] Carmichael's utterance, widely broadcast through national media, was not the earliest expression of the phrase or sentiment, nor did it guarantee a consensus on what "black power" meant in practice. But his use was nothing if not opportune, and it announced a consequential turn from the integrationist efforts Martin Luther King espoused, as well as cynicism over the possibility and desirability of colorblind racial harmony. Its spirit of self-determination and sometimes militancy telegraphed the nationalistic visions of Malcolm X, whose spectacular, contentious, and truncated tenure as a leader in the Nation of Islam bestowed persuasive inspiration and a powerful template for how blacks could direct the course of their own collective fate.

The Black Panther Party, started in Oakland, California, in October 1966, was the most visible symbol and organization of black power and remains a cornerstone of its legacy. Huey P. Newton and Bobby Seale generated the party's ten-point program, which included objectives such as eliminating police brutality, advocating for acceptable housing, and promoting black self-sufficiency.[23] Their radical political objectives, which aligned the black ghetto with other strugglers in the Third World, came packaged in an arresting visual display, a remark scholars often make in commenting on the group's remarkable media savvy.[24] The expert use of media, including its visual elements, was in fact central to their greater cause; it was "not only as a heuristic tool but also a provocation to revolution," meant to activate average black citizens to join their cause.[25] Black power set out to reform black identity and hasten blacks' desire to establish their own institutions.[26]

Black power was an influential shorthand that described a wide range of activities that restructured blacks' relationship to the public sphere. A similar racial awakening permeated the arts of the period. Though the seedlings of an Afrocentric American aesthetic had sprouted long before—recognizable in the Harlem Renaissance, and later in figures such as Lorraine Hansberry, Paul Robeson, and Nina Simone—a self-conscious movement appeared in the mid-1960s, and by 1968 had assumed the moniker the Black Arts Movement. Amiri Baraka (né Leroi Jones) was among the Black Arts Movement's most important leaders. He founded the Black Arts Repertory Theater and School of Harlem with a group of other black artists in 1964, and though the theater folded within the year, he remained a highly visible champion of black creative production. With writer and activist Larry Neal, Baraka co-edited the 1968 volume *Black Fire: An Anthology of Afro-American Writing*, a collection that included prominent figures such as Stanley Crouch, Sun Ra, Sonia Sanchez, and Stokely Carmichael.[27] That same year, Neal explained in *The Drama Review* that "The Black Arts Movement is radically opposed to any concept of the artist that alienates him from his community. Black Art is the aesthetic sister of the Black Power concept. As such, it envisions an art that speaks directly to the needs and aspirations of Black America . . . A main tenet of Black Power is the necessity for Black people to define the world in their own terms. The Black artist has made the same point in the context of aesthetics."[28]

Leaders of the Black Arts Movement advocated for creativity by and for black people and determined the historic distinction between black and white as a source of strength rather than sorrow. Their aesthetic nationalism would come to strongly determine how black people understood, accessed, and performed black identity and black aesthetics moving forward.[29] Moreover, the Black Arts Movement cohered a sense of black popular culture and helped to define it as something separate from the mainstream.[30] This had particular purchase for music, as songs started to reflect the political focus on identity politics and musicians became visible symbols of black power's popularization.

Earlier in the decade, Baraka theorized the significance of black music to black identity. A jazz writer as well as a poet and dramatist, he published *Blues People: Negro Music in White America,* a critical milestone, in 1963. The book chronicles African American music from the times of slavery to Baraka's present, and argues that it is central to any understanding of African American identity—where "American" is not just a throwaway, but a critical addition. "Blues could not exist if the African captives had not become American captives," Baraka writes, and as a result, African Americans are a "blues people."[31] He later explains, "The Negro could not ever become white and that was his strength; at some point, always, he could not participate in the dominant tenor of the white man's culture. It was at this juncture that he had to make use of other resources, whether African, subcultural, or hermetic. And it was this boundary, this no man's land, that provided the logic and beauty of his music."[32]

Like black music itself, Baraka's argument contains much intricacy and paradox. He argues that blacks create "the most expressive art to come out of America, and in essence . . . of the same aesthetic stance as other high art of the period"[33]—as Gennari points out, his antidote to the bland march of midcult plaguing American culture[34]—while also fretting quite candidly about the "dilution" and the subsequent "sterility" of the black essence that results from too much acceptance in the white mainstream.[35] As much as the white world effaced the black one, it was also a critical part of its history and thus its definition. The conceptual and practical difficulties of a productive separation of the races continued to snare Baraka and many of his peers as they later attempted to realize that vision.

Black music in general and the blues in particular remained volatile flashpoints within the greater Black Arts Movement. Just two years after Baraka's study of African Americans as "blues people," he and many of his fellow black artists rejected the genre as a pitiable vestige of black subordination to whites. While not all radical black creative people shared this belief—Larry Neal famously championed the blues as a storehouse of the black spirit—many among the Black Arts movement sought to celebrate forms that blacks could create and possess themselves, with minimal white interference. Thus the revolutionary jazz of Albert Ayler, John Coltrane, Sun Ra, and others took precedence over the blues, generally held to be a "politically more problematic" genre and the object of escalating white interest.[36]

The versions of black power that black popular musicians produced were more potent among the black populace than either blues or jazz, but politically thorny nonetheless. Soul took shape in the mid-1960s, at the juncture of rhythm and blues, gospel, jazz, and the blues; this "blacker" sound differed sharply from the poppier, more palatable music of early Motown sound.[37] Solomon Burke, Aretha Franklin, Curtis Mayfield, Otis Redding, and a number of other black musicians took their music in this direction. As the '60s wore on, the more racially distinct sounds merged with nationalistic sensibilities absorbed from the black power movement and drew black listeners away from the white mainstream and toward a sphere of black musical consumption.[38] Notably, some whites also liked this music, but it did not address or invite them; soul for many black fans was the foil to rock and roll, where their energy and dollars were spent. Yet even as soul was speaking to masses of black people, intellectuals of the Black Arts movement remained unconvinced that black popular musics were where their emphasis should lie.[39]

Black responses to the black music of this moment are varied, shifting, and open as many questions as they answer. Yet black creative, intellectual, and political movements of the period were clear on the centrality of blackness to their production and consumption and worked from an acceptance of a divergence between the races, rather than attempting to bridge or elide that division. As these distinctions manifested themselves through artists as well as within audiences, through sound as well as culture, the mostly white critical establishment were outsiders; this status exacerbated what already felt like a musical and political culture unable to keep yet another revolutionary promise that had seemed to be achievable just a few years before.

We can see this dramatized in the pages of the *Village Voice* and its coverage of black music during this period. Though a few black artists, such as Jimi Hendrix, Otis Redding, and Aretha Franklin achieved acceptance among the overwhelmingly white counterculture, and jazz critics necessarily had to engage with racial difference in their craft, the soul phenomenon went largely unnoticed in the *Village Voice*. Christgau, who wrote for *Esquire* as well as the *Voice* during this time, noted years later that James Brown represented a phenomenon lost on many of the contemporary white critics. "James Brown was really getting his shit together, proving himself the greatest musician in the history of rock and we didn't know, none of the white people knew," he explained. "This bifurcation that happened between white and black music really did not help the general spirit one little bit. It was a genuinely integrated world there for a few years . . . and black power plus funk did that in."[40]

Though uttered years later, his comment underscores the central problematic at work in examining the function, as well as the fallout, of rock criticism's understanding of racial identity. For white critics, race presented a difficult and at times insurmountable challenge, illustrative of broader concerns about the possibilities and impossibilities of music as culture and politics. The sensibility of the Black Arts Movement extolled exclusively black allegiances from cultural producers as well as audiences, and though its discourse circulated mostly in black publications that *Voice* critics did not access, such arguments at the very least contextualize our contemporary understanding of rock critical reactions and, more likely, seeped into *Voice* writers' awareness to provide a cautionary tale. Coupled with the vociferous protests of soul music, then, the message was clear: whites should be careful when dealing with black music. In fact, soul music provoked white listeners to realize just how much they did not know.

Another way to consider the issue that Christgau raised is that, rather than black power, soul, and later funk music literally "doing in" the integrationist spirit, they simply made visible divisions that had always existed between black and white musical experiences. Perhaps white listeners "understood" black rock 'n' roll and R&B, but how they understood it may have varied greatly from ways that blacks listened to the same music. In their work on black music, both Craig Werner and Brian Ward explore how black musicians communicate messages that white audiences might overlook or misinterpret.[41] While I think it is important to caution against essentialist interpretations of their arguments—that blackness offers some key to a "truer" meaning that is necessarily unavailable to whites, a perspective some black cultural nationalists then and now would support—different cultural experiences can and do impact reception practices. White critics had to come to terms with what, if anything, about themselves placed limits on their ability to "hear" for others unlike themselves. Christgau's statement quoted above both acknowledged this (by noting that white critics didn't "get" James Brown) and rejected it (in the reaction that soul ruined integration).

Christgau's declaration that James Brown's music qualified as rock is yet another manifestation of this point. It is not a self-evident statement but rather an argument that contends, in its usual form, that all musical genres that can be linked back to 1950s rock 'n' roll in some fashion are part of rock history. But rock as a commercial and cultural category long has been the province of white musicians and listeners; what is "rock" to whites might constitute something very different for non-whites. It is worth questioning why rock holds a claim to such a wide swath of music when no other term could reasonably be used as a synonym. Bernard Gendron helps to explain this phenomenon of the late 1960s in part; he notes that critics defined white rock as art whereas black soul music was for entertainment. The very whiteness of rock and the perception of it as avant-garde music excused white critics from having to understand black music at all, in Gendron's view.[42] It follows, then, that what they could appreciate, either at the time or in hindsight, would be christened rock music—and the individual or collective understanding (or, in the case of James Brown, the desire to understand) would be a crucial component of knowing what exactly rock was. Partly what is at issue in Christgau's comment is the paradoxical, competing desires characteristic of this moment: on the one hand, wrestling to come away with some unified conception of the musical landscape while at the same time acknowledging the widening diversity and attendant gulfs; at one moment, finding oneself on the leading edge of musical culture and at the next discovering one had lagged behind, fumbling to explain what felt ineffable. What white rock critics could rightly consider as their domain connects to the dance that was occurring at this moment between the modern and the postmodern, the specific and the general, where the desire for universal narratives and all-encompassing categories remained even as the possibility for these things was rapidly diminishing.

While white critics may not have been aware of the influence artists like Brown had on black culture, the relationship between whites and black music did emerge as an issue of heated critical discussion near the end of 1968. In the *Voice,* this developed most clearly in reaction to the blues revival. The blues revival has varied meaning among historians of music. For some, it is a continuation of a folk revival; to others, the influence of the blues resonates throughout 1960s rock.[43] For my purposes, the blues revival refers to a distinct phase in the late 1960s when music "by and for chiefly black Americans [was turned] into a music by black and white Americans primarily for white Americans and Europeans."[44] Traditional blues artists such as B. B. King, Howlin' Wolf, and Muddy Waters began to appeal to white, young, upwardly mobile city dwellers.[45] Yet black artists did not share whites' sudden fascination, as Nelson George explains:

Older black fans, who'd loved Muddy and company at the neighborhood bar, rarely came to these temples of youth culture partly because they didn't feel comfortable among middle class white teens and college students, and partly because they didn't know about the gigs: advertising, in the underground press and progressive rock radio . . . never reached them. To blacks who still valued the blues, it seemed these cultural heroes had been kidnapped by the younger brothers and sisters of the folks who'd led Chuck Berry astray. And to younger blacks—the soul children of the sixties—the blues just wasn't . . . "relevant" in a world of dashikis, Afro picks, and bell-bottoms.[46]

George's observation hints at the complexity among generations of black listeners, who had a range of motivations for keeping their distance from the revival. Understood from the pages of the *Village Voice*, whites also reacted to the music in complicated ways. Often, though not exclusively, rock critics entered the conversation about the blues revival via the white blues practitioners it created—students of the blues who became famous as the music was enjoying its renaissance. Making points about white musicians let them demonstrate increased sensitivity to racial identity while still allowing them to work.

Rock criticism of the late 1960s was neither alone nor original in critically engaging music in terms of race. Race had been an integral yet fraught element of jazz criticism since it began in the 1930s due to the overwhelming whiteness of its writers. According to Perry Meisel, the earliest white jazz critics "celebrated jazz for its redemptive primitivism" and asserted that the blackness of the musicians offered them a direct vector into authenticity—and the blacker they were, the better.[47] The scope of race within critical writing changed in the postwar period; as critics demanded the appreciation of jazz as a significant strand of American art, the music also became a platform to interpret America's multiracial and often racist history.[48] Certain white critics, such as Ralph J. Gleason and Nat Hentoff, eagerly used their criticism toward this end.[49] In the '60s, jazz writers also contended with Civil Rights and black nationalism, resulting in fractious discussions about the centrality of African American identity to musical understanding.[50] But jazz writing was never as solipsistic a genre as rock criticism. The salient devices of rock criticism—New Journalistic tactics of subjectivity and participation, the personal nature of politics, the erotics and emotionality of writing, its singular union of rapture and jeremiad—never dominated jazz writing, a far more technically minded pursuit. In rock criticism, the self was the most supreme and utilized technic, the spindle around which discussion of the music turned—and sometimes, the self was itself the subject.

On a subject as heated as racial politics, writers' mental and emotional states often surfaced. As Richard Goldstein neared the end of his *Voice* tenure, the racial implications of the blues revival weighed on him heavily. A despondent late 1968 column entitled "Electric Minotaur" complained that Albert King, a black blues guitarist, "totes the white man's electric burden" while another, Muddy Waters, "has surfaced as soul guru of the movement." Goldstein intoned that the revival took advantage of these musicians and, rather than fostering racial cohesion, obscured the widening divisions between blacks and whites. "Maybe, we can't overcome," Goldstein quipped. Despite how it might appear, he explained, "I don't think we're ready to dig the same sound on 125th Street and Saint Mark's Place," an allusion to streets that run through the hearts of (black) Harlem and the (white) East Village respectively. He reserved even more pointed words for Jimi Hendrix, whose reception smacked of racism, tokenism, and minstrelsy. Picking up on his "early outrage" at Hendrix's theatrically sexual stage antics, Goldstein wrote, "he does pander to his audience, and it does feel humiliating. Coming from a white man . . . I could have easily accepted that jingle-jangle grace. But I still demand dignity from a black performer."[51]

Many years later, Goldstein remarked that Black Power inspired him, yet he remained incredibly disenchanted with the persecution of black leadership.[52] He also clearly absorbed its lessons that race could neither be denied nor simply appreciated as just another difference. Abandoning an integrationist approach to civil rights, Goldstein leaned heavily toward the idea that permanent, perhaps intractable differences lie between how whites and blacks interacted with music. In that he was a white critic, this perspective exhibited racial sensitivity, but it also raised difficult, barbed questions: Why did he demand different things from black and white performers? What would those demands look like? And who was he, as a white critic, to place those demands anyway?

Goldstein's last music column for the *Voice* was published on January 16, 1969, and he once again addressed this dilemma.[53] Here, he theorized that whites embraced the blues revival because it allowed them escape from the commercialism that had seeped into pop music. "How much more authentic Albert King seems, with his open-collar shirt, sipping orange juice between riffs, than Jim Morrison, who is all leather and lanolin," he wrote. "How much easier it is to adore Ma Rainey, who is black and rural-real, than Janis Joplin, who is white and nearly rich, and who comes from the latter-day Lourdes of dreams that dripped blood and money: San Francisco." Whites flocked en masse to the blues in a manner that was "essentially elitist." Pop, which Goldstein originally conceived as a productive tool, transmogrified from a tool of capitalist exploitation to a modern-day master's whip, enslaving black performers into a power structure that still privileged whiteness, even as it masqueraded as feeding black interests. Down the line, white adoration might strip the blues of its blackness completely. The rich black tradition of blues music "will matter to the bulk of America only in its popularizers," Goldstein opined. "The man who emerges from some cosmic delta to instant acclaim as a superstar will be the one who reconciles blues power with the freaky exhibitionism of rock. I'll wager . . . he'll be a white man. Very white. Maybe, even an albino." His last comment, an aside to albino blues guitarist Johnny Winter who was a rising celebrity of the blues revival, was a sullen declaration that the inevitable had in fact already occurred.[54]

What had been rock, folk, and now this latest trend's open secret—that whites repeatedly borrowed (stole?) black musical forms—had arrived as a matter of public airing in the pages of the *Voice*, and critics did not agree on its meaning. "The blues were developed to accommodate a very special content, and . . . white bands, with no like experience to inform the content, have substituted flash for emotional expression," wrote Annie Fisher a few weeks earlier in "Blues & Blues," an edition of Riffs.[55] Despite the fact that many "black genius[es]" have not received the credit due them for their cultural contributions, Fisher complained that "those who put down white blues as fake make me wonder at what point recognition of the past becomes ancestor worship." As one of the biggest champions of blues music at the paper and a regular reviewer of classic and contemporary blues artists, Fisher saw the blues as living music that should be allowed to transform; skilled performers deserved accolades regardless of color. Still, Fisher admitted that most white musicians suffered from "emotional paucity" and "lack of improvisation." Even in pushing toward colorblind listening, this critic could not only see race, but hear and feel it.

The debate underscored two fundamental problems in using identity as a basis for criticism, and these problems would rear their heads many times over. First, proposing identity as a good approximation for musical expertise and understanding carried alongside it the risk of essentialism—that certain groups had access to experiences, understanding, and cultures that simply were not available to others. For white critics to agree with this belief was as vexing an assertion as for them to deny it, and both bound the critical act. Second, critics had to think about whether identities were fixed entities or deserved the ability to shift over time, and what this meant for musicians' debts to the past. Does Aretha Franklin, as a black soul songstress, have more of an ability (and duty) to channel Bessie Smith or Mahalia Jackson? And if she does not perform in this way, is she adding to the panorama of black music or detracting from it? Critics also had to contemplate how and whether musicians needed to honor their influences, especially when those influences weren't of the same race. Technology factored in greatly here, with critics internalizing the idea that blacks were most authentic when they stayed away from electric and technological musical effects.

Perhaps ironically, the solution to the intellectual quandaries identity presented became identity, as fragmentation so dissected the concept of "the general" for journalists that they increasingly turned inward to find a space from which to write. Many movements that fell under the umbrella of identity politics responded in a similar way, as coherent categories around race, gender, or sexual orientation inevitably faced internal divisions, often also framed in identity terms. Regardless of whether they believed everything that identity movements sought to proffer, critics absorbed the belief that certain kinds of musicians had access to particular styles of playing, genres of music, and the like. This called into question critics' own ability to view and understand diverse musical styles, as well as guided their thinking on possible remedies.

The writing of Carman Moore, the *Voice*'s only black critic writing about rock, provides a telling insight into this shift. Ohio-born Moore was a composer by training who arrived in New York in 1958 to study, first, with renowned composer Hall Overton and later completed his master's at Julliard.[56] He began writing for the *Voice* in 1964, as a contributor with Leighton Kerner to the classically devoted Music column. Moore's beat was new classical music, the emerging "downtown" scene that began in 1960, when a young pianist named Yoko Ono sponsored a concert series in her loft apartment. As the 1960s progressed, and particularly with the release of *Sergeant Pepper's* in 1967, Moore's attention turned toward rock music, particularly to the popularizing blends among rock, classical, jazz, blues, and other musical genres. As opposed to formal classical writing, which tended toward being "mathematical," Moore found it "a relief to just talk almost like just a fan—how you felt about the thing as opposed to trying to take it apart and describe it." Such liberty changed his writing style, and he "found [himself] moving more toward personal statements."[57]

Moore's deeply personal music criticism took on a sociological air as his thinking evolved on whether black musicians owned particular musical styles and how right it was for whites to imitate them. Early on in the blues revival, Moore reviewed in a way that was "encouraging the growth of black music in the white world," in line with the integrationist perspective he held on the Civil Rights movement.[58] For example, in April 1969 Moore wrote a defense of Johnny Winter, noting, "He cannot pretend to be black. He is a white albino from Texas. But his blues is very good" and "he will probably become a legendary bluesman."[59] Moore's stance rejected the vantage black power advocated, where the very idea that a white person could accurately render black music was, in certain circles, tantamount to blasphemy.

Moore spent much of 1969 writing about blues and jazz musicians, often quite glowingly. "The blues revival has done a beautiful thing to popular music," he wrote in a column entitled "Blues and Beautiful" that appeared on November 13, 1969. "It has brought back the jam session."[60] As a composer, Moore could think positively about the musicological affects of music as somewhat distinct from the sociological effects. Alongside Don Heckman, a jazz writer who also penned reviews of rock into the early 1970s, Moore delighted in the musical unions that were thriving as the revival took hold.

This carried over into his assessments of rock music. A Stones show later that year moved Moore to consider the relationship between the band, who had grown rich in their interpretations of black rock 'n' roll, and their lesser known influences and contemporaries. "If you are American it is enough, and if you are also black it is much more to make you reluctant to fall under the ironic spell of British skill in black roots music," he wrote. "Say "rock 'n' roll in free association, and people fire back 'Beatles and Rolling Stones' then and only then in diminuendo procession, you may hear 'Aretha Franklin, Ray Charles, Chuck Berry, Bob Dylan, Elvis, Hendrix, Joplin' . . ."[61] Moore's incredulous set-up then took a turn to assert the "intense pleasure" of experiencing the Stones' music. The Stones could instruct others toward the "path to authentic music power that many American and suburban white singers who love the blues and country might adopt." After laying out the program the Stones had followed to excellence (including "imitate and steal from everywhere for a year or so, then let your subconscious mix it into your own thing"), Moore insisted that doing so was constructive. "America needs you," he wrote, "Or at least music needs you."

The preceding is a rich commentary on the complex, even contradictory, positions that a focus on identity created for critics. Moore simultaneously acknowledged the way that black musicians might be slighted by white stars who shone more brightly, yet arrived at a position that suggested that these stars deserved it precisely because they were ingenious enough to borrow musically from outside their native traditions. More optimistic than Goldstein, Moore championed a great proverbial melting pot of music that allowed white musicians to sample widely in order to create the most interesting music possible.

Moore's thinking took a turn, however, around the concept of authenticity. A few weeks after he had boosted the Rolling Stones—and, in turn, other aspiring white blues rock bands—upon closer inspection, he found them lacking when compared to an artist like Aretha Franklin. "Wealthy modern artists," having not suffered the hardships of poverty or the struggles of racism, could not possibly communicate true struggle, whereas artists who had necessarily did. "When the '20s Mississippi blues genius Robert Johnson comes out of your speaker singing . . . you stone better believe him, because you know he was black, poverty-stricken, and died violently," wrote Moore.[62] "But . . . you can't imagine Ruby Tuesday up and really leaving Mick Jagger, nor would you rush a check to the Beatles because you just heard 'Taxman.' " On the contrary, "Aretha's for real," despite her growing celebrity (and, presumably, growing bank account). He later identified her as "Soul Sister No. 1" whose music "should be piped all day into the halls of black schools as a purveyor of soul subconscious and as a soul purifier."[63] In another instance, when a *New York Times* reporter suggested that "the taint of either racism or bad taste hangs over the national record choices," causing inferior white groups to garner acclaim over superior black ones, Moore claimed to be "buying much of that sentiment."[64] In a piece from later in the year he identified the nature of "black truth" in art, which was evident in the sounds of "the sharecropper" and the "urban man," who were "both committed to life like it is."[65]

Moore's writing demonstrated how authenticity translated into this new context of black power, Black Arts, and identity politics. Previously, in the discourse around folk music, authenticity had been related to a concept of the Other—the idea that music closest to "rural folk" was best. Here, authenticity took on a new meaning. For black performers, being authentic meant displaying one's soul, and creating music that "keeps it real." Certainly, class played into this—the reason that poor blacks, whether in the country or the city, were imagined as especially soulful. Yet authenticity had been transformed into something used to measure oneself not against an Other, but against an essentialized version of one's own identity.

Moore soon earned his own column in the paper where he carried this idea forward. Called New Time and started in late 1970, it was described by its author as "a column devoted to some thoughts on contemporary music" including modern classical, rock 'n' roll, and jazz.[66] It is in this column that Moore truly began to exhibit his feelings about the essence of black music. By this time, white thievery of black music, the lack of outrage about it from blacks in general, and the economic system that enabled such a scenario increasingly disturbed him. Blacks "have let their culture get ripped off without at least showing a little cheek"; whites, in turn, "allowed their mutations of black culture to get exploited." With rock becoming "world geographic music," the stakes were higher than ever. Black America was "the mother of it all"—a fact that most Americans refused to acknowledge. "There are too many success-drunk white musicians who steal the music and run," Moore contended, yet "the world is too small and sharing too necessary for any group of people to shut their culture in and keep the world from partaking on some level." The solution for Moore was giving back, economically and culturally, lest rock become "just another establishment."[67]

The political imperatives on musicians and critics alike had moved away from the possibility of unity and into the realm of separate identities, so much so that even an attempt to bridge that gap would be entangled in the vocabulary of separatism and difference. "I had pointed out to me last week by a brother that that terms 'rock' and 'soul music,' not to mention 'rhythm and blues' are racist labels and contribute to the spiritual separation of peoples, even those of good will and good vibes," he began a column entitled "Call It Soul Music" from the summer of 1971.[68] Moore agreed with his critic "reluctantly, basically because as a scribe I need proper nouns desperately," and noted how these terms contributed to, but also functioned in the service of, differences in demographics, sounds, and producers of various kinds of music. Still, pondering the effects of these terms only served as an "apology" for invoking them, which he then proceeded to do repeatedly over the column's course. How could a critic celebrate difference while at the same time acknowledging differential access?

By the early 1970s, race had arrived at the forefront of thinking for many critics, but it also introduced a host of critical problems that had yet to be overcome. Critics had to make decisions about how, and if, to cover music that was not expressly for themselves, and on what level to defend or chastise the musical miscegenation of others. This issue, initially fairly confined to a discussion of audiences and artists, evolved into an overt conversation about critics themselves through the writing of Robert Christgau. It is in his writing that a postmodern problem was answered with a well-worn solution: "know thyself."

The Critical Self

The growth, diversification, and fragmentation of the popular music market—where rock was still the primary focus of many major labels but was swiftly ceding ground to pop, soul, country, M.O.R, and other genres[69]—paralleled the vast expansion of rock criticism as a profession. In November 1967, Jann Wenner began *Rolling Stone* magazine out of San Francisco, and, as the music's first truly national magazine, it quickly assumed a leadership role in the category.[70] *Creem* magazine started out of Detroit in 1969;

known as the most bombastic of the rock rags, it represented the position that "the inauthentic kitsch of rock music's most cacophonous, unsophisticated bands might serve as a viable source of identity and community."[71] Daily newspapers began to hire rock writers, as did mass market magazines, marking the beginning of the growth of this music as a regular component of mainstream arts criticism. John Rockwell, of the *New York Times*, provides a representative example; he began to write for the newspaper in 1972, and though his beat was classical music, before long he was also writing stories about popular music acts such as Genesis, Jethro Tull, and the New York Dolls.[72] In sum, there were many more rock critics working in the United States in the early 1970s than there had been just a half-decade previously, catering to a much wider and more diversified base of fans. Moreover, it was now possible, in a way it had not been before, for a young person reading the pages of the *Voice* to envision "growing up" to be a rock critic. Indeed, the criticism of writers during this period inspired and instructed many of those who would join the slate of rock writers in the middle-to-late 1970s and early 1980s.

One of these figures who proved inspirational to many was Robert Christgau. Born in 1942, Christgau was raised in a working-class Christian family in the Flushing section of Queens, New York, the child of a firefighter and a housewife.[73] As a youngster, he was an avid fan of sports and music, both of which he examined with almost a statistician's eye for detail. In high school, he often listened to Allan Freed's rock and roll radio show and became an enthusiastic fan of the music. Along with friends, he would "come [into Manhattan] and buy used jukebox 45s down on Forty-Second Street";[74] in his later teens, he became a fan of folk music and jazz. After graduating from Dartmouth in 1962, he returned to the New York City area and began working as a journalist. In 1967, he landed a column in *Esquire* magazine called Secular Music, and came from writing that to the *Village Voice*.

His column, Rock & Roll &, began in March 1969 and essentially replaced Pop Eye, though unlike its predecessor it was never the sole location for rock criticism in the *Voice*'s pages. Rock & Roll & continued in the vein of Pop Eye insofar as it contained thoughtful essays about contemporary musical concerns, but it also broached existential questions about music and criticism itself. "Most of my rockhead friends—especially, but not exclusively, writers—have dissociated themselves from the mainstream rock audience,"[75] Christgau explained in his first column, where he mused about the meaning of aging within rock culture. He was also critical, though, of those who might see the situation as historically unique, quipping "isn't that exactly what our parents said about rock and roll in 1956?" Self-consciousness of this order was a stylistic choice most certainly, but it had intellectual ramifications. Since the onset of New Journalism, critics acted as participant observers and found individual reactions essential to their critical act. Yet Christgau's posture penetrated yet another wall that generally stood between journalistic practice and product by injecting self-consciousness about participation. Christgau knew he was a critic, and he wanted you to know that he knew, too.

In a context fraught with an expanding professional competition, difficult political questions, and blooming identity issues, Christgau's inward gesture was a symptom of, but also a participant in, the postmodern historical moment in which he was writing. It is not simply that he often utilized the first person and considered himself an element of the story—New Journalism likewise used these tropes as a stratagem to transform journalism in general, and Richard Goldstein, in particular, mastered the capacity to reveal himself emotionally through his prose.[76] Yet Christgau's twist on what it meant to be subjective enveloped him within a critical persona, a comment on the very idea of writing as one's "self." Self-awareness necessitated self-criticism and made both central to an honest, disclosing critical act—and Christgau's adeptness at such a leap was both an intervention and a calling card. In ways reminiscent of feminist strategies of consciousness-raising on the one hand and clear declarations of one's social location on the other,[77] Christgau found a method that allowed him work successfully.

By July 1969, Christgau coalesced this method into his new feature, Consumer Guide, which was further evidence of his hyper-awareness of his critical function. In Consumer Guide, Christgau evolved music criticism into service journalism, offering snappy reviews of recent albums to which, in a true academic fashion, he assigned letter grades. Despite their pithy character, Christgau's Consumer Guides heightened the intellectual interrogation of his subject matter through their economy; the condensed form was both a management strategy for contending with the labor that criticism now demanded and a commentary on how to conduct it. The long preface with which he opened his first Consumer Guide is worth quoting at length for the rationale he shared:

> Unless you are very rich or very freaky, your relationship to rock is nothing like mine. By profession, I am surfeited with records and live music. Virtually every rock lp [sic] produced in the country is mailed to me automatically, and I am asked to go to more concerts and clubs that I can bear. I own about 90 per cent of the worthwhile rock albums released since the start of the Beatle era, and occasionally I play every one of them. Nevertheless, I haven't heard half the lps in my collection in six months. All this has a double-edged effect.

On the one hand, I am impatient with music that is derivative and see through cheap gimmicks easily. On the other, I can afford to revel in marginal differentiation, delighting in odd and minor talents that might not be worth the money of someone who has to pay for music.

Rock writers in general are so sick of the mediocrity and the bad hype that they simply don't listen to most of the records they receive. I try to, but my methods are necessarily somewhat mechanical. Even if I spent 16 hours a day listening to music—I would estimate the actual figure, by the way, at around eight—I couldn't give each group the time each group believes its record deserves. So I tend to make a lot of snap judgments . . .[78]

Christgau here made vehemently clear how the form of Consumer Guide supplied a logical and matter-of-fact answer to the potentially unsustainable predicament of how to be a just rock critic in the face of merciless surplus. At the same time, he frankly divulged his own inadequacies in completely achieving the task; there were simply not enough hours in the day to be the perfect critic. In addition, criticism was not the glamorously fun job it might seem to an outsider—often bogged down by "mediocrity" and "bad hype," it was also a careful editorial skill that weighed on even the most fanatical music lover.

Christgau's candidness is even more noteworthy when we consider how much he had to say about exactly how he did his job, and the bias, boredom, or repetitiveness that came along with it. Pauline Kael, the famed film critic whose *I Lost It at the Movies* exerted a strong influence on Christgau's style, set a precedent by placing herself in her stories, reflecting on the state of film, and recognizing divisions between herself and other classes of film viewers or the Hollywood elite. Yet within that volume there simply is not so declarative a statement about what critical work is in general, nor so blatant a declaration of the marked difference between critic and audience.[79] Christgau capitalized on the irreverence that characterized rock criticism as a genre and pointed it at himself. Critical identity—that is, not just the idea that the critic could be subject, but that that subject wore the badge of a critic—was inherent to his practice of music criticism.

It would be rare, from this point forward, for Christgau not to begin a Consumer Guide with an airing of his predispositions or a treatise on why or how critics did what they did. "As you know, we rock critics delight in using our unwonted power irresponsibly," began his sixth Consumer Guide— no doubt a sassy aside, yet also an instance to meditate on the nature and scope of critical authority.[80] He continued: "Especially at night I am tortured by self-doubt, asking what right a parasite like myself has to sit in judgment on creative people, especially the young and disinherited, getting rich on checks from The Voice while artists starve." Clearly, in a column where he commented on bands signed to major labels while earning only $40 himself from the effort,[81] he was targeting those who might consider music critics to be unnecessary, unscrupulous, or unfair. His self-consciousness about the role of critics in the circulation of popular music suggests, in an ironic fashion, that being a rock critic was such a minor endeavor as to ultimately have a negligible effect on rock musicians' livelihoods. At the same time, his humble proclamations of his own social function also accentuate the necessity of the act. Who else but the rock critic can be so honest, so impudent, and still keep his job?

His ability to deal in an upfront, humorous fashion with the ins and outs of his profession rendered critical subjectivity a vital, yet elusive, aspect of writing reviews—one that escaped as soon as it was located, slipped away from firm definitions, and continually mocked itself. His style purposefully took on taboo assertions of rock culture and owned them shamelessly, at once highlighting their importance and deflating the critiques of their sting. The relationship between music and the marketplace was chief among these. "This is business, folks, not criticism," he remarked in December 1969, noting, that "I'm the only Consumer Guide you've got, so love me or leave me."[82] A few weeks later, he made light of those who were too vehemently anti-business, announcing: "Music fans, alphabetization fans, capitalism fans—come gather round while I lend my implicit support to the market economy (hiss! boo!) by suggesting that there are real alternatives within the system."[83] Christgau's sharp introspection acknowledged that reviewing participated in the economic process of music criticism, but also implied that without a market, popular music really does not exist. Rather than let this stymie him, in true postmodern fashion he made the soul-searching his strategy. "I suspect I'll stop doing the CG when I start running out of things to say up here," he began his tenth Consumer Guide, calling the introductory segment "a chore that taxes my ingenuity." Later he picked on his own seemingly cozy relationship to the music business, claiming, "I really am a dupe of the record industry. I grow fond of so many of the records they lay on me that I forget despite myself that you poor people have to buy the fuckers."[84] Christgau could be as conscious as anyone of the business aspect of his practice, and that it had its limitations—of which he was also well aware.

Christgau's most fundamental belief about the nature of rock was that it was rife with contradictions, and critical duty implored him to highlight them, in a manner playfully serious and seriously playful. His July 23, 1970, Rock & Roll & where he praised the publication of *Aesthetics of Rock*, Richard Meltzer's book devoted to a philosophical inquiry on rock music, comes to stand as an emphatic case in point. The book itself is both a defense of the academic study of rock music and a wild, often esoteric, and sometimes loosely coherent manifesto. Calling Meltzer "a brown-belt intellectual, a light-heavyweight up-and-comer with some staying power and a lot of flashy moves," Christgau marveled at Meltzer's intellect and nerve; on the one hand, Meltzer wrote about an album "without listening to it because he dug its cover" and was also able to craft "word objects [that] are also interesting writing." Meltzer was thus "brilliant and full of shit, informative and obscurantist, ungodly rational and stone mad, campy and camp, without gaining or losing interest"—making his "the most insightful book about rock ever published."[85] The absolute absurdity of rock lies at the heart of its most profound sense. Meltzer's values were in many ways Christgau's, and he felt it his duty to explore how they might be included day-to-day in rock criticism. It also highlighted a tactic of not taking rock too seriously, lest he burn out like his predecessor.

Christgau engaged criticism as a professional and intellectual problem, one that the changing environment of capitalism, politics, and musical possibility greatly shaped. In opening his twelfth Consumer Guide, he explained why he wrote the column when, as one reader complained, "absolute ratings encouraged readers to remain passive consumers (as it were) rather than exercise intelligent choice."[86] Pondering this, he made an argument which he called the "Campbell's Soup Perplex" which considered the structure versus agency question of popular culture. The crux of his argument turned on the idea that while sometimes a person wants to cook his or her own soup, at other times that same person will eat it straight out of the can. With cooking soup as an allegory for purchasing music, Christgau explained, "If I weren't professionally involved, my attitude toward music" would mimic his theory on soup. "Most often, I dig on intelligent choice, but I'm also glad that some crass AM programmer pounded 'Sugar, Sugar' and 'Ride Captain Ride' into my head until I dug them."

Christgau's devotion to pop and appreciation of mass culture persisted from the 1960s—indeed, it was an idea that he and Goldstein ruminated on as friends, along with Christgau's then-partner Ellen Willis—but he was also aware that he must make judgments, good and bad, that erected and played on hierarchies as interpreted through himself. This is among the clearest indication of the postmodern impulse in his work. The critical identity, thus, depended on not only the negations of the cultural divide, but ultimately the ability to invert them, to cross verboten boundaries and promote a sense of self-awareness.

In his early work at the *Village Voice*, Christgau engaged in an intellectual exercise about what criticism could and should be. Identity was an important element of this practice because, in a rapidly changing and destabilizing musical and sociocultural context, the self served as knowable, reliable, and admirably—and only—relative. "The interesting thing about any performance is not what it is, but now it is perceived," he explained in column on April 24, 1969. Rather than feel "guilty" that he was a "music critic . . . who knows nothing about music," he instead argued that "to concentrate on the formal elements of music . . . is to make the assumption that has constricted the arts in this century, namely, that a work exists apart from its environment, that it is a thing-in-itself which has to be understood in itself. Bullshit."[87] Such a perspective not only justified his ignorance of pitch, tone, rhythm, key, and other formal musical elements, but also served to rationalize his own knee-jerk reactions and deep-seated biases. "Results are not guaranteed—I change my mind a lot, and I've missed good things in my time," he explained in one Consumer Guide, cautioning readers to "Remember my prejudices, now—I am indifferent to most rock improvisation, dislike white blues, love black blues but can do without many of the second-raters riding the current crest, and am very anti-pretension."[88] A later column continued this explanation, noting, "I'm just like anyone else—I trust the familiar, and tend to give the benefit of the doubt to artists I've liked in the past. Allow for that. Also, when I don't write about a group, it usually means they're not even good enough to worry about."[89]

Christgau's staunch ownership of his own prejudices is, finally, among the most striking elements of his criticism, and one that reminds us of the profound and painful rifts that rang throughout musical and political culture. One of Christgau's most enviable skills was his ability to locate himself—adamantly, repeatedly, without shame or misgiving, and ultimately without permanence. This kind of "strategic essentialism"[90] actually inverts the essentialism discussed in the earlier portion of this chapter, using the idea of being one thing only momentarily in order to work, but never actually pinning down one's subjectivity completely. Yet that essentialized Christgau still functioned as an explanation, and maybe an excuse, for not being otherwise. He was, after all, a white, male critic with a host of proclivities and biases. Subjectivity in this instance actually always evades, and never fully justifies.

It is thus both ironic and fitting, then, that one of Christgau's final actions before departing the *Village Voice* for *Newsday* in mid-1972 was to put together the first critics' poll, Pazz & Jop, the results of which were unveiled with a front-page teaser on February 10, 1972. Despite using rather hazy criteria to determine entry (Christgau noted that "anyone with the temerity to enter the poll obviously had interest and arrogance, that made anyone who entered a critic"), Pazz & Jop ultimately presented readers, writers, and aspiring critics with empirical proof of a critical consensus—thereby, a means to determine whether one stacked up.[91] Presiding above this codification in myriad ways was Christgau himself, who explained:

> The Pazz & Jop Critics Poll has convinced me—for the first time really—that I have an audience. I'm not sure how we related to each other—that is the central mystery of all popular culture, even a modest rock and roll column—but that we do relate is obvious. For one heady period, eight of my own selections were also in the Pazz & Jop Top 10 . . . no other entry in the poll was so representative. Spiritual synchronicity? Authority tripping? I don't really know, but it feels good, and for the moment I'll settle for that.[92]

Christgau, wearing his self on his sleeve in all its postmodern agitations, at the end of the day had landed in the kingly position of being able to stand for all. Certainly, an element of this was that Christgau already spoke to an audience of believers, either self-selected or converted by his writing, which offers much to consider in terms of what kind of critical authority critics possess. Yet, it is equally important to recognize what an affirmation of Christgau's critical persona this Pazz & Jop outcome turned out to be. Having carved his way through the difficult terrain of this fragmentary period, Christgau emerged a force with which to be reckoned and an architect to be mimicked. No one else could be a Christgau, but plenty would without a doubt try.

CHAPTER 5
Mattering

The 1970s secured Christgau's standing as one of rock criticism's most perspicacious observers as well as its eagerest workhorse. As editor of the *Voice* music section, he steered the writing of numerous prominent critics; his tireless effort at the Consumer Guide, for a number of years printed in the *Voice* as well as *Creem,* guaranteed that his writing style and taste preferences would mold countless other aspiring music journalists and connoisseurs. More than any other individual, it was Christgau who solidified the reputation of the post-'60s *Voice* as the preeminent music writers' paper and a launching pad for up-and-coming scribes, and his labors as what writer Greg Tate affectionately called "a one-man affirmative action committee"[1] recruited women and black writers into the critical ranks who, in turn, stretched the borders of "rock criticism" to embrace a wider range of perspectives, styles, and genres. And in 1981, with the publication of his guide to the previous decade's albums (a task he'd revisit again at the end of the '80s and the '90s) Christgau created rock crit's premier encyclopedia and its de facto bible—irreproachable evidence that he knew more, had heard more, and had more to say about popular music than possibly any other person alive.

Yet his ascendance as the Dean of American Rock Critics only accentuated his wrangle with how to be a critic. Not only was the amount of music released changing the *how* of doing criticism—by the 2000s, Christgau estimated that there were more hours of music recorded every year than there were hours in the year to listen to it—but criticism's social function, its *why,* also needed revisiting.[2] In the '70s, this meant contending with how rock could both be "a multibillion-dollar industry" and at the same time have "suffered a loss of cultural prestige" as it shrank to occupy a mere "subcultural life."[3] Ten years later, " '70s fragmentation became a way of life"; in another ten, even a strong distaste for '60s exceptionalism did not preclude him from observing that "the popular music we call rock did once galvanize social forces in a way it hasn't since."[4] He encapsulated these and related concerns in a simple phrase: "The Mattering."

I have used these pages to tell the early history of music criticism at the *Village Voice* in an effort to make popular music criticism more connected to, and meaningful within, American intellectual history and life. As a class of New York pop intellectuals, *Voice* critics of the 1960s turned to mass culture, previously considered a wasteland, and found reason for serious conversation and invested study. Motivating them was that rock music had assumed an awesome stature in their everyday lives, articulating a new sensibility not only within mass culture, but also in the political, cultural, and economic zeitgeist. With rock music an ample and undefined canvas, the new critical venture allowed young writers to tell stories that were not only relevant and legitimating, but also uniquely, powerfully theirs.

Yet as the '70s progressed, an expanding music industry, fragmenting audiences, a growing critical cohort, and the increasing recognition of diversity in both music and demography made for a context quite distinct from the one the first-generation rock critics had entered. With these changes replicating across the media landscape, both the idea and the promise of "mass culture"—already uncertain owing to what some saw as overzealous, adulterating commercialism—further destabilized, providing both the seed for criticism's explosive growth and the crack that threatened its very foundations. In the mire of these changes, prominent critics at the *Voice* and beyond found themselves pondering the existential: Does it matter?

Matters to Whom?

To wonder whether criticism matters in the "grand scheme of things" is as exaggerated as it is fundamentally human. Whether and how we matter energizes us during moments of triumph and grips us during moments of dread; it helps to guide and frame the decisions we make for ourselves, our loved ones, and our communities. And for better or worse, for many of us our livelihoods offer a way for us to matter across those boundaries, giving the question of mattering not just magnanimity, but also a practicality. Whatever its motive—glory or infamy, justice or power, the rewards of an afterlife or of this one—doing work that matters is an avenue toward finding a purpose for individual existence, and for human existence as a whole.

The question of mattering is therefore a social and cultural question deeply caught up in the lives and the judgments of others. Certain kinds of work rarely have to justify that they matter, and that has everything to do with cultural values; the doctor who works with cancer patients seldom has to argue that her work matters, nor does the police officer who patrols the neighborhood, the mayor who governs the metropolis, or the kindergarten teacher who helps a five-year-old learn to read. But those of us whose work addresses what appear to be less essential needs—leisure, entertainment, delights of the mind—have a trickier case to make, one we're generally not very good at making, either. There's an economics to mattering, too, that aggravates these concerns. Lamentable as it may be, it is often easier to matter when a direct link can be shown between work and our own or someone else's money.

During the moment of introspection of the 1970s, did rock criticism matter in any of these ways? Economically, the answer is yes: by early in the decade, the vocation had been elevated as a promotional tool for the recording and concert industries, a stepping stone for a successful career in journalism, and a vital part of moneymaking for magazines and newspapers. There were also tales, some taller than others, of music critics making or breaking musical acts, with Cream and Bruce Springsteen just two of the most fabled examples.[5] Countercultural types were no longer its lone peddlers, either. From regional newspapers such as *Newsday* to general interest magazines such as *Newsweek,* and at many points in between, more editorial space devoted to rock music meant plenty of venues for critics to sell their work and variety in the kinds of writers that would be able to join the ranks.[6] For many aspiring writers, the field was open, alluring, even romantic; as Patti Smith noted of her own music writing in the early '70s, "this was a time when the vocation of a music journalist could be an elevated pursuit."[7]

What might in retrospect appear to be the zenith of rock criticism didn't feel that way to a number of writers who had been in the thick of it since its earliest days, though. Mattering economically or promotionally would never suffice if rock and its criticism lacked substantive cultural value, and a number of critics harbored suspicions that such a devaluation had arrived. In a *Rolling Stone* article from 1971, Jon Landau wrote that "rock music, drugs, communes, astrology, etc. are too insubstantial to form the core of a durable culture and so they too passed from their role as primary elements to secondary ones"[8]; the comment sharply contrasts with what his critical peers were saying just a few years earlier. In another essay, Landau suggested that professionalization sapped critics of their verve and spirit, so most might as well call it quits after a few years. "Their inspiration recedes, their ambition expands, and we are left with another critic whose career outlasts his commitment by several decades or so," he surmised.[9] "There is seldom any thought, only the axiomatic repetition of ideas that once upon a time and long ago were fresh and stimulating but, through their interminable repetition by hacks, and by the constantly fixed expression of them in print, have become as hollow as whatever they replaced."[10]

Chet Flippo, a contributor to *Rolling Stone,* agreed. "Rock writing at one time attracted some of the brightest talents of the Sixties generation of writers; it is now obvious that it draws only opportunists," he noted in a 1974 master's thesis devoted to the subject. Alas, "without exception, every magazine piece that appears about rock writing is written in the past tense: everything that is going to happen has already happened. Rock writing, in short, is an idea whose time has passed."[11] That same year, the inimitable *Creem* contributor Lester Bangs took a more chaffing but no less emphatic position on music writing in *Shakin' Street Gazette,* calling it "a big ruse from the word go" that "don't mean shit except exploitatively and in the zealotic terms of wanting to inflict your taste on other people."[12] Ever the jester, Bangs was of course joking, but what he said was also true enough to sting. In the end, could a critic be anything but a zealot imposing his taste on whoever would listen?

Not all critics were ready to think about music writing quite so nihilistically, even if they conceded that their contemporary moment necessitated at least a modicum of musical solipsism. Greil Marcus, a *Rolling Stone* editor who started to write books of cultural criticism during the 1970s, addressed these issues in a 1979 collection he edited, devoted to the albums writers would want were they to be stranded on a desert island:

> Rock and roll has never been remotely monolithic—there have always been countless performers to pin your hopes on; though one may have found identity as a member of an audience, one also found it by staking a place in that audience, defining one's self against it—but in 1965 virtually no one who cared about rock and roll could fail to care about the Beatles . . . For a long time now, there has been no single figure one has felt compelled to celebrate or denigrate. People have staked out their territory in rock and roll, but they don't feel much like members of anything big enough to take over the world . . . The objects of the obsessiveness that has always been part of being a rock and roll fan, or a rock and roll critic, are no longer obvious."[13]

Marcus claimed that the vanishing of universal musical obsessions rendered "the rest of rock more visible—and more compelling." Nonetheless, multiplicity created other predicaments for critics. On the one hand, "albums become less touchstones than companions," moments of esoteric passion that might or might not be shared far and wide. On the other hand, "of course writers and fans continue to turn [albums] into touchstones,"[14] compelled, by habit or hope, to extrapolate one's own likes and dislikes beyond oneself. This conundrum finds Marcus both ecstatic about the possibilities of fragmentation and at the same time mindful of the challenge criticism's operating premise would undergo as a result. This is not to say that prior to this, critics always concurred on musical choices, but instead that what disappeared with the '60s was a confidence that they were part of the same conversation. Ellen Willis, in a *New Yorker* piece a few years earlier, touched on some of these issues in writing about the divided critical response to Grand Funk Railroad. For proponents of the band, there was "the hope that [their] enormous success . . . can re-create a cohesive rock community by polarizing what has become an amorphous, fragmented audience." But instead, she concluded, "I doubt whether one person or one band, no matter how potent, can put it back together."[15]

And this, too: everyone was getting older, in a scene where youth had served as a filter through which to listen and interpret musical meaning. How would aging reframe the critical act? Christgau considered this in his first *Voice* Rock & Roll & column, when he poked fun at Berkeley radical Jack Weinberg, famous for the advice "never trust anyone over 30"—who had, of course, neared the dreaded age in the years since. Christgau observed that "various generation gaps" had emerged among those younger than thirty, showing that even slightly older fans related to the music in ways distinct from their younger brethren. The remembrance of "pre-Dylan" rock—and more, the ability to remember—inevitably colored Christgau's experience of succeeding music, and while he did not begrudge getting older, he did lament the changes to music that time had wrought.[16] "In my glum conservative moments, I often wonder why they can't just make music like . . . Carl Perkins and the Marvelettes and the Hollies and Chuck Jackson," he stated in a later column. Though he drew a line between nostalgia and what he deemed his "conscious aesthetic preference" for older music, he still found it "culturally impossible" for those styles to be repeated because new musical creators are "pretentious" and, for older groups who attempt to create their own sounds, "inspiration has been lost."[17]

Given these pressures of the "post-'60s" as well as those outlined earlier in this book, criticism adapted in both overt and more subtle ways. Christgau, for one, admitted to developing a critical disposition toward "semipopular music" in the late '60s and early '70s, which he described as "arcane stuff with limited mass potential"[18]—an evolution mirrored in the growth in small-scale, genre-specific music publications, especially in the 1980s. In response to this greatly enlarged critical scene, during the '80s and '90s it became commonplace for many critics, by necessity or proclivity, to seek out corners where they could differentiate themselves, sometimes focusing solely on one or a few genres of expertise. For example, for former *Voice* editor and longtime critic Chuck Eddy, an ability to write engagingly about hair metal—a genre that "nobody was writing about"[19] in the '80s—allowed him to carve out a niche for himself that branded him as a creative, iconoclastic critical voice. The same might be said for writers such as Joan Morgan, Greg Tate, and Nelson George, who made their names writing intelligently about hip hop when few others were doing so. All of this foreshadows not only the seemingly infinite specialization of a large number of music bloggers today, but also the economic strategy of segmentation and fragmentation which supplies its structuring logic. What requires answering in the mire of these dynamics is whether they have resulted in a corrosion of criticism's efficacy—that what was once useful, read, and part of "what people are talking about" is no longer in a position to make those claims.

Over the years, Christgau has proposed that the eclipse of self-evident mattering is a result of the disappearance of "monoculture." The term is a synonym for a world un-fragmented, when a limited number of popular artists united a wide listening audience under a more or less common banner. In a 2006 interview, he explained that "everybody listened to the same music on the radio . . . I think it's good for people to have a shared experience."[20] I have already discussed how rock's status as mass music was central to why critics wanted to write about it; it had a sizeable community responding to its rhythms, and a potentially even larger one who might be taken in. But, to follow out this logic, no matter whether rock produced any tangible change or articulated any meaningful community, at the very least it created common roots; to write about rock was a way of participating in and recording that experience. Monoculture thus attached popularity and value, implicating critical and musical practice in equal measure.

The decentralization of the contemporary musical environment emblematized in the shift toward digital music and Internet distribution shines a spotlight on the striking contrasts between monoculture and contemporary conditions. Even some younger critics, who did not live through the 1960s, feel this acutely. "I always felt the monoculture helped make better art because there was something to rebel against," noted Chris Weingarten, a widely published music critic and blogger who gained some notoriety in 2010 as the first critic to successfully profit from Twitter.[21] "Now everything is so splintered that [critics] don't even have to engage with what's popular."[22] Other writers working in this environment share Weingarten's perspective. Upon Michael Jackson's 2009 death, for instance, music critic

Michaelangelo Matos mourned the loss of monoculture that his death signified. "Michael Jackson is the final pop star of seeming consequence to *everyone*—not just people who don't normally care about music, but people who don't care about culture, period" (emphasis in original).[23] Another critic, Ryan Bigge, noted in the *Toronto Star* that "the infrastructure that made the winner-take-all monoculture possible during the mid-to-late twentieth century—the radio-MTV-record store monopoly of music distribution—is gone forever, thanks to the Internet."[24] Even writers picking up on the potentialities laden in the passage of monoculture nonetheless took the idea for granted. "The old musical monoculture seems more obsolete than ever," wrote Kelefah Sanneh in a 2006 *New York Times* article on the CMJ music festival. In its place, he argues, is a "mini-monoculture" that looks "less like a wide-open space and more like a well-organized market."[25]

Of course, not all contemporary pop music critics romanticize monoculture or believe that it once existed. It's a conceptual pillar ripe for dismantling: for its selective memory; for its reliance on an oligarchic corporate control over both music and journalism; for its inherently rockist disposition (meaning that it privileges rock music to the dismissal of other genres, especially pop, country, and R&B, and all the bias that entails); or for its convenient masking of how diverse musical culture really was in the 1960s and beyond (again, to the detriment of other genres and audiences). Each of these critiques raises crucial issues that should caution us against believing how "shared" the experience of musical culture was during the mid-twentieth century. Nevertheless, it is relatively easy to dismiss the idea of monoculture as a remnant of an era when universality felt empowering rather than oppressive, buoyed by the privileges of whiteness, masculinity, and/or access. It is much more difficult to take it seriously as a way of seeing. The idea of monoculture exposes the rifts that exist between early rock critics, still shaped by modernism, and their more fully postmodern offspring. "We were coming from an era where the order was still intact," Goldstein noted to me in a recent conversation. "We were rebelling against it, but we knew what the order was." In contrast to the canons and systematicity of the past, today such concepts are at best debatable, at worst anathema.

The passage of monoculture, as a rhetorical tool or a historical fact, means that the question of whether music or its criticism matters must be followed closely with a second question: matters to whom? A number of music critics have become deft at parsing the infinite diversities that organize the listening and creative publics and seek instances in which they merge, blend, or overlap. More crucial and far more humbling than this work is recognizing that even if "popular music" has numerous sites of production and appeal, thinking seriously about it might not. Modesty about what music criticism might do and for whom is the beginning of any serious conversation about its responsibilities and potential as a form of public intellectualism.

Becoming (Counter) Public

In the midst of completing this manuscript, I attended the joint conference of the International Association for the Study of Popular Music (IASPM) and the Experience Music Project, which convened during the late spring of 2012. IASPM is an organization primarily composed of scholars of popular music, most of whom teach in universities, while the Experience Music Project is a Seattle-based museum that sponsors the conference as an annual educational program, opening its admissions and presentation slots to a mix of musicians, fans, academics, and popular music writers. The 2012 event gathered several hundred panelists and more than a thousand registrants over the course of several days. Both of these entities and conferences such as this one owe their existence in large part to the work of the rock critics I have chronicled in this book, and the conference serves as strong evidence that serious thinking about popular music has an audience.

Many might recognize the conference as the embodiment of public intellectualism in its truest sense. Prominent music writers, teenage fans, students and professors, and legendary musicians mingled during the panels, keynotes, and other events, generating ideas and excitement about the many different aspects of popular music. None of the attendees had to pay, so anyone with the means to get there was welcome to attend. Yet in another way, while the conference certainly celebrated intellectualism, its public credentials are not so certain. Many if not most of the attendees could be aptly described as "music geeks," a subculture that often irritates, intimidates, or is simply of no consequence at all to more casual music listeners. The gathering took place on the campus of a private university, in the heart of a very expensive city, and in part during the hours of a regular workday. In contrast to classic examples of public space such as parks or schools, the "public" of this conference was not a cross-section of the general populace. While diverse topics, perspectives, and identities were represented, it's arguable that those in attendance had more similarities than differences. Was the conference less meaningful, less important, or less defendable if it wasn't exactly "public"?

In order to make sense of music criticism as a form of public intellectualism, it is necessary to think about how and why "public" becomes a meaningful claim. Most obviously, the mantle of the "public" imbues something with a collective sensibility and a democratic ethos—the sense that it is of broad concern, that it harbors political implications. In a classic conception, John Dewey defined the public as "a state [that] springs from the fact that all modes of associated behavior may have extensive and enduring consequences which involve others beyond those directly engaged in them."[26] The definition is concise and self-evident, but it opens up as many questions as it answers; "public" remains a complicated and contested term, used to signal many different things. In its most broad conception, everyone is part of the public, especially in those instances when we act as a polis or citizenry. The public can also refer generically to an audience, such as the readers of this book;[27] this is what we generally mean when we say a novelist, singer, or sports figure has a public. Third, public is a mode of address and space of being, in opposition to the idea of the private. From this last definition stems the notion of publicity, which connotes both the state of being public and the intentional means one might use in order to become public. These shades of meaning regularly bleed into one another, as the latter is a de rigueur path toward achieving the former and in many senses has replaced any other motivation for being public.

Media are increasingly important to each of these interpretations of public. As spaces of deliberation, the media house and frame public debates. The media are also where many of us get a sense of what "the public" is beyond everyday encounters; media coverage is one of the prime distinguishing factors between public and private citizens. The increasing role of media in everyday life has an enormous part to play in understanding our contemporary sense of the public, regularly characterized as in crisis. We live in a time of diminishing belief and investment in public institutions of all stripes, and in the United States at least, public dialogue on many issues veers toward polarization and ugliness. Coupled with dwindling spheres of private action and increasingly capricious tools for public address, the presence of "the public" feels both omnipresent and tenuous. Media alert us to these issues as much as they exacerbate and inflame them.

Though media, especially print media, have been central to determining what counts as public intellectualism, all mediation raises the problems presented in the varied understandings of the public and publicity as described above. Is public intellectualism necessarily for "everyone," or is it simply public in its posture or to its intended audience? Does public intellectualism play a vital role in democracy, alerting a general audience to issues of mass concern and, if so, how does that stand up against (and prevent falling into) the fragmentation and distrust that seem endemic to our over-mediated age? Michael Warner's insightful book *Public and Counterpublics* helps to ground some of these questions. Focused especially on writing, Warner explores publics as phenomena of written communication; when we write, he argues, we anticipate our public but cannot will it into being. "The work to which one belongs, the scene of one's activity, will be determined at least in part by the way one addresses it," Warner writes. "In modernity, therefore, an extraordinary burden of world making comes to be borne above all by style."[28]

If how we communicate determines who might encounter our message (including catalyzing any action that might arise from it), the public is less a concrete entity than a promise: a wish that we might articulate what we intend to the people we want to reach. The inimitable Jonathan Lethem quips about this in his collection of essays *The Ecstasy of Influence,* noting in the introduction that he's guilty of "addressing you before you've been quite willing to arrive, pretending you've arrived in order to have someone to gab with until you get here."[29] The hope and anxiety at the center of writing to a/the public is especially important in thinking about intellectual publics, Warner argues, for they often communicate in ways difficult or even inaccessible to a general reader, a fact for which they receive much disapproval. Yet Warner suggests that "we begin to normalize intellectual work whenever we suppose a direct equation between value and numbers—imagining that a clear style results in a popular audience and therefore in effective political engagement."[30] Arguing for realism pertaining to "complicated" and "clear" writing styles alike, he usefully names the audience for intellectual work a counterpublic: people who are "socially marked by their participation in this kind of discourse; ordinary people are presumed not to want to be mistaken for the kind of person who would participate in this kind of talk or be present in this kind of scene."[31]

Counterpublicity is a useful idea in identifying the style of rock criticism's public intellectualism. We are living in the world rock critics created for us, where popular music has made enormous strides in terms of respect and recognition and where it is far more common for music to be discussed and debated as a significant sociological, cultural, and political object. At the same time, while scribes writing in the mid-twentieth century changed public dialogue, their success at doing so also birthed a robust counterpublic sphere—a world in which the Experience Music Project hosts a pop conference teeming with eager participants; where intelligent books are written about My Bloody Valentine, Prince, and Celine Dion; where music blogs enjoy passionate readerships; where universities offer courses in the history of blues or the genres of popular music. Naming this dynamic sphere a counterpublic does not resign popular music criticism to forever languishing on the margins. It does not mean that publics or counterpublics are static or self-contained; it does not mean that nothing unites us. On the contrary, counterpublicity is a style of publicity that mounts a strategic defense against the vulgar populism that equates reach with importance. In a world far too complicated and diverse to be understood as if a winner takes all, the intellectualism of pop music critics is well equipped to both model and teach the importance and range of critical thinking.

These aspects of popular music criticism should be of strong interest to academics, not only for study but also as relatives to our own practice as (counter)public intellectuals. Though our ways of doing so differ and we have different social and professional responsibilities, academics and critical journalists aspire to many of the same things, such as communicating ideas, advancing knowledge, and preserving history. We also face many of the same dilemmas—adapting to new technology, countering business decisions driven by the bottom line, and trying to be heard within deaf political structures—and these are dilemmas we ought to be thinking about together. It is our task to make the argument and frame the questions that will allow us both to advocate for the greatly enlarged space for critical public intellectualism and to argue for the use value of the counterpublics we need in order to nourish ourselves and generate meaningful knowledge.

One way to begin tackling this work is to consider how the legacy of rock criticism endures despite, or even because of, the rapidly changing media and social landscape of our times. The most apparent, if prosaic, of these is the durability of the critical impulse itself. However discounted it might be monetarily, the desire to provide written commentary on popular culture and especially music has democratized and, in that sense, become more valuable. For instance, the explosion of music blogs might seem to indicate that professional criticism has no purpose, but their language is often imbued with tropes long common to music journalism. Moreover, online all of us are perpetually asked to like, respond, and review, and while our efforts may be exploited at times, they remain instances that confirm the importance of critique.

Many people also continue to care about music, that most mysterious of the human arts, even as the traditional industries that were built around it crumble and morph. It hardly needs repeating that some of the biggest success stories of recent web and computer history—the invention of Napster, the ascendance of Apple, the rise of social networking sites in the image of MySpace, the popular release of cloud computing—have done so with music as a lynchpin of their business models. Dynamic popular music communities have flourished online, many of them around sites of criticism, highlighting a range of possibilities for new kinds of musical publics and counterpublics. Those of us who care about popular music and its criticism should not just be heartened by these developments; we should lay claim to them as indications of the continuing relevance and power of our work.

Communal Experts

Robert Christgau shepherded in a different kind of watershed moment for rock criticism in 2006 when he lost his job as the *Village Voice*'s Senior Music Editor, leaving the self-proclaimed Dean of American Rock Critics without an institution. He had been a fixture at the paper for most of the previous thirty-seven years, and his termination was part of yet another overhaul-cum-identity crisis for the newspaper, whose buy-out that year by New Times Newspaper Company would be the seventh of its half-century existence. So much upheaval over the years had exacted its toll time and again on the paper's staff—as early as 1974, when *New York* magazine pioneer Clay Felker acquired full control of the paper from its founders, staff members bemoaned the loss of the publication's spirit. But this time, observers lamented, the venerated tradition of rock criticism seemed to go down with it. *Slate*'s Jody Rosen eulogized that Christgau's dismissal left "a big hole in the pop critical community" and that "all rock critics working today . . . are in some sense Christgauians."[32] The *New York Times* quoted despondent staffer Tom Robbins, who noted that Christgau "helped put the *Voice* on the map."[33] A number of prominent rock critics lodged their protest by refusing to participate in the *Voice*'s annual Pazz & Jop, the critics' poll Christgau debuted in 1972, with *New Yorker* critic Sasha Frere-Jones proclaiming "when you fire Bob Christgau, you know, it's a slap in the face to so many of us in so many ways."[34] That proverbial slap foreshadowed the numerous music critics' jobs that have been shed in the years since and the changing realities of newspaper and magazine publishing, from which alternative weeklies like the *Voice* have not been spared.

Nevertheless, as economic realities and historical circumstances conspired to the contrary, Christgau continued to flex his relevance. By the end of 2006, he had begun to contribute a monthly version of his Consumer Guide to the MSN Network and to write reviews for Barnes and Noble; he was freelancing for NPR's *All Thing Considered;* and he licensed a storehouse of Consumer Guides to Rhapsody, a web-based subscription music service. The monthly Consumer Guide existed until July 2010, when it morphed into a more frequently updated blog entitled Expert Witness. Expert Witness has become Christgau's latest signature, a revamp of the Consumer Guide named for the niche he sees it filling in popular music discourse. "Expert Witness is not a joke," he noted in the blog's inaugural post. "It's a boast that in criticism, knowledge counts, and that I have a load and a half."[35] At the time of this writing, Christgau also was working on another expression of his incommensurable knowledge—a book dedicated to the story of his life with popular music.

Christgau's impact is visible not just in his indefatigable presence within popular music journalism but also in the standing of his protégés and colleagues from the *Voice*—figures such as Ann Powers, Chuck Eddy, Joe Levy, Nelson George, and Joan Morgan, who rank among the nation's most prominent music and cultural critics. However, merely cataloging this influence does not in itself make an adequate case for the role of expertise in contemporary life. On the contrary, "expertise" as a way of claiming authority over knowledge can seem everyday more antiquated, too autocratic and not as scientific as crowdsourcing, data mining, reputation scores, or taste algorithms. Placed alongside these "social" tools in which all of us provide the inputs as we benefit from the output, what Christgau represents, even its new media installments, can feel very much of another era, one we could periodize as moving toward closure the day he stopped writing at the *Voice*. There's a way in which this is true, at least in part. There will only ever be one Robert Christgau, and it's possible if not probable that no one else will be able to have the longevity, centrality, and clout that he has. And the *Voice*, while still a significant presence, did hold a unique position as a force that might be difficult if not impossible to reassume, were that the paper's objective—and for good reason, it very well might not be.

Yet all of this mourning and lionization can start to resemble cartoon or hagiography, not only in how it represents and fossilizes Christgau's role but also for how it misunderstands the real spirit, and the enduring life, of expertise. Just as our contemporary new media tools are not as perfectly democratic as we might hope, intellectual experts have seldom been the individual, despotic authorities of our contumely (or, for that matter, our imaginations). Expertise is, rather, a powerful symbol of communion, social not only in the work required to assume it but also in the way it is adjudicated and circulated. This makes experts into sparks where conversation begins, one node of many around which meaning may grow. The reach of Christgau's career is therefore not an end that can be pointed to or counted up. Instead, it is a process that continues to move, reform, and attach, dynamically realized as long as anyone feels compelled to think seriously about popular music.

As new media forms reshape popular music and its criticism, this social, communal element is not new, but it is newly apparent. When music writers first turned to blogs in the mid-2000s, they confronted the challenges and opportunities the dynamic form provided, allowing writers to be deliberately intertextual and commenters more readily engaged. Newer social media tools, such as Pandora, Last.FM, Twitter, and Facebook, do even more to diversify both methods and access points for discussing popular music, amping up the speed and ease of sharing, response, and feedback. These communitarian impulses have also been detectable in some recent, concentrated attempts to rethink what it means to criticize popular music. At the University of Southern California, for instance, Doug McLellan runs the Engine projects, annual collectives tasked to develop innovative models for what arts journalism might look like in the twenty-first century. At the time of this writing, the most recent iteration was Engine29, which began in the fall of 2011 and proposed six projects to redefine arts journalism; they ranged from critics taking to the streets of Los Angeles on bikes to get more in touch with the art of their communities, to the creation of an interactive game allowing players to create their own "arts and entertainment meccas." Also in 2011, the National Endowment for the Arts partnered with the Knight Foundation to fund projects in arts journalism in municipalities around the country, including Philadelphia, Detroit, Macon, Georgia, and Miami. These formal projects, as well as the grassroots experiments going on around the country and globe, suggest that while the model for arts criticism, including popular music criticism, is in a state of flux, the need for such journalism remains. Art helps to create meaning in our lives,[36] and journalism is the space in which that meaning is recorded, for now as well as for the future.

The ability to listen, write, and read together—with music as our muse, our riddle, our antagonist—deserves unwavering faith and resolute defense. Making an argument for why music criticism matters, then, should be of a piece with invigorating conversations about and continuing to persuade others as to why cultural production or art matter at all. Every one of us who is a cultural worker has a stake in making this claim, because not only the solvency of our labor depends upon it, but so does the vitality of our culture itself. To live in a world that cares about music and culture, that creates musical citizens, demands that we are loud and clear in these beliefs. It also requires being proud of what criticism does well—that is, that we champion its ability to start conversations, catalyze interest in music, and produce knowledge. A robust critical sphere is good for all of us less because it has mass appeal than because it is representative of the salience of music in American culture. And that matters.

NOTES

Introduction: Criticism

1. Bernard Gendron and Stanley Aronowitz briefly touch on the intellectual nature of rock criticism their works, but it is one of myriad points in books devoted mostly to other cases. See Stanley Aronowitz, *Roll Over Beethoven: The Return of Cultural Strife* (Hanover, CT: Wesleyan University Press, 1993) and Bernard Gendron, *Between Montmartre and the Mudd Club: Popular Music and the Avant-Garde* (Chicago: University of Chicago Press, 2002). In addition to this, anthologies of rock criticism or tributes to rock writers often discuss the critics' intellectual chops, but do not engage in historical analysis or embark on the kind of detailed textual analysis that this book seeks to present. For examples, see Nona Willis-Aronowitz, ed., *Out of the Vinyl Deeps: Ellen Willis on Rock Music* (Minneapolis: University of Minnesota Press, 2011); and Tom Carson, Kit Rachlis, and Jeff Salamon, *Don't Stop 'til You Get Enough: Essays in Honor of Robert Christgau* (Austin, TX: Nortex Press, 2002).

2. Lisa L. Rhodes, *Electric Ladyland: Women and Rock Culture* (Philadelphia: University of Pennsylvania Press, 2005), 90.

3. Sasha Frere-Jones, introduction to Willis-Aronowitz, *Out of the Vinyl Deeps*, xi; Alice Echols, *Daring to Be Bad: Radical Feminism in America, 1967–1975* (Minneapolis: University of Minnesota Press, 2011), 267.

4. The book received a 2011 National Book Critics' Circle nomination as well as scores of favorable reviews, and was the subject of a well-attended conference/book launch held at New York University in April 2011.

5. Jim Wayne, "Music Criticism 2.0?" *Online Journalism Review*, 18 December 2007. www.ojr.org/ojr/stories/071218wayne/.

6. National Arts Journalism Program, *Reporting the Arts II: News Coverage of Arts and Culture in America*, 2004, 10.

7. Pew Project for Excellence in Journalism, *The State of the News Media: An Annual Report on American Journalism, 2010*, 15 March 2010, www.stateofthemedia.org/2010/index.php.

8. Many stories have chronicled the dour fate of music and entertainment journalists in the softened economy of recent years. The worst years in recent memory were 2008 and 2009, when a number of media publications lost significant staff of all kinds; as of 2011, the number of newsroom employees is slightly up, but lower than it was in 1978, according to an annual survey conducted by the American Society of Newspaper Editors. The downturn has not spared music critics: over the last five years, *Blender* went to an online-only format and *Spin* and *Rolling Stone* fired several staff; publications including *Newsweek*, the *Tampa Tribune*, the *Atlanta Journal-Constitution*, the *Baltimore Sun*, the *Fort Worth Star-Telegram*, and the

Dallas Morning News, to name just a few examples, cut their music coverage or laid off music writers. See Martin Bernheimer, "Critics in a Hostile World," *Financial Times,* 5 July 2008; "Over 100 Staffers Leave Newsweek," *Radar Online,* 27 October 2008, www.radaronline. com/exclusives/2008/03/newsweek-buyouts-writers-david-ansen-gates.php; Eric Deggans, "Tampa Tribune Pop Music Critic Curtis Ross among Media General Staffers Laid off Today," *Tampa Bay Tribune,* 6 June 2011, www.tampabay.com/blogs/media/content/tampa-tribune-pop-music-critic-curtis-ross-among-media-general-staffers-laid-today; Stephanie Clifford, "Print Version of Blender Magazine Will Cease Publication," *New York Times,* 27 March 2009; Andy Rosen, "Baltimore Sun Cuts 27% of Newsroom," *The Daily Record,* 30 April 2009; Anick Jesdanun, "Former Newspaper Rivals Cooperate as Jobs Are Cut," Associated Press, 5 January 2009; Ryan Tate, "Fresh Rolling Stone Layoffs Pave Way For Clueless Web Strategy," *Gawker.com,* 8 December 2008, www.gawker.com/5105038/fresh-rolling-stone-layoffs-pave-way-for-clueless-web-strategy.

9. Bernheimer, "Critics."

10. Simon Frith, *Sound Effects: Youth, Leisure, and the Politics of Rock 'n' Roll* (New York: Pantheon, 1981), 165.

11. For examples of work on rock criticism and taste, see Motti Regev, "Producing Artistic Value: The Case of Rock Music," *Sociological Quarterly* 35, no. 1 (1994): 85–102; and John M. Sloop, "The Emperor's New Makeup: Cool Cynicism and Popular Music Criticism," *Popular Music and Society* 23, no. 1 (1999): 51–73. For examples of work on the relationship between rock criticism and ideology, particularly along lines of race and gender, see Kembrew McLeod, "'*1/2': A Critique of Rock Criticism in North America," *Popular Music* 20, no. 1 (2001): 47–60; Chris Atton, "Writing about Listening: Alternative Discourses in Rock Journalism," *Popular Music* 28, no. 1 (2009): 53–67; and Daphne Brooks, "The Write to Rock: Racial Mythologies, Feminist Theory, and the Pleasures of Rock Music Criticism," *Women and Music* 12 (2008): 54–62. For examples of work on how rock criticism produces value for music and shapes its political reception, see, inter alia, Steve Jones, *Popular Music and the Press* (Philadelphia: Temple University Press, 2002). For examples of work on how rock criticism operates as a journalistic field with its own norms, see Ulf Lindberg et al., *Rock Criticism from the Beginning: Amusers, Bruisers, and Cool-Headed Cruisers* (New York: Peter Lang, 2005); Jason Toynbee, "Policing Bohemia, Pinning up Grunge: The Music Press and Generic Change in British Pop and Rock," *Popular Music* 12, no. 3 (1993): 289–300; Bethany Klein, "Dancing about Architecture: Popular Music Criticism and the Negotiation of Authority," *Popular Communication* 3, no. 1 (2005): 1–20; Gendron, *Between Montmartre,* 161–224; Devon Powers, "'Bye Bye Rock': On the Possibility of an Ethics of Rock Criticism," *Journalism Studies* 10, no. 3 (2009): 322–36.

12. In addition to the writing that will be discussed in detail throughout this book, writers whose careers began in the '60s and '70s, such as Ellen Willis, Lester Bangs, Richard Meltzer, and Greil Marcus, have been known to reflect on criticism in their writing; this practice continues among contemporary writers such as Ann Powers, Jody Rosen, and Douglas Wolk, among numerous others.

13. Michael Bull and Les Back, introduction to *The Auditory Culture Reader* (New York: Berg, 2003); Valentin Mottier, "'Talking about Music Is like Dancing about Architecture': Artspeak and Pop Music," *Language and Communication* 29 (2009): 127–32; Steven Feld and Aaron A. Fox, "Music and Language," *Annual Review of Anthropology* 23 (1994): 25–53.

14. Morris Dickstein, *Double Agent: The Critic and Society* (New York: Oxford University Press, 1992), 55–57.

15. Robert Christgau, "Yes, There Is a Rock Critic Establishment (But Is That Bad for Rock?)" *Village Voice,* 26 January 1976.

16. Thomas Bender, *New York Intellect: A History of Intellectual Life in New York City, from 1750 to the Beginnings of Our Own Time* (New York: Knopf, 1986); Russell Jacoby, *The Last Intellectuals: American Culture in the Age of Academe* (New York: Basic Books, 1987); Richard

Posner, *Public Intellectuals: A Study of Decline* (Cambridge: Harvard University Press, 2001); Dickstein, *Double Agent.*

17. Jacoby, *Last Intellectuals,* 7.

18. Posner, *Public Intellectuals,* 167–220.

19. Michael Warner, *Publics and Counterpublics* (New York: Zone Books, 2005), 90.

20. Dickstein, *Double Agent,* 55, 53.

21. For a more in-depth look at the journalism of some of the classic New York intellectuals such as Dwight Macdonald, see Robert Vanderlan, *Intellectuals Incorporated* (Philadelphia: University of Pennsylvania Press, 2011).

22. Eleanor Townsley, "The Public Intellectual Trope in the United States," *American Sociologist* 37, no. 3 (2006): 40.

23. Christopher Lasch, *The New Radicalism in America, 1889–1963: The Intellectual as Social Type* (New York: Knopf, 1965), x.

24. David Hollinger, *In the American Province: Studies in the History and Historiography of Ideas* (Baltimore: Johns Hopkins University Press, 1989), 145.

25. Steve Jones and Kevin Featherly, "Re-Viewing Rock Writing: Narratives of Popular Music Criticism," in *Pop Music and the Press,* ed. Steve Jones (Philadelphia: Temple University Press, 2002), 23; John Gennari, *Blowin' Hot and Cool: Jazz and Its Critics* (Chicago: University of Chicago Press, 2006), 171, 271–79.

26. Chester Flippo, "Rock Journalism and *Rolling Stone*" (M.A. thesis, University of Texas at Austin, 1974), 7.

27. See Gestur Gudmundsson et al., "Brit Crit: Turning Points in British Rock Criticism, 1960–1990," in *Pop Music and the Press,* ed. Jones, 41; and Jim DeRogatis, *Let It Blurt: The Life and Times of Lester Bangs, America's Greatest Rock Critic* (New York, Broadway Books, 2000), 48–49.

28. Maureen Cleave, "All About the Beatles," *Datebook,* September 1966, 11.

29. Robert Milliken, *Lillian Roxon: Mother of Rock* (New York: Thundermouth Press, 2005), 165.

30. For more extensive discussion on this point, see Linda Martin and Kerry Seagrave, *Anti Rock: The Opposition to Rock 'n' Roll* (Hamden, CT: Archon Books, 1988). In this book, I consider rock and roll to be guitar-based music that grew directly out of rhythm and blues during the late 1940s and early 1950s; black and white performers were both common in rock and roll. Rock music, by contrast, emerged in the mid-1960s and was primarily the province of white performers. See my discussion of these points in chapter 2.

31. Gudmundsson, "Brit," 45.

32. Paul Williams, *Crawdaddy! Book: Writings (and Images) from the Magazine of Rock* (Milwaukee: Hal Leonard Corp., 2002), 7–10.

33. Flippo, "Rock Journalism," 14.

34. Lindberg, *Rock Criticism,* 73–74.

35. Williams, *Crawdaddy! Book,* 11.

36. Robert Draper, *Rolling Stone Magazine: The Uncensored History* (New York: Harper Perennial, 1990), 8.

37. Ben Fong-Torres, introduction to *The Rolling Stone Rock 'n' Roll Reader* (New York: Bantam Books, 1974), xiv.

38. Draper, *Rolling Stone,* 25.

39. Ibid., 120.

40. Ellen Willis, "My Grand Funk Problem—and Ours," in *Out of the Vinyl Deeps,* ed. Willis-Aronowitz 112.

41. DeRogatis, *Let It Blurt,* 75; Draper, *Rolling Stone,* 113.

42. Draper, *Rolling Stone,* 27, 283.

43. Thurston Moore, as quoted in Robert Matheu and Brian Bowe, Creem: *America's Only Rock 'n' Roll Magazine* (New York: Collins, 2007), 10.

44. Gendron, *Between Montmartre,* 231.

45. DeRogatis, *Let It Blurt,* 76–79.

46. Michael J. Kramer, "'Can't Forget the Motor City': *Creem* Magazine, Rock Music, Detroit Identity, Mass Consumerism, and the Counterculture," Michigan Historical Review 28, no. 2 (2002): 43–44.

47. DeRogatis, *Let It Blurt,* 71, 126, 172.

48. Louis Menand, "It Took a Village: How the *Voice* Changed Journalism," *New Yorker,* 5 January 2009, 37.

49. Kevin McAuliffe, *The Great American Newspaper: The Rise and Fall of the* Village Voice (New York: Charles Scribner's Sons, 1978), 135.

50. John McMillian, *Smoking Typewriters: The Sixties Underground Press and the Rise of Alternative Media in America* (New York: Oxford University Press, 2011), 33, 39.

51. Geoffrey Stokes, *The Village Voice Anthology: Twenty-five Years of Writing from the Village Voice* (New York: Morrow, 1982).

52. McMillian, *Smoking Typewriters,* 121.

53. Tom Robbins, "Ron Plotkin," *Village Voice,* 13 August 2002, www.villagevoice.com/2002-08-13/news/ron-plotkin/1/.

54. Stokes, *Village Voice,* 8.

1. Village

1. Village Voice Plans to Use the 'Neighborly' Approach," *New York Times,* 30 October 1955.

2. Ibid.

3. "Miss Isabel Bryan, Publisher, Dead; Co-Founder of The Villager Was 83," *New York Times,* 12 October 1957.

4. "W. G. Bryan is Dead; Founded Villager," *New York Times,* 2 March 1941.

5. Emma Harrison, "Folksy Publisher of Villager Is 82," *New York Times,* 2 January 1956.

6. This is the motto that ran on the front of *The Villager* of the period.

7. Abe Peck, *Uncovering the Sixties: The Life and Times of the Underground Press* (New York: Citadel, 1985), 9–10, 22.

8. Benedict Anderson, *Imagined Communities: Reflections on the Origin and Spread of Nationalism* (New York: Verso, 1993).

9. Dan Wakefield, *New York in the Fifties* (Boston: Houghton Mifflin, 1992), 20.

10. Christine Stansell, *American Moderns: Bohemian New York and the Creation of a New Century* (New York: Henry Holt, 2000), 43.

11. Milton Klonsky, "Greenwich Village: Decline and Fall," in *The Scene Before You: A New Approach to American Culture,* ed. Chandler Brossard (New York: Rinehart, 1955), 19, 21.

12. Thomas Frank, *The Conquest of Cool: Business Culture, Counterculture, and the Rise of Hip Consumerism* (Chicago: University of Chicago Press, 1997), 11–13. Frank explains this obsession as apparent through the work of David Riesman, John Kenneth Galbraith, and William H. Whyte, as well as shared by their wide readership.

13. Stansell, *American Moderns,* 2–3, 43, 150; Mark Morrison, *The Public Face of Modernism: Little Magazines, Audiences, and Reception, 1905–1920* (Madison: University of Wisconsin Press, 2000), 5, 9; Aaron Jaffe, *Modernism and the Culture of Celebrity* (Cambridge: Cambridge University Press, 2005), 3.

14. Steven Watson, *The Birth of the Beat Generation, 1944–1960* (New York: Pantheon, 1995), 40.

15. Clellon Holmes, "This Is the Beat Generation," *New York Times,* 16 November 1952.

16. Ann Charters, *The Portable Beat Reader* (New York: Viking, 1992); and Barry Miles, "The Beat Generation in the Village," in *Greenwich Village: Culture and Counterculture,* ed. Rick Beard and Leslie Berlowitz (New Brunswick, NJ: Rutgers University Press, 1993), 165–80. Charters and Miles disagree somewhat on the exact amount of time the Beats spent in the Village.

17. Miles, "The Beat Generation," 168.

18. Dore Ashton, "The City and the Visual Arts," in *New York: Culture Capital of the World, 1940–1965*, ed. Leonard Wallock (New York: Rizzoli, 1988), 133, 135, 145. Serge Guilbaut also makes this point; he notes the central role of abstract expressionism in delivering the seat of the art world from Paris to New York. See Serge Guilbaut, *How New York Stole the Idea of Modern Art: Abstract Expressionism, Freedom, and the Cold War* (Chicago: University of Chicago Press, 1983), 1, 3–4.

19. Bradford R. Collins, "Life Magazine and the Abstract Expressionists, 1948–1951: A Historiographic Study of a Late Bohemian Enterprise," *The Art Bulletin* 73, no. 2 (1991): 283–308.

20. John Rockwell, "New York's Music," in *New York: Culture Capital of the World, 1940–1965*, ed. Wallock, 226–28.

21. Ted Gioia, *History of Jazz* (New York: Oxford University Press, 1997), 205.

22. John Gennari, *Blowin' Hot and Cool: Jazz and Its Critics* (Chicago: University of Chicago Press, 2006), 179–80, 210.

23. Julie S. Price, *The Off-Broadway Theatre* (New York: Scarecrow Press, 1962), 35; Richard Gilman, "The City and the Theater," in *New York: Culture Capital of the World*, ed. Wallock, 206.

24. Gilman, "The City," 206.

25. Price, *Off-Broadway*, 136–37, 39, 175. This period is also, ironically, when the *Voice* began writing about Off-Broadway and when the Obies were created.

26. John McMillian, *Smoking Typewriters: The Sixties Underground Press and the Rise of Alternative Media in America* (New York: Oxford University Press, 2011).

27. Nigel Fountain, "A Vision of the Village," *Guardian*, 13 April 1996.

28. Kevin McAuliffe, *The Great American Newspaper: The Rise and Fall of the* Village Voice (New York: Charles Scribner's Sons, 1978), 10; Adele Mailer, *The Last Party: Scenes from My Life with Norman Mailer* (New York: Barricade Books, 1997), 29, 38; Ed Fancher, interview by author, 31 May 2006, New York, tape recording, subject's office, New York.

29. Carl E. Rollyson, *The Lives of Norman Mailer: A Biography* (New York: Paragon Books, 1991), 72.

30. Ibid., chap. 4.

31. Mailer, *Last Party*, 57–59.

32. Mailer, *Last Party*; Mary V. Dearborn, *Mailer: A Biography* (Boston: Houghton Mifflin, 1999), 82; "Dan Wolf, 1915–1996," *Village Voice*, 23 April 1996; Fountain, "A Vision."

33. Dearborn, *Mailer*, 88. Other notable figures such as Clellon Holmes, Herman Wouk, and Rosalind Drexler also participated.

34. Jarrett Murphy, "Paper Route," *Village Voice*, 26 October 2005, www.villagevoice.com/2005-10-18/specials/paper-route/. McAuliffe, *Great American Newspaper*, 13–14.

35. McAuliffe, *Great American Newspaper*, 15.

36. Ibid., 11.

37. It also speaks to the neighborhood's diverse populations and the *Voice*'s ability—and sometimes inability—to serve them all. This point will be discussed more fully in the subsequent chapters.

38. "Our Policy (?)," *Village Voice*, 30 November 1955.

39. Fancher, "Interview."

40. Ibid.; McAuliffe, *Great American Newspaper*, 15.

41. "Editorial No. 1," *Village Voice*, 26 October 1955.

42. Dan Wolf and Edwin Fancher, introduction to *The Village Voice Reader: A Mixed Bag from the Greenwich Village Newspaper* (Garden City, NY: Doubleday, 1962), 5.

43. Fancher, "Interview."

44. "The First Six Months," *Village Voice*, 18 April 1956.

45. Norman Mailer, "The Hip and the Square," *Village Voice*, 25 April 1956.

46. Fancher, "Interview."

47. Jack Newfield, "An Inner Voice," *Village Voice*, 23 April 1996.

48. Richard Goldstein, interview by author, 26 May 2006, New York, tape recording, subject's home, New York.

49. Marc Weingarten, *The Gang That Wouldn't Write Straight: Wolfe, Thompson, Didion, and the New Journalism Revolution* (New York: Crown, 2006), 21–24; Ann Douglas, *Terrible Honesty: Mongrel Manhattan in the 1920s* (New York: Farrar, Straus, and Giroux, 1995), 35.

50. Weingarten, *The Gang*, 47–66; Kenon Breazeale, "In Spite of Women: *Esquire* Magazine and the Construction of the Male Consumer," *Signs: The Journal of Women and Culture in Society* 20, no. 1 (1994): 1.

51. McAuliffe, *Great American Newspaper*, 149.

52. Aurora Wallace, *Newspapers and the Making of Modern America* (Westport, CT: Greenwood Press, 2005), 132.

53. This idea builds upon the arguments in John J. Pauly, "The Politics of New Journalism," in *Literary Journalism in the Twentieth Century*, ed. Norman Sims (New York: Oxford University Press, 1990).

54. Geoffrey Stokes, *The Village Voice Anthology: Twenty-five Years of Writing from the Village Voice* (New York: Morrow, 1982), 8.

55. "Leighton Kerner, 79, Classical Music Critic." *New York Times*, 4 May 2006.

56. Sally Banes, *Greenwich Village 1963: Avant-Garde Performance and the Effervescent Body* (Durham, NC: Duke University Press, 1993), 73; Judith Briggs, *Jonas Mekas* (Minneapolis: Walker Art Center, 1980), 2.

57. Fancher, "Interview"; Emmanuel Levy, *Citizen Sarris, American Film Critic* (Lanham, MD: Scarecrow Press, 2001), 1–2.

58. Banes, *Greenwich Village 1963*, 264 n. 3.

59. Ibid., 71–72; McAuliffe, *Great American Newspaper*, 268.

60. As quoted in Banes, *Greenwich Village 1963*, 80.

61. Fred Goodman, *The Mansion on the Hill: Dylan, Young, Geffen, Springsteen, and the Head-on Collision of Rock and Commerce* (New York: Vintage, 1998), 3–4; Frith, *Sound Effects*, 29; and Ronald Cohen, *Rainbow Quest: The Folk Music Revival and American Society* (Amherst: University of Massachusetts Press, 2002), 13–14.

62. Cohen, *Rainbow Quest*, 145, 159.

63. Ibid., 108, 138.

64. Ibid., 157–60, 212–13.

65. John Wilcock, "Music Makers Quit the Square (But Only for the Wintertime)," *Village Voice*, 26 October 1955. Also, the portion of Greenwich Village in question had been home to Italians since the late nineteenth century. See Terry Miller, *Greenwich Village and How It Got That Way* (New York: Crown, 1990), 198–200; and Donald Tricarico, *The Italians of Greenwich Village: The Social Structure and Transformation of an Ethnic Community* (Staten Island, NY: Center for Migration Studies of New York, 1984), 1–4.

66. Letter to the Editor, *Village Voice*, 11 May 1961.

67. "Two-Way Street," *Village Voice*, 15 April 1965.

68. Devon Powers, "The 'Folk Problem': The *Village Voice* Takes on Folk Music, 1955–1965," *Journalism History* 33, no. 4 (2008): 209–10.

69. Bob Reisner, "The Menace of Folk," *Village Voice*, 24 February 1960.

70. Bob Shelton was one of folk music's most vociferous boosters. See David Hajdu, *Positively 4th: The Life and Times of Joan Baez, Bob Dylan, Mimi Baez Fariña and Richard Fariña* (New York: North Point Books, 2001), 37.

71. Bob Shelton, "Listen, Mr. Reisner!" *Village Voice*, 2 March 1960.

72. J. R. Goddard, "Two Folk-Singers." *Village Voice*, 24 August 1961.

73. J. R. Goddard, "Records: A Summer's Crop of Folk Discs," *Village Voice*, 14 September 1961.

74. J. R. Goddard, "Bobby Dylan," *Village Voice*, 26 April 1962.

75. Jack Newfield, "Blowin' in the Wind: A Folk Music Revolt," *Village Voice*, 14 January 1965.

76. J. R. Goddard, "Dylan Meets the Press," *Village Voice*, 25 March 1965.

77. Simon Frith, *Sound Effects: Youth, Leisure and the Politics of Rock 'n' Roll* (New York: Pantheon, 1981), 48.

78. Steve Waksman has explained that Dylan's use of the electric guitar raises a host of questions about the significance of that instrument to both the "folk purists" who shunned Dylan and rock fans, noting that the electric guitar, having emerged from black rock and roll, carried along with it those signifiers that might have intensified the purist reaction. See Steve Waksman, *Instruments of Desire: The Electric Guitar and the Shaping of Musical Experience* (Cambridge: Harvard University Press, 1999), 1, 4, 6.

79. Jack Newfield, "Mods, Rockers Fight Over New Thing Called 'Dylan,'" *Village Voice*, 2 September 1965.

80. Cohen, *Rainbow Quest*, 242.

2. Pop

1. Richard Goldstein, "Evaluating Media," *Village Voice*, 14 July 1966.

2. For further discussion, see for example Paul R. Gorman, *Left Intellectuals & Popular Culture in Twentieth-Century America* (Chapel Hill: University of North Carolina Press, 1996); Andreas Huyssen, *After the Great Divide: Modernism, Mass Culture, Postmodernism (Theories of Representation and Difference)* (Bloomington: Indiana University Press, 1986); Pierre Bourdieu, *Distinction: A Social Critique of the Judgment of Taste* (Cambridge: Harvard University Press, 1984), 485–500; Jürgen Habermas, *The Structural Transformation of the Public Sphere: An Inquiry into a Category of Bourgeois Society* (Cambridge: MIT Press, 2001), 159–75.

3. Raymond Williams, "The Masses," in *The Raymond Williams Reader*, ed. John Higgins (Oxford: Blackwell, 2001), 42.

4. Gorman, *Left Intellectuals*, 2.

5. Gorman, *Left Intellectuals*.

6. Ibid., 34–37; Mark Pittenger, "A World of Difference: Constructing the Underclass in Progressive America," *American Quarterly* 49, no.1 (1997): 56 n. 13; R. A. Peterson, "The Rise and Fall of Highbrow Snobbery as a Status Marker," *Poetics* 25, no. 2 (1997): 84.

7. Pittenger, "A World of Difference," 29.

8. James Carey, "Commentary: Communications and the Progressives," *Critical Studies in Mass Communication* 6 (1989): 266–67.

9. Here I am informed by the argument put forward in Mark Goodman and Mark Gring, "The Radio Act of 1972: Progressive Ideology, Epistemology, and Praxis," *Rhetoric & Public Affairs* 3, no. 3 (2000).

10. Gorman, *Left Intellectuals*, 91; Garth Jowett, Ian Charles Jarvie, Kathryn H. Fuller, *Children and the Movies: Media Influence and the Payne Fund Controversy* (Cambridge: Cambridge University Press, 2007), 11.

11. Michael Pollak, "Paul F. Lazarsfeld: A Sociointellectual Biography," *Science Communication* 2, no. 2 (1980): 163.

12. Jefferson Pooley, "The New History of Mass Communication Research," in *The History of Media and Communication Research*, ed. David W. Park and Jefferson Pooley (New York: Peter Lang, 2008), 49–52.

13. Van Wyck Brooks, *America's Coming of Age* (New York: Octagon Books, 1975), 7.

14. Gorman, *Left Intellectuals*, 111.

15. Michael Denning, *The Cultural Front: The Laboring of American Culture in the Twentieth Century* (New York: Verso, 2011), xviii.

16. Denning, *Cultural Front*, xvi–xx, 107–14.

17. Ibid., 109; Gorman, *Left Intellectuals*.

18. Lawrence Levine, "Jazz and American Culture," in *The Unpredictable Past: Explorations in American Cultural History* (New York: Oxford University Press, 1993), 179.

19. Ibid., 174.

20. Denning, *Cultural Front,* 311–33; Gorman, *Left Intellectuals,* 133–34; Theodor Adorno, "On the Fetish Character in Music and the Regression in Listening," in *The Culture Industry: Selected Essays on Mass Culture,* ed. J. M. Bernstein (New York: Routledge, 1991), 49, 53.

21. Gilbert Seldes, *The Seven Lively Arts* (New York: Harper & Brothers, 1924), 84, 93, 95.

22. John Gennari, *Blowin' Hot and Cool: Jazz and Its Critics* (Chicago; University of Chicago Press, 2006), 28–29; John Leland, *Hip: The History* (New York: Perennial Books, 2004), 81–84.

23. "Our Country and Our Culture," *Partisan Review,* 19, no. 3 (1952): 285.

24. Bernard Rosenberg, "Mass Culture in America," in *Mass Culture: The Popular Arts in America,* ed. Bernard Rosenberg and David Manning White (New York: Free Press, 1957), 5.

25. "Panel Discussion: The Mass Media," in *Culture for the Millions?: Mass Media in Modern Society,* ed. Norman Jacobs (Boston: Beacon Press, 1965 [1961]), 167, 169.

26. Paul Lazarsfeld, "Mass Culture Today," in *Culture for the Millions?* xiv.

27. For instance, Frank Stanton, president of CBS and a one-time colleague of Paul Lazarsfeld at Columbia, critiqued the intellectuals for misunderstanding mass culture while noting that mass media "have shown themselves inefficient warriors, and on the whole have tended to be too little concerned with what the intellectuals have had to say." See Frank Stanton, "Parallel Paths," in *Culture for the Millions?* 85.

28. Edward Shils, "Mass Society and Its Culture," in *Culture for the Millions?* 12.

29. Landon Y. Jones, *Great Expectations: America and the Baby Boom Generation* (New York: Coward, McCann, & Geoghegan, 1980), 17–19, 20.

30. William Boddy, "The Beginnings of American Television," in *Television: An International History,* ed. Anthony Smith and Richard Patterson (Oxford: Oxford University Press, 1998), 26, 37.

31. Jones, *Great Expectations,* 42–46.

32. Walter Benjamin and Dwight Macdonald both expressed some fascination with film.

33. Bernard Rosenberg and David Manning White, "Television and Radio," in *Mass Culture: The Popular Arts in America,* 342.

34. Jones, *Great Expectations,* 42–46; Aniko Bodroghkozy, *Groove Tube: Sixties Television and the Youth Rebellion* (Durham, NC: Duke University Press, 2001), 25–29.

35. Bodroghkozy illustrates this point by quoting a Yippie activist who in 1967 said to a police officer, "We grew up in the same country, and we're about the same age. We're really brothers because we grew up listening to the same radio programs and TV programs, and we have the same ideals. It's just this fucked-up system that keeps us apart. I didn't get my ideas from Mao, Lenin, or Ho Chi Min. I got my ideals from the Lone Ranger." See Bodroghkozy, *Groove Tube,* 31–32 for quote; see also 24–29, 33.

36. Gary Cross, *An All-Consuming Century: Why Commercialism Won in Modern America* (New York: Columbia University Press, 2000), 104–5.

37. Jim Curtis, *Rock Eras: Interpretations of Music and Society, 1954–1984* (Bowling Green, OH: Bowling Green State University Popular Press, 1987), 44; and David Sanjek, *From Print to Plastic: Publishing and Promoting America's Popular Music (1900–1980)* (Brooklyn: Institute for Studies in American Music, 1983), 38–39.

38. Keir Keightley, "Long Play: Adult-Oriented Popular Music and the Temporal Logics of the Post-War Sound Recording Industry in the USA," *Media, Culture, and Society,* 26, no. 3 (2004): 377.

39. Brian Moon, paper delivered at Experience Music Project Pop Conference, 21 April 2007.

40. Susan Douglas, *Listening In: Radio and the American Imagination from Amos 'n' Andy and Edward R. Murrow to Wolfman Jack and Howard Stern* (New York: Times Books, 1999), 222.

41. Andre Millard, *America on Record: A History of Recorded Sound* (New York: Cambridge University Press, 1995), 174; Richard Peterson, "Why 1955? Explaining the Advent of Rock Music," *Popular Music* 9, no. 1 (1990): 105.

42. Peter Fornatale and Joshua E. Mills, *Radio in the Television Age* (Woodstock, NY: The Overlook Press, 1980), 11, 15; Douglas, *Listening In,* 221.

43. Fornatale and Mills, *Radio,* 18–20; Millard, *America,* 208.

44. Douglas, *Listening In,* 226.

45. Ibid., 228–39; Charlie Gillett, *The Sound of the City: The Rise of Rock and Roll* (New York: Pantheon, 1983 [1970]), 1–49, 167; and Phillip Ennis, *The Seventh Stream: The Emergence of Rocknroll in American Popular Music* (Hanover, NH: Wesleyan University Press and the University Press of New England, 1992), 124–28; 171–76. The most categorical example of this kind of DJ is Alan Freed.

46. Gillett, *Sound of the City,* 11, 14, 22, 38.

47. Diane Pecknold, *The Selling Sound: The Rise of the Country Music Industry* (Raleigh, NC: Duke University Press, 2007), 88–89.

48. Gillett, *Sound of the City,* 65, 67–68; Steve Chapple and Reebee Garofalo, *Rock 'N' Roll Is Here to Pay* (Chicago: Nelson-Hall, 1977), 44.

49. Ennis, *Seventh Stream,* 259.

50. Ernest A. Hakanen, "Counting Down to Number One: The Evolution of the Meaning of Popular Music Charts," *Popular Music,* 17, no. 1 (January 1998): 104; Sanjek, *From Print to Plastic,* 23.

51. Ennis, *Seventh Stream,* 259–60, 261.

52. Douglas, *Listening In,* 249.

53. Gillett, *Sound of the City,* 17.

54. David Szatmary, *Rockin' in Time: A Social History of Rock-and-Roll* (Upper Saddle River, NJ: Prentice Hall, 2000), 47.

55. Gennari, *Blowin' Hot and Cool,* 169.

56. Adorno, "Fetish Character in Music," 29–60.

57. Ennis, *Seventh Stream,* 261–65, 270; Christgau, "Chuck Berry," and Jim Miller, "Jerry Lee Lewis," both in *The Rolling Stone Illustrated History of Rock and Roll,* ed. Anthony DeCurtis (New York: Random House, 1992), 64 and 75 respectively. The next chapter will focus particularly on industry tactics that accomplished much the same goals.

58. Szatmary, *Rockin' in Time,* 54.

59. Ennis, *Seventh Stream,* 270; Chapple and Garofalo, *Rock 'N' Roll,* 50; Laura E. Cooper and B. Lee Cooper, "The Pendulum of Cultural Imperialism: Popular Music Interchanges between the United States and Britain, 1943–1967," *Journal of Popular Culture* 27, no. 3 (Winter 1993): 64; Szatmary, *Rockin' in Time,* 97–125.

60. Szatmary, *Rockin' in Time,* 97–100; Devin McKinney, *Magic Circles: The Beatles in Dream and History* (Cambridge: Harvard University Press, 2003), 51–57.

61. Szatmary, *Rockin' in Time,* 99, 107–8.

62. Greil Marcus, "The Beatles," in *The Rolling Stone Illustrated History of Rock and Roll,* ed. DeCurtis, 11.

63. Steven H. Madoff, "Wham! Blam! How Pop Art Stormed the High Art Citadel and What the Critics Said," in *Pop Art: A Critical History,* ed. Steven H. Madoff (Berkeley: University of California Press, 1997), xiv; Sara Doris, "Pop Art and the Contest over Culture" (Ph.D. diss., Northwestern University, 1999).

64. Doris, "Pop Art," 87–94.

65. Ibid., 87–88; Gorman, *Left Intellectuals,* 183–85.

66. Lawrence Alloway, "Pop Culture and Pop Art," in *Pop Art: A Critical History,* ed. Madoff, 7.

67. Ibid.

68. Susan Sontag, "One Culture and the New Sensibility," in *Against Interpretation and Other Essays* (New York: Picador, 1966), 300, 304.

69. Susan Sontag, "Notes on Camp," in *Against Interpretation and Other Essays,* 289, 288.

70. Doris, *Pop Art,* 111, 118.

71. Ibid., 96.

72. Susan Sontag, "Against Interpretation," in *Against Interpretation and Other Essays*, 14, emphasis in original.

73. Ibid., 13.

74. Robert Genter, *Late Modernism: Art, Culture, and Politics in Cold War America* (Philadelphia: Oxford University Press, 2010), 4.

75. Howard Brick, *Age of Contradiction: American Thought & Culture in the 1960s* (Ithaca: Cornell University Press, 1998), 59.

76. Ibid., 63; Fred Turner, *From Counterculture to Cyberculture: Stewart Brand, the Whole Earth Network, and the Rise of Digital Utopianism* (Chicago: University of Chicago Press, 2006), 53–54.

77. Marshall McLuhan, *Understanding Media: The Extensions of Man* (Cambridge: MIT Press, 1994 [1964]), 57.

78. Philip Marchand, *Marshall McLuhan: The Medium and the Messenger* (Cambridge: MIT Press, 1989), 160; Turner, *From Counterculture to Cyberculture*, 54.

79. Marchand, *Marshall McLuhan*, 200; Bodroghkozy, *Groove Tube*, 38–39; Goldstein, "May 26 Interview."

80. Barry Katz, *Herbert Marcuse and the Art of Liberation* (London: Verso Editions and NLB, 1982), 173–74.

81. Herbert Marcuse, *One Dimensional Man* (Boston: Beacon, 1964), 250.

82. Ibid., 256.

83. Katz, *Herbert Marcuse*, 162–63; Marianne DeKoven, *Utopia Limited: The Sixties and the Emergence of the Postmodern* (Raleigh, NC: Duke University Press, 2004), 27.

84. Ulf Lindberg, Gestur Gudmundsson, Morten Michelsen, and Hans Weisethaunet, *Rock Criticism from the Beginning: Amusers, Bruisers, and Cool-Headed Cruisers (Music/Meanings)* New York: Peter Lang, 2005), 66.

85. Julie Stephens, *Anti-Disciplinary Protest: Sixties Radicalism and Postmodernism* (Cambridge: Cambridge University Press, 1998), 96, 98.

86. Herbert Marcuse, *Essay on Liberation* (Boston: Beacon Press, 1969), 27.

87. Genter, *Late Modernism*, 123–24, 319–20; Norman O. Brown, *Love's Body* (New York: Vintage, 1966).

88. Lindberg et al. also discuss the relationship between the work of Marcuse and McLuhan regarding the utopian aspects of both writers. See Lindberg, *Rock Criticism*, 65–68.

89. Robert Christgau, interview by author, 4 October 2006, tape recording, subject's home, New York.

90. Richard Goldstein, interview by author, 2 February 2012, tape recording, telephone interview.

91. Brian Kellow, *Pauline Kael: A Life in the Dark* (New York: Viking, 2011), 3, 23, 106, 344, 41–43, 49–50.

92. Greil Marcus and Robert Christgau have both noted the influence of Kael during interviews; see Greil Marcus, interview by author, 2 February 2007, New York, tape recording, telephone interview; Christgau, "Interview; see also Stanley Aronowitz, *Roll Over Beethoven: The Return of Cultural Strife* (Hanover, NH: Wesleyan University Press, 1993), 175; Kellow, *Pauline Kael*, 81–83.

93. Kellow, *Pauline Kael*, 106, 278.

94. Pauline Kael, *I Lost It at the Movies* (Boston: Little, Brown, 1965), 7.

95. Ibid., 25.

96. Aronowitz, *Roll Over Beethoven*, 174.

97. Lewis J. Gould, *Watching Television Come of Age: The New York Times Reviews* (Austin: University of Texas Press, 2002), 2–4.

98. Gould, *Watching Television*, 10.

99. Gould, *Watching Television*, 75–93, 139–58, 122–25; Eric Burns, *Invasion of the Mind Snatchers: Television's Conquest of America in the Fifties* (Philadelphia: Temple University Press, 2010), 23.

100. Gould, *Watching Television*, 11.

101. Ibid., 234.

102. Elizabeth Weinstein, "Married to Rock and Roll: Jane Scott, Grandmother of Rock Criticism," *Journalism History* 32, no. 3 (2006): 148; Margalit Fox, "Jane Scott Is Dead at 92; Veteran Rock Music Critic," *New York Times*, 6 July 2011.

103. Weinstein, "Married to Rock and Roll," 147.

104. Gennari, *Blowin' Hot and Cool*, 3.

105. Ibid., 210; Ted Gioia, *History of Jazz* (New York: Oxford University Press, 1997), 199.

106. Gennari, *Blowin' Hot and Cool*, 77–78, 294.

107. Steve Jones and Kevin Featherly, "Re-Viewing Rock Writing: Narratives of Popular Music Criticism," in *Pop Music and the Press*, ed. Steve Jones (Philadelphia: Temple University Press, 2002), 23.

108. Marc Weingarten, *The Gang That Wouldn't Write Straight: Wolfe, Thompson, Didion, and the New Journalism Revolution* (New York: Crown, 2005), 89, 100.

109. Tom Wolfe, *The New Journalism* (New York: Harper and Row, 1973), 35.

110. Aronowitz makes a similar point; see Aronowitz, *Roll Over*, 188.

111. John Pauly, "The Politics of New Journalism," in *Literary Journalism in the Twentieth Century*, ed. Norman Sims (New York: Oxford University Press, 1990), 116. Pauly here focuses specifically on the effect New Journalism had on "hard" news, but I find his arguments are appropriate for the field of cultural journalism as well.

112. Goldstein, "May 26 Interview."

113. Aronowitz, *Roll Over*, 171.

114. Brick, *Age of Contradiction*, 24.

115. Goldstein, "May 26 Interview."

116. Brick, *Age of Contradiction*, 54.

117. Goldstein, "May 26 Interview."

118. Paul Schindler, "Village Voice fires Richard Goldstein," *Gay City News*, August 12, 2004; Goldstein, "May 26 Interview."

119. Richard Meltzer, *The Aesthetics of Rock* (New York: Da Capo, 1970), x; Paul Williams, *Crawdaddy! Book: Writings (and Images) from the Magazine of Rock* (Milwaukee: Hal Leonard Corp., 2002), 7.

120. Kevin McAuliffe, *The Great American Newspaper: The Rise and Fall of the* Village Voice (New York: Charles Scribner's Sons, 1978), 123, 127–28.

121. "Newspapers: Voice of the Partially Alienated," *Time*, 11 November 1966.

122. McAuliffe, *Great American Newspaper*, 130.

123. Richard Goldstein, "The Soul Sound from Sheepshead Bay," *Village Voice*, 23 June 1966.

124. Richard Goldstein, "Evaluating Media," *Village Voice*, 14 July 1966.

125. Ibid.

126. Goldstein, "May 26 Interview."

127. Ibid.

128. Richard Goldstein, "The Fugs Go Pro," *Village Voice*, 21 July 1966.

129. Ibid.

130. Richard Goldstein, "Beyond the British," *Village Voice*, 4 August 1966.

131. Ibid.

132. Richard Goldstein, "On Revolver," *Village Voice*, 25 August 1966.

133. Jules Siegel, "Requiescat in Pace—That's Where It's At," *Village Voice*, 1 September 1966.

134. James Kempton, "John, Paul, George, Ringo: Cool Duel with the Press," *Village Voice*, 25 August 1966.

135. Goldstein, "On Revolver."

136. Richard Goldstein, "69 with a Bullet," *Village Voice*, 24 November1966.

137. Richard Goldstein, "Flak," *Village Voice*, 12 January 1967.

138. Richard Goldstein, "Phillers," *Village Voice,* 23 February 1967.

139. Richard Goldstein, "Inside the Psychedelic Pshell," *Village Voice,* 20 October 1966.

140. "Pops and Boppers," *Newsweek,* 19 December 1966, 66.

141. Goldstein, "Evaluating."

142. Goldstein, "69."

3. Hype

1. Richard Goldstein, "Giraffe Hunters," *Village Voice,* 27 October 1966.

2. Richard Goldstein, interview by author, 8 August 2006, phone conversation, New York.

3. Lawrence Grossberg, "Reflections of a Disappointed Music Scholar," in *Rock over the Edge: Transformations in Popular Music Culture,* ed. Roger Beebe, Denise Fulbrook, and Ben Saunders (Raleigh, NC: Duke University Press, 2002), 32.

4. Howard Brick, *Age of Contradiction: American Thought & Culture in the 1960s* (Ithaca: Cornell University Press, 1998), 99.

5. Timothy Miller, *The Hippies and American Values* (Knoxville: University of Tennessee Press, 1991), 74–75, 88–89.

6. Simon Frith, *Sound Effects: Youth, Leisure, and the Politics of Rock 'n' Roll* (New York: Pantheon, 1981), 50, 53.

7. Roy Shuker, *Popular Music: Key Concepts* (New York: Routledge, 2002), 133–34.

8. Jon Landau as quoted in Frith, *Sound Effects,* 49.

9. Richard Goldstein, "Evaluating Media," *Village Voice,* 14 July 1966.

10. T. J. Jackson Lears, "From Salvation to Self-Realization: Advertising and the Therapeutic Roots of Consumer Culture, 1880–1930," in *The Culture of Consumption: Critical Essays in American history, 1880–1930,* ed. Lears and Richard W. Fox (New York: Pantheon, 1983); and Doug Rossinow, *The Politics of Authenticity: Liberalism, Christianity, and the New Left in America* (Chicago: University of Chicago Press, 1998), 4–5.

11. Rossinow, *Politics of Authenticity,* 6.

12. Hans Weisethaunet and Ulf Lindberg, "Authenticity Revisited: The Rock Critic and the Changing Real," *Popular Music and Society* 33, no. 4 (2010), 465.

13. Lawrence Grossberg, *We Gotta Get Out of This Place: Popular Conservatism and Postmodern Culture* (New York: Routledge, 1992), 207.

14. Frith, *Sound Effects,* 38.

15. In her landmark discussion on underground U.K. club cultures in the 1990s for instance, Sarah Thornton views "various media and businesses as integral to the authentication of cultural practices," while also noting a strong resentment within the underground for positive media coverage in mass market publications. See Sarah Thornton, *Club Cultures: Music, Media, and Subcultural Capital* (Middletown, CT: Wesleyan University Press, 1996), 9, 117, 122–29.

16. Steve Chapple and Reebee Garofalo, *Rock 'N' Roll Is Here to Pay* (Chicago: Nelson-Hall, 1977), 3.

17. Ibid., 82–85.

18. Ibid., 76; Goldstein, "8 August Interview"; Jim DeRogatis, *Let It Blurt: The Life and Times of Lester Bangs, America's Greatest Rock Critic* (New York: Broadway Books, 2000), 208; Fred Goodman, *The Mansion on the Hill: Dylan, Young, Geffen, Springsteen, and the Head-on Collision of Rock and Commerce* (New York: Vintage, 1998), 166–69; Devon Powers, "Long-Haired, Freaky People Need to Apply: Rock Music, Cultural Intermediation and the Rise of the 'Company Freak,'" *Journal of Consumer Culture* 12, no. 3 (2012): 3–18; Alice Echols, *Scars of Sweet Paradise: The Life and Times of Janis Joplin* (New York, Metropolitan Books, 1999), 185; Devon Powers, "Bruce Springsteen, Rock Criticism, and the Music Business: Towards a Theory and History of Hype," *Popular Music and Society* 34, no. 3 (2011): 205.

19. Chapple and Garofalo, *Rock 'N' Roll,* 138–41.

20. Ibid., 141; Goodman, *Mansion on the Hill,* 28.

21. Goodman, *Mansion*, 23–24, 53.

22. Chapple and Garofalo, *Rock 'N' Roll*, 141.

23. Pete Johnson, "Hippies at Their Happiest at Monterey Pop Festival," *Los Angeles Times*, 20 June 1967.

24. Chapple and Garofalo, *Rock 'N' Roll*, 143.

25. Goodman, *Mansion on the Hill*, 43, 77.

26. Susan Douglas, *Listening In: Radio and the American Imagination from Amos 'n' Andy and Edward R. Murrow to Wolfman Jack and Howard Stern* (New York: Times Books, 1999), 247, 253.

27. Chapple and Garofalo, *Rock 'N' Roll*, 98–101; Douglas, *Listening In*, 252.

28. Douglas, *Listening In*, 263.

29. Chapple and Garofalo, *Rock 'N' Roll*, 75.

30. Robert Draper, *Rolling Stone Magazine: The Uncensored History* (New York: Harper Perennial, 1990), 74.

31. Powers, "Long-Haired Freaky People Need to Apply," 15.

32. Labels also made their own attempts to mimic the underground press with psychedelic promotional materials aimed at radio stations. See Chapple and Garofalo, *Rock 'N' Roll*, 75; Goodman, *Mansion on the Hill*, 78; David Armstrong, *A Trumpet to Arms: Alternative Media in America* (Los Angeles: J. P. Tarcher, 1981), 171.

33. Robert Christgau, interview by author, 4 October 2006, tape recording, subject's home, New York.

34. DeRogatis, *Let It Blurt*, 54.

35. Ibid.

36. A notable proponent of this stance was Richard Meltzer, who explained in his 1970 tome *Aesthetics of Rock*, that "operating under the premise that 'high mischief' was the basic, irreducible nub of any 'true' rock experience, and that if I didn't commit it with ongoing frequency no one else would (so, uh, BYE BYE ROCK), I'd do things like jump in the fountain at a Rolling Stones press party, throw chicken bones at some annoying singer at the Bitter End, review (harshly) albums I'd obviously never listened to (or concerts I'd never attended), reverse the word sequence of a text to make it read backwards (or delete, for no particular reason, every fourth word)." See Richard Meltzer, *The Aesthetics of Rock* (New York: Da Capo, 1970), xiv–xv.

37. Christgau, "Interview"; Goldstein, "August 8 Interview".

38. Goldstein, "May 26 Interview."

39. Goodman, *Mansion on the Hill*, 301–6.

40. Marilyn Bender, "How to Be Profitably Hip," *New York Times*, 14 February 1971.

41. Ibid.

42. Craig Karpel, "Das Hip Kapital," *Esquire* magazine, December 1970, 185.

43. Ibid., 275.

44. Ibid., 279.

45. Ibid., 282.

46. Ibid., 275, 282.

47. Joel Rosenbaum, John Roberts, and Robert Pipel, *Young Men with Unlimited Capital: The Inside Story of the Legendary Woodstock Festival Told by the Two Who Paid for It* (New York, Harcourt Brace Jovanovich, 1974).

48. John C. McWilliams, *The 1960s Cultural Revolution (Greenwood Press Guides to Historic Events of the Twentieth Century)* (Westport, CT: Greenwood Press, 2000), 74–75.

49. Rosenbaum, Roberts, and Pipel, *Young Men with Unlimited Capital*.

50. This conception of the original Woodstock can perhaps be seen most clearly in the discourse that surrounded the 25th anniversary concert held in 1994. As Klein notes, "the baby-boomer pundits and aging rock stars posture about how the $2 cans of Woodstock Memorial Pepsi, festival key chains and on-site cash machines betrayed the anti-commercial spirit of the original event." See Naomi Klein, *No Logo: Taking Aim at the Brand Bullies* (New

York: Picador, 2000), 65. Klein fails to engage with the fact that the original Woodstock was itself an incredibly commercial enterprise.

51. Thomas Frank, *The Conquest of Cool: Business Culture, Counterculture, and the Rise of Hip Consumerism* (Chicago: University of Chicago Press, 1997); Sam Binkley, "Cosmic Profit: Countercultural Commerce and the Problem of Trust in American Marketing," *Consumption, Markets, and Consumer Culture* 6, no. 4 (2003): 231–49; Joe Turow, *Breaking Up America: Advertisers and the New Media World* (Chicago: University of Chicago Press, 1998), 31; Douglas Holt, "Why Do Brands Cause Trouble? A Dialectical Theory of Consumer Culture and Branding," *Journal of Consumer Research* 29, no. 1 (2002): 82.

52. Michael Grieg, "Death of the Hippies: A Sad, Solemn Ceremony," *San Francisco Chronicle*, 7 October 1967; Don McNeill, "Autumn in the Haight: Where Did the Love Go?" *Village Voice*, 30 November 1967.

53. Grieg, "Death of the Hippies."

54. "Death Notice for Hippie," *Village Voice*, 30 November 1967. All typos are in the original.

55. Richard Goldstein, "Mover," *Village Voice*, 19 January 1967.

56. Charles Perry, "The Sound of San Francisco," in *The Rolling Stone Illustrated History of Rock and Roll*, ed. Anthony DeCurtis (New York: Random House, 1992), 362–69.

57. Richard Goldstein, "Flak," *Village Voice*, 12 January 1967.

58. Richard Goldstein, "The Flourishing Underground," *Village Voice*, 2 March 1967.

59. Goldstein, "May 26 Interview"; Richard Goldstein, *Reporting the Counterculture* (Boston: Unwin Hyman, 1989), xiii.

60. Goldstein, "Flourishing."

61. Richard Goldstein, "Albumin," *Village Voice*, 13 April 1967.

62. Kevin McAuliffe, *The Great American Newspaper: The Rise and Fall of the* Village Voice (New York: Charles Scribner's Sons, 1978), 122.

63. Richard Goldstein, "The New Jazz: San Francisco Bray," *Village Voice*, 22 June 1967.

64. Richard Goldstein, "Blossomings," *Village Voice*, 27 April 1967.

65. Ibid.

66. Allan F. Moore, "The Brilliant Career of Sgt. Pepper's," *Windows of the Sixties: Exploring Key Texts of Media and Culture*, ed. Anthony Aldgate, James Chapman, and Arthur Marwick (London: I. B. Tauris, 2000), 139.

67. Ibid., 143; Andre Millard, *America on Record: A History of Recorded Sound* (New York: Cambridge University Press, 1995), 331; Les Roka, "A Day in the Life of American Music Criticism: The Sergeant Pepper Debate of 1967–1969," *Journalism History* 30, no. 1 (2004): 20–30.

68. Moore, "Brilliant," 139.

69. Tom Phillips, "Beatles 'Sgt. Pepper': The Album as Art Form." *Village Voice*, 22 June 1967.

70. Richard Goldstein, "We Still Need the Beatles, But . . . ," *New York Times*, 18 June 1967.

71. Richard Goldstein, "I Blew My Cool Thru the New York Times," *Village Voice*, 20 July 1967.

72. Ibid.

73. Richard Goldstein, "The Hip Homunculus," *Village Voice*, 29 June 1967.

74. Ibid.

75. Richard Goldstein "Autohype," *Village Voice*, 18 July 1968.

76. Goldstein, "May 26 Interview."

77. Ibid.

78. Richard Goldstein, "Pop Poll," 11 January 1968.

79. McAuliffe, *Great American Newspaper,* 154.

80. Annie Fisher, "Interpreting," *Village Voice*, 27 June 1968.

81. Goldstein, "May 26 Interview."

82. Richard Goldstein, "Homecoming," *Village Voice*, 26 September 1968.

83. Richard Goldstein, "CJ Fish on Saturday," *Village Voice*, 3 October 1968.

84. Ibid.

85. Annie Fisher, "Hookered," *Village Voice*, 26 September 1968.

86. Robert Christgau, "Rock Is Obsolescent, But So Are You," *Village Voice*, 7 November 1970.

4. Identity

1. Robert Christgau, "Being . . . ," *Village Voice*, 3 July 1969.

2. Lucian Truscott IV, "How Sexy Is Rock?" *Village Voice*, 10 July 1969.

3. Sandy Pearlman, "Revolutionary Moments," *Village Voice*, 2 January 1969.

4. Christgau, "Being . . ."

5. Peter Tschmuck, *Creativity and Innovation in the Music Industry* (Dordrecht, The Netherlands: Springer, 2006), 136, 140.

6. See Lizabeth Cohen, *A Consumer's Republic: The Politics of Mass Consumption in Postwar America* (New York: Vintage, 2003), 292–98.

7. Marilyn Halter, *Shopping for Identity: The Marketing of Ethnicity* (New York: Schocken Books, 2000), 6–7.

8. David Harvey, *The Condition of Postmodernity: An Enquiry into the Origins of Cultural Change* (Cambridge, MA: Blackwell, 1990), 328.

9. Marianne DeKoven, *Utopia Limited: The Sixties and the Emergence of the Postmodern* (Raleigh, NC: Duke University Press, 2004), 229.

10. Ibid., 250.

11. For more on this argument, see Todd Gitlin's *Twilight of Common Dreams: Why America Is Wracked by Culture Wars* (New York: Henry Holt, 1995). Gitlin, a prominent 1960s activist, argues that the Left has been plagued by internal divisions since the late 1960s moment when identity-based movements emerged.

12. Alix Kates Shulman, "Ellen Willis: A Feminist Iconoclast Who Challenged Conservatism in All Its Forms," *The Guardian*, 13 November 2006; Alice Echols, *Daring to Be Bad: Radical Feminism in America, 1967–1975* (Minneapolis: University of Minnesota Press, 1989), 101.

13. Echols, *Daring to Be Bad*, 186. This is also a consistent theme in Ellen Frankfort, *Life at the Village Voice: An Unauthorized Account* (New York: William Morrow, 1976).

14. Robert Christgau, "Look at That Stupid Girl," *Village Voice*, 11 June 1970.

15. Robert Christgau, "The Joy of Joy," *Village Voice*, 15 April 1971.

16. Carman Moore, "What if Joan Had Called Judy & Grace?" *Village Voice*, 23 September 1971.

17. Echols, *Daring to Be Bad*.

18. Nelson George, *The Death of Rhythm and Blues* (New York: Penguin, 1988), 103.

19. Jon Pareles, "James Brown, the 'Godfather of Soul,' Dies at 73," *New York Times*, 26 December 2006; Craig Werner, *A Change Is Gonna Come: Music, Race, & the Soul of America* (Ann Arbor: University of Michigan Press, 2006), 221.

20. James Maycock, "'Godfather of Soul' Who in the Culturally Explosive Sixties Became an Icon for Black America," *The Independent*, 26 December 2006.

21. See Emily Bernard, "A Familiar Strangeness: The Spectre of Whiteness in the Harlem Renaissance and the Black Arts Movement," in *New Thoughts on the Black Arts Movement*, ed. Lisa Gail Collins and Margo Crawford (New Brunswick, NJ: Rutgers University Press, 2006). Bernard extends a version of this argument when she writes that "intimate relationships . . . with whiteness are not extraneous or even peripheral to authentic black experience, they are defining aspects *of* that experience" (emphasis hers, 256). Here, we can consider that songs that celebrated black culture also purposefully confronted white culture—that the assertion of blackness was always also a rejection of whiteness.

22. Peniel E. Joseph, *Waiting 'til the Midnight Hour: A Narrative History of Black Power in America* (New York: Henry Holt, 2006), 142, 163–64; Lisa Gail Collins and Margo Crawford,

"Power to the People! The Art of Black Power," in *New Thoughts on the Black Arts Movement,* ed. Collins and Crawford, 3; Jane Rhodes, *Framing the Black Panthers: The Spectacular Rise of a Black Power Icon* (New York: The New Press, 2007), 60–64.

23. Joseph, *Waiting 'til the Midnight Hour,* 208.

24. Ibid., 209; Amy Abugo Ongiri, *Spectacular Blackness: The Cultural Politics of the Black Power Movement and the Search for a Black Aesthetic* (Charlottesville: University of Virginia Press, 2009); Rhodes, *Framing the Black Panthers.*

25. Ongiri, *Spectacular Blackness,* 34.

26. William Van Deburg, *New Day in Babylon: The Black Power Movement and American Culture, 1965–1975* (Chicago: University of Chicago Press, 1992), 9.

27. Ongiri, *Spectacular Blackness,* 88–90.

28. Larry Neal, "The Black Arts Movement," *The Drama Review* 12, no. 4 (Summer 1968): 29.

29. Ongiri, *Spectacular Blackness,* 93–94.

30. Collins and Crawford, "Power to the People," 8.

31. Leroi Jones (Amiri Baraka), *Blues People: Negro Music in White America* (New York: Quill Press, 1999 [1963]), 17.

32. Ibid., 80.

33. Ibid., 231.

34. John Gennari, *Blowin' Hot and Cool: Jazz and Its Critics* (Chicago: University of Chicago Press, 2006), 271–79.

35. Jones (Baraka), *Blues People,* 131, 169.

36. Adam Gussow, "'If Bessie Smith Had Killed Some White People': Racial Legacies, the Blues Revival, and the Black Arts Movement," in *New Thoughts on the Black Arts Movement,* ed. Collins and Crawford, 228.

37. Werner, *A Change Is Gonna Come,* 72–73, 76–77; Van Deburg, *New Day in Babylon,* 195–207; Brian Ward, *Just My Soul Responding: Rhythm and Blues, Black Consciousness, and Race Relations* (Berkeley: University of California Press, 1998), 3.

38. Ward, *Just My Soul Responding,* 3–4, 282–90.

39. Ongiri, *Spectacular Blackness,* 131.

40. Robert Christgau, interview by author, 4 October 2006, tape recording, subject's home, New York.

41. Werner, *A Change Is Gonna Come,* 6; Ward, *Just My Soul Responding,* 244.

42. Bernard Gendron, *Between Montmartre and the Mudd Club: Popular Music and the Avant-Garde* (Chicago: University of Chicago Press, 2002), 187, 221. Gendron's argument about race and rock music criticism goes on to say that this explains why black music was generally not talked about in white criticism. While in some instances that is true, this chapter seeks to show that the critics were in fact talking about it.

43. Mike Daley, "Why Do Whites Sing Black?: The Blues, Whiteness, and Early Histories of Rock," *Popular Music and Society,* 26, no. 2 (2003): 161–68.

44. Jeff Titon, as quoted ibid., 163.

45. Ibid.; George, *Death of Rhythm and Blues,* 107.

46. George, *Death of Rhythm and Blues,* 107.

47. Perry Meisel, "From Bebop to Hip Hop: American Music after 1950," in *A Concise Companion to Postwar American Literature and Culture,* ed. Josephine Hendin (Malden, MA: Blackwell, 2004), 95.

48. Gennari, *Blowin' Hot and Cool,* 169; Steve Jones and Kevin Featherly, "Re-Viewing Rock Writing: Narratives of Popular Music Criticism," in *Pop Music and the Press,* ed. Steve Jones (Philadelphia, Temple University Press, 2002), 22–23.

49. Jones and Featherly, "Re-Viewing Rock Writing," 22–23.

50. Gennari, *Blowin' Hot and Cool,* 251–53, 297.

51. Richard Goldstein, "Electric Minotaur," *Village Voice,* 24 October 1968.

52. Goldstein, "August 8 Interview"; Goldstein, "May 26 Interview."

53. Goldstein would return to the *Voice* several years later.

54. Richard Goldstein, "Why the Blues?," *Village Voice,* 16 January 1969.

55. Annie Fisher, "Blues and Blues," *Village Voice,* 28 November 1968.

56. Carman Moore, *Crossover: An American Bio* (Rochester Hills, MI: Grace Publishing, 2001), 33–34.

57. Carman Moore, interview by author, 21 October 2006, subject's home, tape recording, New York.

58. Ibid.

59. Carman Moore, "Blacks and Blue Winter," *Village Voice,* 24 April 1969.

60. Carman Moore, "Blues and Beautiful," *Village Voice,* 13 November 1969.

61. Carman Moore, "Stone Soul Show," *Village Voice,* 4 December 1969.

62. Carman Moore, "Aretha on Time," *Village Voice,* 5 February 1970.

63. Carman Moore, "Soul Purifier," *Village Voice,* 29 April 1971.

64. Carman Moore, "Tomorrow's Tithe Today," *Village Voice,* 2 April 1970.

65. Carman Moore, "Blues Truth," *Village Voice,* 18 June 1970.

66. Carman Moore, "New Time," *Village Voice,* 29 October 1970.

67. Carman Moore, "Banking on Rock," *Village Voice,* 11 February 1971.

68. Carman Moore, "Call It Soul Music," *Village Voice,* 24 June 1971.

69. R. Serge Denisoff, *Solid Gold: The Popular Record Industry* (New Brunswick, NJ: Transaction Books, 1975), 463–67.

70. Robert Draper, *Rolling Stone Magazine: The Uncensored History* (New York: Harper Perennial, 1990).

71. Michael J. Kramer, "'Can't Forget the Motor City': *Creem* Magazine, Rock Music, Detroit Identity, Mass Consumerism, and the Counterculture," *Michigan Historical Review* 28, no. 2 (2002): 46.

72. John Rockwell, "Kristoffersen in Song Program," *New York Times,* 5 December 1972; John Rockwell, "Two British Bands, New Here, Indicate Evolution in Rock," *New York Times,* 15 December 1972; John Rockwell, "Dolls 'Revive' Rock in an Uptown Debut," *New York Times,* 3 February 1973.

73. Barbara O'Dair, "A Conversation with Robert Christgau," in *Don't Stop til You Get Enough: Essays in Honor of Robert Christgau,* ed. Tom Carson, Kit Rachlis, and Jeff Salamon (Austin, TX: Nortex Press, 2002), 156.

74. Christgau, "Interview."

75. Robert Christgau, "Gap Again," *Village Voice,* 27 March 1969.

76. Christgau himself has meditated on the preponderance of subjectivity and the usage of I in his volume *Any Old Way You Choose It*—yet further evidence of his unyielding self awareness. He writes that "'New Journalism' with which rock criticism was associated was notorious for its subjectivity" and claims that "the editorial 'I' is still a valuable tool, especially in criticism, so much of which is rationalized opinion." See Robert Christgau, *Any Old Way You Choose It: Rock and Other Pop Music, 1967-1974* (New York: Cooper Square Press, 2000), xiv–xv.

77. Echols, *Daring to Be Bad,* 4, 203; Anita Shreve, *Women Together, Women Alone—The Legacy of the Consciousness Raising Movement* (New York: Viking, 1989), 11.

78. Robert Christgau, "Consumer Guide (1)," *Village Voice,* 10 July 1969.

79. For example, Kael's first essay in *I Lost It at the Movies* details her alienation from the Los Angeles film scene, but she does not go so far into detail about how she actually produces criticism. See Pauline Kael, "Zeitgeist and Poltergeist; Or, Are Movies Going to Pieces? Reflections from the Side of the Pool at the Beverly Hills Hotel," in *I Lost It at the Movies* (Boston: Little, Brown, 1965), 3–27.

80. Robert Christgau, "Consumer Guide (6)," *Village Voice,* 15 January 1970.

81. Christgau, "Interview."

82. Robert Christgau, "Consumer Guide (5)," *Village Voice,* 11 December 1969.

83. Robert Christgau, "Consumer Guide (8)," *Village Voice,* 26 February 1970.

84. Robert Christgau, "Consumer Guide (10)," *Village Voice,* 28 May 1970.

85. Robert Christgau, "R. Meltzer," *Village Voice,* 23 July 1970.

86. Robert Christgau, "Consumer Guide (12)," *Village Voice,* 30 July 1970.

87. Robert Christgau, "New Thing," *Village Voice,* 24 April 1969.

88. Christgau, "Consumer Guide (1)."

89. Robert Christgau, "Consumer Guide (3)," *Village Voice,* 14 August 1969.

90. I am here referring to Gayatri Spivak's conception of strategic essentialism in which, in true deconstructionist fashion, an essentialized position is put forward by a group temporarily in order to achieve a political goal.

91. Robert Christgau, "Pazz & Jop Critics Poll," *Village Voice,* 10 February 1972.

92. Robert Christgau, "What Does It All Mean?" *Village Voice,* 10 February 1972.

5. Mattering

1. Greg Tate, interview by author, 19 July 2010, tape recorded phone interview, Philadelphia.

2. Robert Christgau, introduction to *Christgau's Consumer Guide: Albums of the '90s* (New York: St. Martin's Griffin, 2000), ix.

3. Robert Christgau, introduction to *Rock Albums of the '70s: A Critical Guide* (New York: Da Capo Press, 1981), 10, 12.

4. Robert Christgau, introduction to *Christgau's Record Guide: The '80s* (New York: Pantheon, 1990), 3; Christgau, *Christgau's Consumer Guide,* x.

5. For more on the role of rock critics in the success of Bruce Springsteen, see Devon Powers, "Bruce Springsteen, Rock Criticism, and the Music Business: Toward a Theory and History of Hype," *Popular Music and Society* 34, no. 2 (2011): 203–19. The role of negative reviews in the breakup of Cream is common folklore, though to my knowledge not confirmed.

6. Don McLeese, "Straddling the Cultural Chasm: The Great Divide between Music Criticism and Popular Consumption," *Popular Music and Society* 33, no. 4 (2010): 433–47.

7. Patti Smith, *Just Kids* (New York: Ecco, 2010), 178.

8. Jon Landau, "The Cooling of America," in *It's Too Late to Stop Now: A Rock and Roll Journal* (San Francisco: Straight Arrow Books, 1972), 215.

9. Jon Landau, "Confessions of an Aging Rock Critic," in *It's Too Late to Stop Now,* 219.

10. Ibid., 222. Perhaps voicing his own frustrations with criticism, Landau would soon make a move to musical production.

11. Chester Flippo, "Rock Journalism and *Rolling Stone*" (M.A. thesis, University of Texas at Austin, 1974), 162.

12. Jim DeRogatis, *Let It Blurt: The Life and Times of Lester Bangs, America's Greatest Rock Critic* (New York: Broadway Books, 2000), 250.

13. Greil Marcus, introduction to *Stranded: Rock and Roll for a Desert Island* (New York: Da Capo, 1979), xx.

14. Ibid., xx–xxi.

15. Ellen Willis, "My Grand Funk Problem—and Ours," in *Out of the Vinyl Deeps: Ellen Willis on Rock Music,* ed. Nona Willis-Aronowitz (Minneapolis: University of Minnesota Press, 2011), 112–14.

16. Robert Christgau, "Gap Again," *Village Voice,* 27 March 1969.

17. Robert Christgau, "Consumer Guide (21)," *Village Voice,* 2 December 1971.

18. Christgau, *Rock Albums,* 6.

19. Chuck Eddy, interview by author, 19 July 2010, tape recorded phone interview, Philadelphia.

20. Steve Horowitz, " 'My Tastes Don't Evolve; They Broaden': An Interview with Robert Christgau," Popmatters.com, www.popmatters.com/pm/feature/my-tastes-dont-evolve-they-broaden-an-interview-with-robert-christgau.

21. Justin Peters, "Stayin' Alive," *Columbia Journalism Review,* May/June 2010.

22. Chris Weingarten, interview by author, 14 July 2010, tape recorded phone interview, Philadelphia.

23. "Don't Stop Til You Get Enough," *Salon,* 26 June 2009.

24. Ryan Bigge, "The Loudness War Is to Blame," *Toronto Star,* 20 July 2008.

25. Kelefah Sanneh, "In a World of Cacophony, Experience Is Sharing," *New York Times,* 6 November 2006.

26. John Dewey, *The Public & Its Problems* (Athens: Swallow Press/Ohio University Press, 1991 [1927]), 27.

27. Michael Warner, *Publics and Counterpublics* (New York: Zone Books, 2005), 65–66.

28. Ibid., 129.

29. Jonathan Lethem, *The Ecstasy of Influence: Nonfictions, Etc.* (New York: Doubleday, 2011), xvi.

30. Warner, *Publics and Counterpublics,* 138.

31. Ibid., 120.

32. Jody Rosen, "X-ed Out: The *Village Voice* Fires a Famous Music Critic," *Slate,* 5 September 2006.

33. Motoko Rich, "Village Voice Dismisses 8, Including Senior Arts Editors," *New York Times,* 1 September 2006.

34. Jacob Gans, "*Voice* Music Poll Undermined by Internet," NPR, 5 January 2007. www.npr.org/templates/story.php?storyId=6727764.

35. Robert Christgau, "This Blog: The Whats, Whys, and Wherefores," *Expert Witness,* 22 November 2010, social.entertainment.msn.com/music/blogs/expert-witness-blogpost.aspx?post=258264de-2519-4d38-a469-ca4742b3bf29&_blg=7#ic-anchor.

36. The Knight Foundation conducted a report, published in 2010, that noted that a key driver of people's attachment to their community is its "social offerings"—that there are things to do, and spreading awareness and interpretation of those things when they are art is important. See The Knight Foundation, "Soul of the Community" 2010, www.soulofthecommunity.org/sites/default/files/OVERALL.pdf

INDEX

Devon Powers is an assistant professor of communication at Drexel University. A former rock critic, her research and teaching explores popular music, twentieth-century history, media industries, and promotional culture. With Melissa Aronczyk, she co-edited *Blowing Up the Brand: Critical Perspectives on Promotional Culture.* She is an alumna of Oberlin College (BA) and New York University (PhD), and currently lives in Philadelphia.

WRITING THE RECORD

A volume in the series

American Popular Music

Edited by Rachel Rubin and Jeffrey Melnick